D1535291

VANDERBILT STUDIES IN THE HUMANITIES

Vanderbilt Studies in the Humanities

Volume 1

Edited by
Richmond C. Beatty
J. Philip Hyatt
and
Monroe K. Spears

NASHVILLE
VANDERBILT UNIVERSITY PRESS
1951

PREFACE

THE present volume is the first of a contemplated series that will be published, whenever justified, under the sponsorship of the Vanderbilt Humanities Area Committee. This Committee consists of representatives of the departments of English, Romance Languages, Germanic Languages, Classics, History, Philosophy, and Religion. The grouping here indicated reflects a view on the part of the administration that the interests of faculty members cannot and should not be defined in terms of specific subjects they may happen to be teaching. One professor of Ethics of the Faculty of the School of Religion, for example, is currently offering a course in Jurisprudence jointly with the Dean of the School of Law. The range and quality of work in the Humanities at Vanderbilt must be seen in a collection of this sort to be fully appreciated. Its unity is a growing experience. We hope, moreover, that the appearance of this and future collections will encourage at Vanderbilt—and elsewhere—scholarship which goes beyond the limitations of single disciplines, which crosses freely departmental boundaries and demonstrates the essential unity of all studies dealing with man.

The volume has been edited by a committee composed of Professors Richmond C. Beatty, J. Philip Hyatt, and Monroe K. Spears, to whom, on behalf of the University, I hereby express thanks.

HARVIE BRANSCOMB
Chancellor
Vanderbilt University

April 1, 1951

TABLE OF CONTENTS

I. Why the Modern South Has a Great Literature 1
   DONALD DAVIDSON

II. Christopher Fry: The Redemption of Joy 18
   MONROE K. SPEARS

III. Sir Edward Coke: Advocate of the Supremacy of Law 34
   SAMUEL E. STUMPF

IV. Shepherd of Hermas, Parable II 50
   KENDRICK GROBEL

V. The Consistence and Qualities of Milton's Chaos 56
   WALTER CLYDE CURRY

VI. The Deuteronomic Edition of Jeremiah 71
   J. PHILIP HYATT

VII. Thomas Lodge's Use of Agrippa's Chapter on Alchemy 96
   EDGAR HILL DUNCAN

VIII. Revelation in the Short Story: A Note on Methodology 106
   WALTER SULLIVAN

IX. The Friendship Motif in Middle English Literature 113
   ROB ROY PURDY

X. The Poetry and Novels of Robert Penn Warren 142
   RICHMOND C. BEATTY

XI. The Happy Captivity of Francisco Núñez de Pineda
   y Bascuñán 161
   MAXWELL LANCASTER

XII. Keats's Philosophy of Negative Capability in Its Philosophical Backgrounds 174
   CLAUDE LEE FINNEY

XIII. The Nature of the Conflict in Jonson's *Sejanus* 197
   JOSEPH ALLEN BRYANT, JR.

XIV. Judaism, Jesus, and Paul: Some Problems of Method
   in Scholarly Research 220
   SAMUEL SANDMEL

XV. Petrarch's Doctrine of Meditation 251
   DAYTON PHILLIPS

I

WHY THE MODERN SOUTH HAS A GREAT LITERATURE [1]

By DONALD DAVIDSON

(Professor of English)

FOR a thematic text I ask you to consider a famous passage from Vergil's second "Georgic":

> Felix, qui potuit rerum cognoscere causas,
> Atque metus omnes et inexorabile fatum
> Subjecit pedibus strepitumque Acherontis avari.
> Fortunatus et ille, deos qui novit agrestes
> Panaque Silvanumque senem Nymphasque sorores.
> Illum non populi fasces, non purpura regum
> Flexit et infidos agitans discordia fratres,
> Aut conjurato descendens Dacus ab histro,
> Non res Romanae perituraque regna; neque ille
> Aut doluit miserans inopem aut invidit habenti.
> Quos rami fructus, quos ipsa volentia rura
> Sponte tulere sua, carpsit, nec ferrea jura
> Insanumque forum aut populi tabularia vidit.

Vergil, like us, lived at a time when republican institutions had been undermined by those who were responsible for upholding them. Skepticism and materialism were destroying religion. A New Deal, headed by a dictator on the make, was pretending to restore the republic, but was actually subverting it. Foreign and civil war had produced economic and administrative chaos. The urban proletariat was being bribed into complacency by a program of bread and circuses. Veterans of the Roman armies were being subsidized. Tax burdens were enormous. Armies of occupation had to be maintained in various parts of the world, yet the threat of war in the direction of what is now Germany, the Balkans, and the Near-East remained continuous. Since these, Vergil's circumstances, were much like ours, I trust I may be pardoned if I offer a free modern paraphrase of Vergil's Latin rather than a literal translation:

> Happy (no doubt) is the man who believes that science has the answer to everything, and so thinks that he no longer need fear any-

---

1. An address delivered April 21, 1950, at Mississippi State College, for the annual meeting of The Southern Literary Festival.

thing—such as hell, which must be a mere superstition, or even death itself.

But blessed, too, (if not happy) is the man who knows that the God of his fathers is still manifest in the fields, woods, and rivers. That man does not have to cater to the urban masses of New York and Detroit. He does not need to beg favors from Roosevelt or Truman. He has nothing to do with the jealous and traitorous schemes that split our parties in fratricidal strife. He doesn't spend his time worrying over where the Russians will strike next, or about Washington politics, or over whether the French or British cabinet will again have to resign. He may be one of the "have not's," but he doesn't envy the "have's." He just knows that country ham and fried apples are mighty good eating, especially when they come off your own land; and that "parity prices" don't have anything to do with their essential goodness. Knowledge of such things is his safeguard against the tediousness of bureaucrats, the madness of Washington, and statistics.

My answer to the question, "Why does the modern South have a great literature?" could easily hinge upon Vergil's deliberate contrast between two words, *felix* and *fortunatus*. To understand that, we must understand the two kinds of knowledge that Vergil associates with the intellectually "happy man" *(felix)* and the "blessed man" *(fortunatus)*. But we cannot understand Vergil's meaning until we have examined our own condition of knowledge.

The man of our time who "knows the causes of things" is of course the scientist. We generally turn to the scientist for explanations of physical or social phenomena. We do not any longer ask a philosopher for explanations, and least of all a novelist or a poet— that is, if a public policy that will cost us money and trouble is to be based upon the answer. We live under the rule of scientific expertism. The President does not dare send a message to Congress, nor does Congress dare pass a law, without at least going through the motions of consulting scientific experts and bolstering up the "program" with an array of statistical information that they have compiled.

The Church itself—especially the Protestant church—no longer relies exclusively upon Scriptures and church doctrine. It still reads "lessons" from the Holy Scriptures as a part of its ritual, but the commentary upon the Scriptures avoids the Church Fathers and draws heavily upon social science. The Cole Lectures at Vanderbilt University, for example, were founded as religious lectures, to be delivered by clergymen. But in this, the seventy-fifth year of Vanderbilt University, those Cole Lectures, offered under the auspices of the

Vanderbilt School of Religion, were given by the famous White Russian sociologist, Piritrim Sorokin. He was assisted by two or three prominent ministers who, if they are not as good sociologists as Sorokin, are just as sociological-minded.

So the official, the really valid answer to my question, "Why does the modern South have a great literature?" ought to come from modern science, which is supposed to know the answer to everything. I do not expect the physicist or chemist to deal with it, since as yet there does not seem to be a physics or chemistry of literature. The answer must come from the social scientist. Since literature is some-how or other related to the cultural condition of a people, I turn hope-fully to the sociologist, for he makes it his business to deal with all cultural matters whatsoever.

My question contains two assumptions, which are implied in the terms "modern South" and "great literature." I hasten to explain that by "modern" I mean "contemporary" and perhaps a little more —in point of time the South of the past thirty years, but also the South which in various ways seems consciously striving to be "mod-ern." By "great literature" I mean "great" in the sense of being generally accepted by distinguished critics as of highest quality and most serious import.

One of the Southern writers thus accepted is William Faulkner of Mississippi. Suppose, then, I turn to sociology and ask whether it can account for the appearance in Mississippi, of all places, of Wil-liam Faulkner, in the three decades between 1920 and 1950. My question has a corollary which I believe I am entitled to state: Can sociology also explain why William Faulkner, or some novelist of comparable stature, did *not* appear, during this period, somewhere north of the Ohio—say, in Massachusetts or Wisconsin?

For convenience, I shall seek my answer in the statistical tables assembled from various sources and approvingly published by How-ard W. Odum and his associate, Harry Estill Moore, in a compen-dious book entitled *American Regionalism: a Cultural-Historical Approach to National Integration.* The authors are sociologists of unchallenged eminence. Their book is a synthesis of information gathered from many fields of inquiry over a long period. I assume that it is authoritative and reliable.

The focal point of my inquiry is the decade from 1920 to 1930, for if any cultural factors determined the performance of William

3

Faulkner, they must have been the factors prevalent at about this time, when the new Southern literature was beginning to emerge. No figures are available in this book for the previous decade, but I believe we may safely assume that the decade from 1920-1930 is good enough for our purpose, since that was William Faulkner's formative period.

Now in the formative period of William Faulkner—and, if you wish, of his contemporaries—what cultural factors, exactly, were at work in the Southern scene?

I am very sorry to have to report to you that during William Faulkner's formative period the cultural factors were extremely forbidding in the State of Mississippi. I can hardly see how Mr. Faulkner survived, much less wrote novels. On the evidence of Mr. Odum's tables, culture was at a very low ebb in Mississippi—so low that, if I had only these tables to depend upon, I would confidently assert, as a devoted follower of sociology, that a William Faulkner in Mississippi would be a theoretical impossibility; and that, if he emerged at all, he would have to originate in, say, Massachusetts, where the cultural factors were favorable to literary interests.

Here is the picture. In Mississippi, in 1920, the per capita wealth, as estimated by bank resources, was under $250, and Mississippi, in this respect, was in the lowest bracket in the nation. In Massachusetts, on the other hand, which was in the highest bracket, the per capita wealth by the same measurement was $1,000 and up.

In this decade, too, Mississippi had a very small urban population. In 1930 it was less than 20 per cent despite a small recent increase. Mississippi was almost entirely rural, while Massachusetts was just the other way—90 per cent urban. Most of the South was nearly as rural as Mississippi. The point is important. It has often been thought that cities foster the literary arts, while the country does not. Lack of cities has frequently been assigned as the reason for the lack of a flourishing Southern literature.

As to "plane of living" (Mr. Odum's term) Mississippi by 1930 was about as low as a state can get. "Plane of living" in Mr. Odum's terminology refers to a composite figure calculated from per capita income, tax returns, residence telephones, ownership of radios, and the like. Well, Mississippi by this standard was on a plane of living described as 15 to 40 per cent of the national average—but much nearer to 15 than to 40 per cent. It was in the low bracket. In comparison, Massachusetts was in the high bracket, 70 per cent and above.

Mississippi was in the lowest bracket in nearly everything as compared with Massachusetts and most of the Northern, Midwestern, and Western states. In ownership of automobiles per farm, it was 26.5 per cent as compared with Massachusetts' 61.9 per cent. In average value of farms Mississippi was in the lowest bracket, except for the Delta, which was in the next to the lowest bracket. In "farms with water piped into the house" Mississippi offered a pitiful 5 per cent in comparison with Massachusetts' grand 79 per cent. Mississippi farmhouses were almost without plumbing fixtures. Mississippi spent only a lean 7 and a fraction cents per capita for libraries, the lowest expenditure in the nation, while Massachusetts, home of the Pilgrim Fathers and of Harvard University, spent $1.18 per capita, the highest in the nation. Mississippi was in the lowest bracket, too, in expenditures for public education. Only Georgia was lower. And Massachusetts in this respect was of course very high, though not quite as high as New York.

Mr. Odum offers no tables in this book as to religious belief, but we all know that Mississippians in the 1920's were mostly conservative, true-believing Christians rather Fundamentalist in tendency. On the other hand Massachusetts, except for its Catholic population, would certainly be rather heavily liberal, progressive, skeptical, as to religion, and perhaps even atheistical. If liberalism in religion is an index of cultural welfare—and it is often so regarded—then Massachusetts during this period would again be in a very high bracket, despite its Catholic Irish and its Italians, and Mississippi would be rated very low by modern standards.

We need not continue with Mr. Odum's interesting tables. By every cultural standard that the sociologist knows how to devise Mississippi rates low in the national scale during William Faulkner's formative period. The only bracket in which it would stand high would be in ratio of farm tenancy to population. Its proportion of farm tenants would be very high—but that fact would put it low in Mr. Odum's cultural ratings, for he would take it to indicate a bad economic condition and hence a bad cultural condition.

So it would go for all the Southern states at the time of the emergence of the new Southern literature. All would rank low by the sociologist's measurements. The *highest*-ranking one would be

5

North Carolina, which has long been heavily industrialized and fanatically liberal, and which, interestingly enough, has not contributed nearly as profusely to the new Southern literature as have Mississippi and other Southern states.

But we are perfectly familiar with the picture of the South that has been built up during the past three decades. It has been dinned into us—and into the nation—through newspapers, magazines, books, moving pictures, radio broadcasts, political speeches, and quasi-religious preachments that we are a backward area in an otherwise progressive nation. We have lacked everything, it seems, that makes Massachusetts and Wisconsin great: educational facilities, factories, libraries, hospitals, laboratories, art museums, theatres, labor unions, publishing houses, accumulations of wealth, high dams, electric power, agricultural machinery, birth control. Some of these material deficiencies have been corrected during recent years, but the South is still "backward" in most of the categories named. "Backward," however, is one of the mildest terms used to describe us. In more common use are such terms as "bigoted," "intolerant," "reactionary," "ignorant," "uncivilized." We have been reproached for being lynchers and Ku-Kluxers; for living in the past rather than in the future; for passing anti-evolution laws and electing to office Huey Long, Bilbo, Talmadge.

Nevertheless, we have produced William Faulkner, and the literary intellectuals of Harvard University are reading Faulkner, studying Faulkner, writing essays and books about Faulkner. It is a dead certainty that they are not reading with equally serious attention the current fictional product of Massachusetts, for they are smart men, and they know that in our day Massachusetts has not produced a novelist comparable to William Faulkner. To find a novelist comparable to Faulkner in all New England they have to go to more backward times and read Henry James.

Let us look at some of the queer conjunctions of events that ought to be illuminated by the sociologists.

In 1925 the Dayton trial took place in Tennessee. In the light of the famous Monkey Law, Tennessee was immediately judged to be one of the most notorious spots of cultural depravity in the whole world. But in those same years the Fugitive group of poets emerged in Tennessee and soon, broadening their activities, became the Southern Agrarians. The same cultural factors that produced the so-called

6

Monkey Law must surely have operated upon the Fugitive-Agrarian writers. Did this condition of cultural depravity produce them? At any rate, the influence of this group now seems to have become so pervasive, even in the civilized North, that the defenders of Northern civilization have been thrown into a virtual panic. A flood of articles, many of them denunciatory, has suddenly appeared in the literary magazines. The most hysterical of all, written by Robert Hillyer, former professor of poetry at Harvard, though primarily directed at Pound and Eliot, wildly accused Allen Tate, Robert Penn Warren, and others of this group of organizing a kind of conspiracy to use the prestige of the national government in order to advance their "idiom."[2] This foolish charge might be interpreted to mean that Mr. Hillyer belatedly waked up to the fact that his own folks in the North liked the writings of the uncivilized Southerners better than they liked the writings of Mr. Hillyer and his party. Naturally, that was upsetting to a Harvard man.

But we do not have to stay at the high level of symbolist fiction, modern poetry, and the new criticism, to get comparative examples. How did it happen that the State of Georgia, a very backward state, which has distressed the liberals by steadfastly keeping the Talmadge regime in power, also produced Margaret Mitchell, whose *Gone With the Wind,* as a book and as a movie, has won and kept the attention of the whole world?

How does it happen that Kentucky, the home of feudists, night riders, and julep-sipping colonels, produced that marvelous phenomenon, Jesse Stuart? How does it happen that that same Kentucky, with cultural factors of very low grade by Mr. Odum's indexes, produced Robert Penn Warren, whose most recent novel has shaken the seats of the mighty and, incidentally, won just about every award that it is possible for a novel or a movie to win?

Examples might be multiplied indefinitely. I must now strive to answer the original question—in scientific terms if possible; in other terms if science fails.

The cultural factors described by Mr. Odum either had a causal influence on William Faulkner or they did not.

If they did have a causal influence, we must, under the rigorous impulsion of sociology, reach an astonishing conclusion: namely,

2. Robert Hillyer, "Treason's Strange Fruit," *Saturday Review of Literature,* June 11, 1949.

that the way for a society to produce a William Faulkner is to have him born in a thoroughly backward state like Mississippi, of a chivalrously inclined, feudal-minded, landed Southern family that was ruined by the Civil War and later dipped, not very successfully, into modern business. In other words, a prevalence of rural society, devoted to cotton-growing, afflicted by sharecropping, rather poverty-stricken, conservative in religion and politics, prone to love the past rather than the future, chockful of all the prejudices and customs of the South—that is what it takes to produce a William Faulkner.

Contrarily, a prevalence of material progress, great wealth, modern institutions such as libraries and art museums, factories, industrial gimcracks, liberalism, science, political radicalism—that is the way *not* to produce a William Faulkner. If it were otherwise, Massachusetts and Wisconsin by this time would have produced not one but a couple of dozen William Faulkners.

This conclusion may be discomforting to all who argue that material improvements, liberalism, industrialism, science, and so on are what Mississippi and the South need to attain a high culture. If the appearance of a master artist is an indication of a high culture, they are wrong. Our sociological study clearly indicates either that material improvements, liberalism, industrialism of the order and scale prevalent in Massachusetts are not necessary to produce a master artist; or else—horrible thought—these factors have a negative, blighting effect, and *prevent* his appearance. And without master artists, especially literary artists, how can you have a high culture? I am not the one who proposes that test of a high culture. Our friends of the North have insisted upon it. The British, the French, the Italians, the Germans for centuries have held that view. For a hundred years, too, it has been said, over and over, that that test, above all, was the test the South failed to pass.

The critics of the South might perhaps feel more comfortable if they could argue that Mr. Faulkner's writings are in some sense a *reaction against* the backwardness of his Southern origin and situation. But there is not a solitary hint of such a reaction against backwardness in his novels and stories. Whatever Mr. Faulkner may be against, he is not in his novels against the so-called backwardness of the South. He is simply a novelist whose subject is found in the South. In his novels he has not advocated or even implied an advocacy of any social reform. He does not rush around issuing pronouncements and indictments. He does not join propagandist movements. He doesn't even write literary criticism.

All the same he is as completely Southern as Shakespeare is completely English. So, too, in their various ways are his Southern contemporaries whose works the nation has been reading. They, too, have emerged from backward Southern states in which the cultural factors, by Mr. Odum's ratings, were most forbidding. We must then conclude that the way to produce a John Ransom, an Allen Tate, a Robert Penn Warren, a Julia Peterkin, a Stark Young, a Eudora Welty, a Thomas Wolfe, a Jesse Stuart, an Elizabeth Roberts, is to have them be born and grow up in a backward Southern community that loves everything that Massachusetts condemns and lacks nearly everything that Massachusetts deems admirable and necessary. Let us concede that some of the Southern writers have been more openly sensitive to Northern criticism of the South than Mr. Faulkner has been and that the sensitivity has affected their writing. But the literature of social protest, represented in the North by such men as Theodore Dreiser, Sinclair Lewis, John Dos Passos, is so uncommon among the distinguished Southern writers of our day as to be hardly worth comment. At its substantial best—which is indeed very substantial and momentous—the new literature of the South is not a literature of protest but a literature of acceptance which renders its material as objectively and seriously as any great literature has ever done. It also displays a sense of form, a vitality, a grace, a power, and often a finality of treatment that are remarkably scarce in American literature elsewhere.

But suppose we take the other horn of the dilemma. Suppose the cultural factors described by Mr. Odum did *not* operate in a causal way upon Mr. William Faulkner and his contemporaries. Where are we, in that case?

In that case, I should say, we are nowhere as social scientists. The social scientist must necessarily hold that human phenomena result from causal factors which may be broadly described as heredity and environment. At present he tends to favor environment over heredity, because heredity inevitably gets you into matters of race, and under-present circumstances the social scientist does not enjoy discussing race and heredity together. At any rate, unless the social scientist can prove that cultural factors, mostly environmental, do determine human phenomena, his statistics have no more value than crossword puzzles, and he is not entitled to give expert advice on our social arrangements. If the sociologist admits that, *because* of its very "backwardness," the South produced a William Faulkner, he is in an uncomfortable plight, because that is something he didn't intend to prove. If he admits, on the other hand, that William Faulkner developed regardless of the backwardness or even in spite of it, he is still in a painful plight, because he must then admit that the cultural factors affect some people but not others, especially not high-class literary artists like William Faulkner—which is a very damaging admission.

Or else he must break down and say that, perhaps, after all, he has not yet been inclusive enough. There must be some cultural factors that he left out; but if he can get a large financial subsidy from the Social Science Research Council, he will assign a squad of graduate students to the job, and start punching cards and running the calculating machines, and in a few more years he will have some more indexes to round out the picture. . . .

But I believe we have reached the point where we can dispense with his services. Let us turn back to Vergil, who knew a lot about people and society, as all great artists must.

Vergil's "happy man" who "knows the causes of things" is really a philosopher, not in any way like our modern experimental scientist. His knowledge, which includes a knowledge of science, results from a very lofty intellectual effort that lifts him far above human passions and fears. This knowledge is a sublime, most admirable attainment, and in Vergil's day it was not in conflict with poetry. In fact, the passage under discussion is thought to be a tribute to the Roman poet Lucretius whose *De Rerum Natura* is perhaps the only completely successful "scientific epic" ever written. The happiness associated with this knowledge, however, must be considered a state of intellectual being so very sublime and abstract that few could ever attain it. In our day, it would be almost impossible for a modern experimental scientist to attain it, since he is a specialist and cannot in one operation combine the functions of philosopher, scientist, and poet. Whatever happiness the modern scientist attains is a negative rather than a positive state. His knowledge does not so much exalt him as it dissociates him, because it is exclusive and special rather than inclusive and general. This characteristic has made modern science the enemy rather than the friend of poetry and other literary arts. And any literature that accepts modern scientific knowledge as being an ultimate and complete knowledge is certain to be an incomplete, distorted literature.

But there is another kind of knowledge, which makes men "blessed"—for so I translate Vergil's *fortunatus*. It is the knowledge enjoyed by Vergil's countryman. In the context of the passage I have read, Vergil says that if he cannot have the high philosophic knowledge that makes men "happy" *(felix)* he would next choose the knowledge that makes men "blessed" *(fortunatus)*. This is a stage lower than the very highest knowledge, but it is very admirable and desirable, and it, too, is a high form of knowledge. It rests upon traditional religion—or, in Vergil's exact language, "the rustic gods, Pan and old Silvanus, and the sister Nymphs," which I have freely translated "the God of his fathers." It is a knowledge that possesses the heart rather than a knowledge achieved merely by the head—a knowledge that pervades the entire being, as the grace of God pervades the heart and soul. In the phrase of Allen Tate's famous poem, "Ode to the Confederate Dead," it is "knowledge carried to the heart." Negatively, it relieves the individual from the domination of the mob, the insolence of rulers, the strife of jealous factions, the horrible commotion of foreign wars and domestic politics, the vice of envy, the fear of poverty. Positively, it establishes the blessed man in a position where economic use, enjoyment, understanding, and religious reverence are not separated but are fused in one.

The picture in Vergil is idealized, of course. Nevertheless, that is the kind of knowledge that the South has faithfully cultivated throughout its history. Devotion to such knowledge, knowledge "carried to the heart," is the dominant characteristic of Southern society. Through the influence of Thomas Jefferson and his great contemporaries, it has been woven into our political institutions.

Devotion to this knowledge, I would contend, is the great, all-pervasive "cultural factor" for which the sociologists have neglected to provide data. Therefore they cannot account for William Faulkner and other writers, and their diagnosis of Southern society is untrustworthy.

Furthermore, in viewing Southern society as "backward," they make a false and misleading assumption. In number and size of cities, in number of factories, in number of farmhouses with modern plumbing, the South may be "backward" as compared with a national average calculated from such data. That does not mean that Mississippi or any other state is, for that reason, socially, culturally, intellectually backward. In terms of the standard I have proposed, I can easily argue the contrary and assert that Southern society in the 1920's and 1930's was the most "advanced" in the United States. If "indexed" according to the quality and consistency of its literary performance, it would be indeed very advanced.

But I prefer to describe the South of the past three decades as, on the whole, a traditional society which had arrived at a moment of self-consciousness favorable to the production of great literary works. A traditional society is a society that is stable, religious, more rural than urban, and politically conservative. Family, blood-kinship, clan-ship, folkways, custom, community, in such a society, supply the needs that in a non-traditional or progressive society are supplied at great cost by artificial devices like training schools and government agencies. A traditional society can absorb modern improvements up to a certain point without losing its character. If modernism enters to the point where the society is thrown a little out of balance but not yet completely off balance, the moment of self-consciousness arrives. Then a process begins that at first is enormously stimulating, but that, if it continues unchecked, may prove debilitating and destructive in the end.

Greece in the fifth century B.C., Rome of the late republic, Italy in Dante's time, England in the sixteenth century, all give us examples of traditional societies invaded by changes that threw them slightly out of balance without at first achieving cultural destruction. The invasion seems always to force certain individuals into an examination of their total inheritance that perhaps they would not otherwise have undertaken. They begin to compose literary works in which the whole metaphysic of the society suddenly takes dramatic or poetic or fictional form. Their glance is always retrospective, but their point of view is always thoroughly contemporary. Thus Sophocles, in his *Oedipos Tyrannos,* looks back at an ancient Greek myth, but he dramatizes it from the point of view of a fifth-century Athenian who may conceivably distrust the leadership of Pericles. This is what I mean by the moment of self-consciousness. It is the moment when a writer awakes to realize what he and his people truly are in comparison with what they are being urged to become.

Such a writer is William Faulkner, and such are many of his

Southern contemporaries. In sixteenth-century England there was also a kind of William Faulkner—a country boy from the insignificant village of Stratford, handicapped from the beginning by his ridiculous countrified name, William Shakespeare. That he also had a country accent, not unlike a Southern accent, seems apparent from what the printers have left of his original spelling. He did not have a college education. In the words of his rival and friend, Ben Jonson, he had small Latin and less Greek. But whatever new learning he needed he readily acquired, perhaps in the very process of composing poems and plays. And all the time he had—as Ben Jonson never did —that second kind of knowledge that Vergil praises, that knowledge "carried to the heart" which London and university education could not give, but which he inherited by natural right through Stratford. Ben Jonson, a city boy, schooled by a famous master, William Camden, could never get out from under the weight of his learning. Jonson was always more the critic than the poet, more the adapter and copyist than the original dramatist. But Will Shakespeare, the country boy from a backward region, became one of the world's incomparable originals. London alone could never have produced him.

Prior to the Civil War the entire United States, in greater or less degree, was a traditional society. But the decision of the North to force war upon the Confederacy and the subsequent victory of the Northern armies threw the traditional society of the North into a state of disequilibrium so profound and so rapid in its development that Northern society has never recovered from the shock. The moment of self-consciousness that I have described could therefore not be utilized except by scattered individuals like Henry James, who had to flee to Europe to get his bearings. The Northern writer had scanty opportunity to consult the knowledge in the heart that was his original right. The Northern triumph over the South meant the unchallenged rule in the North of science, industrialism, progressivism, humanitarianism. For Northern writers this rule was disastrous, since it meant that the kind of knowledge chiefly recommended to them was the kind that accomplishes material results—the limited, special knowledge of the scientist and technologist. The result has been that the works of the great Northern writers tend to be all head and no heart. Or else they bear the marks of a lamentable conflict between head and heart. Out of the schism between head and heart arises the literature of realism, of protest, of social criticism. Or else

13

a literature all too evidently determined to be artistic, no matter whether the art has any real subject-matter to exhibit.

Among Northern writers, therefore, a rich subject-matter and a sense of form rarely go together. Sinclair Lewis has an excellent subject-matter, but as to form he is still a cub-reporter with a good memory, hacking out copy to catch the 2 o'clock edition. Dreiser impresses us with the mass of his enormous case histories, but they are written in laborious prose and have apparently been organized with a meat-saw and a butcher knife. On the other hand, Thornton Wilder has a beautiful, though somewhat precious prose style, but he has no subject-matter for the prose to use. One notable instance of a contemporary Northern writer in whom subject and form support each other perfectly is the poet Robert Frost; but Robert Frost rejects the orthodox modern knowledge of the progressive North and adheres to rural New England, which preserves the remnants of its old, traditional society. Beyond these selected examples, the North shows a hodgepodge of experimentalists, propagandists, plausible but empty Book-of-the-Month Club specials, a vast number of scholars and critics, but very few writers of first rank who are not injured by the fearful imbalance of Northern civilization. The Northern writer cannot trust the knowledge in his heart, even when he has it, because he has allowed his civilization to discredit that knowledge. There are too many people looking over his shoulder as he writes—too many college professors, social welfare workers, atomic scientists, pressure groups, librarians, editors of slick magazines, impatient publishers, and seductive subsidizers.

In the South this destructive process has been slow to take hold. Defeated and ravaged in war, the South put up fierce underground resistance to the Reconstruction and thus emerged at the turn of the century, poor in money and what money will buy, but rich in what money can never buy, in what no science can provide, for the South was still a traditional society, injured but very much alive, and by this time wise and experienced in ways of staying alive. The advocates of a New South of industrialism and mass education, though eloquent and powerful, and heavily backed by Northern money, were not able to alter the traditional South very much. So it was not until the latter part of the Roosevelt administration that the South began to receive the full shock of modernism.

What the future offers, I do not know. In the immediate past it

14

seems obvious that Southern writers have not generally been confused by the division between head and heart that is the great problem of Northern writers. The case of Thomas Wolfe offers an
interesting exception to the general rule. From traditional sources
Thomas Wolfe inherited a remarkably rich subject-matter, but he
was utterly incapable of reducing it to coherent form and without
the aid of his editor, Maxwell Perkins, might never have been able to
publish even the somewhat formless books that he did publish. I
suggest that his trouble was that he had been taught to misunder-
stand with his head what he understood with his heart. Thomas
Wolfe had a divided sensibility which very likely resulted from his
education at Mr. Howard Odum's citadel, the progressive University
of North Carolina, and from his subsequent unfortunate experience
at Harvard.

But most of our abler Southern writers, unlike Thomas Wolfe,
seem to be born in possession of an endless store of subject-matter
and also a sense of the form that belongs to the subject-matter. I do
not know how to explain this except by saying that the person who
is born of a traditional society, if he is not corrupted, will act as a
whole person in all his acts, including his literary acts. The truth of
experience that fills his emotional being is not at war with the truth
of his intellectual judgments, but the two, as he writes, are one. His
apprehension of his subject-matter, which is intuitive and comes from
"knowledge carried to the heart," moves hand in hand with his composition, which derives from his intellectual judgment, his sense of
fitness and order. Thus an act as cold-blooded as deliberate literary
composition must be is redeemed and assisted by the warm-blooded
knowledge of the heart. It is natural for a Southern writer to compose that way, as it is natural for him to ride a horse with his whole
heart as well as with his controlling intelligence.

It is also natural for him to see men in their total capacity as persons and to see things in all their rich particularity as things and to
understand that the relationships between persons and persons, and
between persons and things are more complex and unpredictable
than any scientific textbook invites one to think. He needs no literary
critic to tell him that, for his traditional society has already taught
him to look at the world in such a way. It has also impressed upon
him that the world is both good and evil. Toward nature, toward
his fellow creatures, toward the historic past, he has learned to exer-

15

cise that piety which Mr. Richard Weaver, in his book, *Ideas Have Consequences,* has praised as the virtue most needed in the modern world.

Thus it is that in the moment of self-consciousness the Southern writer is able to bring to bear, not only his personal view, but also the total metaphysic of his society. He is therefore unlikely to indulge in the exaggerations and over-simplifications that are the mark of a divided sensibility. For him the people in the bend of the creek are not only sharecroppers representing a certain economic function. They are complete persons with significant personal histories. In fact, they are Joe and Emma, who used to work on old man Brown's place, but left him for reasons well-known. The banker is not merely a banker. He is Mr. Jim, whose wife's mother was somebody's grandmother's double first cousin.

The difference between Southern and Northern writers is the difference it would make if Sinclair Lewis instead of Robert Penn Warren had written *All the King's Men.* In Sinclair Lewis's hands that same material would take on the exaggeration and over-simplification that we are familiar with in Mr. Lewis's novels. Willie Stark would be the caricature of a demagogue—he would be Babbitt recast as a politician. Hunks of satirical realism would be relieved by chunks of humor in the style of the sports page. Mr. Lewis could not achieve the intricate complexity of Mr. Warren's design in which every seeming elaboration proves in the end to be, not an elaboration after all, but a supporting element of the grand scheme. Nor could Mr. Lewis achieve the ethical meaning of Mr. Warren's narrative. Mr. Lewis cannot do such things because he cannot use the knowledge of the heart, if he has it. He cannot use it because he belongs to an anti-traditional society which gives its allegiance to a different sort of knowledge. Perhaps Mr. Lewis is in rebellion against that society; but in his novel about Willie Stark we would never be able to discover just why Willie Stark misbehaves. Willie Stark would of course misbehave in Sinclair Lewis's novel, but it would be only misbehavior, not evil behavior, not sin. For Sinclair Lewis, as for most Northern writers, evil and sin were abolished by Grant's victory over Lee at Appomattox, since which time the North has proceeded on the assumption that there is no defect or irregularity in human nature and human affairs that cannot be remedied by the application of money, science, and socialistic legislation. Therefore, in reading Mr. Lewis's novel about Willie Stark we would inevitably feel that there was no defect in Willie Stark that could not be remedied by a visit to a psychoanalyst or an amendment to the United States Constitution. But it is quite different in the novel that Mr. Warren has written about Willie Stark. We are there confronted with the ancient problem of evil and its manifestations. We must contemplate the imperfection of man, for whatever it is worth of good and bad. For Willie Stark, for the Compsons of Faulkner's novels, for the characters bad or good of most serious Southern novels, there is no remedy in law or sociology, and no reward but the reward of virtue and the hope of heaven.

The point of this discourse is a difficult one. I hope, in seeking to bring it to your attention, that I have not overstated it. At any rate it is the point I would be most anxious to make at this time before any group of Southern writers.

In summation I would say: study your art, all you can. It is indispensable, and no opportunity should be lost to master it. But it is not really the gravest problem, since whatever can be studied can surely be learned. The gravest problem is how and where to apply the art, once it is learned. No textbook, no school, no writers' conference can solve that problem for you. You only can solve it. To solve it you must become aware of the difference between what you think you know, and what you really know. The latter, what you really know, in your bones as much as in your brain, is what I mean by "knowledge carried to the heart." Only that will lead you to your real subject and release you from the false knowledge that brings imitation, subservience, and distortion.

For you as Southern writers that great problem—the problem of discovering your real subject—is easier to solve than if you were Northern writers. But even for Southern writers it is more difficult than it was thirty years ago. The regime of false knowledge has invaded us and threatens still heavier invasions. Therefore, as writers, we have not only a private interest to defend but also a public duty to perform. What that duty is I surely do not need to say, this morning in the State of Mississippi, which in 1948 cast its electoral vote for Thurmond and Wright. I trust you will understand that I have been attempting to define not only a principle of literature but also a principle of life. Out of the knowledge carried to the heart let us defend it, as the true source of virtue and liberty.

II

CHRISTOPHER FRY AND
THE REDEMPTION OF JOY [1]

By MONROE K. SPEARS

(Associate Professor of English)

That same laughter, madam, is an irrelevancy
Which almost amounts to revelation.
—Thomas Mendip, in *The Lady's Not for Burning*

VERSE drama seems now the one hope of regaining any large audience for poetry and the most promising source of new inspiration for the theater. Christopher Fry appears well equipped to restore this long-moribund art to flourishing health and popular favor, for he is prodigally talented: a genuine poet, with a true sense of comedy, an authentic theatrical craft, and abounding vigor and energy. If the revival is to be permanent, however, we must not let our eagerness to welcome again a thriving poetic drama betray us into failure to perceive exactly what we are being offered. For Mr. Fry has serious weaknesses, which are not to be explained by either youth or inexperience. Because of his recent rise to fame, we tend naturally to think of Mr. Fry as a young poet; but he is actually forty-three—the same age as W. H. Auden—and his first play was produced in 1935. If he goes on developing, he may become a great comic dramatist; but his promise is less likely to be realized if critics and audiences ignore his faults or admire him for the wrong reasons. I wish, therefore, to render him grateful tribute by taking his work seriously and examining it closely.

Mr. Fry himself has described the nature and intention of his comedies. They are a protest against "the domestication of the enormous miracle," against the false god of reality as seen by "the dull eye of custom." [2] Comedy, he says, affirms instead the true and joyous reality; it is "an escape, not from truth but from despair: a narrow escape into faith." The comic faith is based not upon naïve optimism, but upon the perception

---

1. This article first appeared in *Poetry* (Chicago), April, 1951 (LXXVIII, 28-43), and is reprinted by kind permission of the editor.
2. As quoted by William Arrowsmith in his excellent essay on Fry, *Hudson Review*, III (1950), 203-216.

that there is an angle of experience where the dark is distilled into light: either here or hereafter, in or out of time: where our tragic fate finds itself with perfect pitch, and goes straight to the key which creation was composed in. And comedy senses and reaches out to this experience. It says, in effect, that, groaning as we may be, we move in the figure of a dance, and, so moving, we trace the outline of the mystery.

In the experience of tragedy we strive against the conditions of our animal life; in the intuition of comedy we laugh at them, knowing that man is essential spirit. Mr. Fry comments that he always thinks of his plays first as tragedies; if "the characters were not qualified for tragedy there would be no comedy, and to some extent I have to cross the one before I can light on the other." To cross the precarious bridge from tragedy to comedy, the characters

> have to unmortify themselves: to affirm life and assimilate death and persevere in joy. Their hearts must be as determined as the phoenix; what burns must also light and renew: not by a vulnerable optimism but by a hard-won maturity of delight, by the intuition of comedy, an active patience declaring the solvency of good.

Whether or not comedy is greater than tragedy, it is, Mr. Fry believes, of special value in times like the present, when

> the loudest faith has been faith in a trampling materialism, when literature has been thought unrealistic which did not mark and remark our poverty and doom. Joy (of a kind) has been all on the devil's side, and one of the necessities of our time is to redeem it.

For laughter "is a truth, not a fantasy, a truth voluble of good which comedy stoutly maintains." [3]

This definition is the reverse of the traditional concept of comedy as ridicule of vices and follies, upholding the civilized norm against the individual's wilful departures from it (egoism, eccentricity, affectation, hypocrisy). The debasement of this traditional theme into ridicule of virtue and idealism as against cynical "realism" and worldly materialism seems to be Mr. Fry's specific target. In contrast, he wishes to make custom, convention, common sense, worldly wisdom ridiculous, to redeem joy from these low companions and associate it with the spiritual and idealistic. This purpose must be applauded by all who are on the side of the angels; but it involves grave difficulties and dangers. The theme cannot well be embodied

---

3. The preceding quotations are all from Mr. Fry's essay, "Comedy," *Adelphi* (London), November, 1950 (Vol. 27, pp. 27-29).

on the level of reality on which comedy normally operates; one must go not only "beyond tragedy" but "beyond comedy" to attain a cosmic or mystical perspective. If the conditions of our animal life are not taken seriously enough, one has *fantasy* rather than comedy. The danger is, also, that the mockery of worldly wisdom will misfire, that the cosmic joy which is the norm will become merely naïve by mundane standards. This comedy which has ceased to be "critical" in order to be "free" may become too free; it may go not only beyond tragedy and comedy but beyond human life; in attempting to be affirmative rather than, as comedy traditionally is, negative and concerned with man's limitations, it may go so far beyond the realm of good and evil that it either falsifies reality or appeals to no standards that are generally acceptable. Romantic admiration for "strangeness and wonder," sentimental denial of the existence of evil, are not what Mr. Fry means; but they are perilously close to it.

The great problem, then, is to embody this admirable theme in an adequate dramatic and poetic structure, so that the higher innocence does not appear sentimental or ingenuous, so that the higher comedy does not transcend the stage. The easiest way to express the theme is to write a play dealing with literal miracles; and three of Mr. Fry's four one-act plays do exactly this. *Boy with a Cart,* produced in 1938 by a group of Sussex villagers, is a pageant-play celebrating the founding of a church by Cuthman, Saint of Sussex. The peasants' simple faith in the "joint action of root and sky, of man/ And God" triumphs; the Saint and his followers are helped and the villains (practical, matter-of-fact people) who attempt to interfere are foiled, by miracle. Mr. Fry uses a Chorus—the first and only time he has done so—and his verse is obviously derivative, reminiscent sometimes of Eliot and sometimes of Auden ("Is God still in the air/ Now that the sun is down?/ They are afraid in the city,/ Sleepless in the town,/ Cold on the roads,/ Desperate by the river,/ Can faith for long elude/ Prevailing fever?"). The technique is simple and unpretentious, largely that of the medieval mysteries, with no attempt to be dramatic in the modern sense. There is some amusing dialogue between the Saint and the practical people, and broad humor in some of the miracles; but the play is primarily an attempt to express the simple faith of medieval peasants and hagiographers, and as such is pleasantly successful.

The Firstborn (1946), Mr. Fry's one tragedy, is a remarkable rendering of a Biblical miracle in vivid and plausible modern terms. The theme—bearing out Mr. Fry's remarks about the narrow bridge between tragedy and comedy, which this play has not crossed—is exactly the same as that of the comedies; it is here embodied in the conflict between Pharaoh, slave to everyday, common-sense, practical "reality" and Moses, representing the plane of miraculous true reality, and instrument of a God who transcends human reason. Moses states the theme explicitly:

> Can you comprehend
> That we're sometimes hoisted by the unbelievable
> On to the shoulders of truth? Our custom is
> To live backward of reality. When it turns its face
> How can it be recognized? But a refusal
> Of recognition is like a cancellation
> Of our existence. Do you deny voice
> To that power, the whirler of suns and moons, when even
> Dust can speak, as it does in Moses now?
> ... Tonight, at midnight,
> God will unfasten the hawk of death from his
> Grave wrist, to let it take our world ...

The conflict, however, attains little dramatic tension because Mr. Fry seems to be unable to make either Pharaoh or the attitude he represents plausible or convincing; thus he never becomes an antagonist to be taken seriously. Another disadvantage is probably unavoidable in the use of such material: in a play involving the direct intervention of an omnipotent God, and in which the outcome is scripturally recorded, there can be no suspense. This handicap Mr. Fry attempts to overcome by inventing minor characters to complicate the action, the most notable being Ramases, Pharaoh's firstborn but an admirer of Moses, and Shendi, Moses' nephew who goes over to the Egyptians. But the dramatic climax, when Moses attempts to save Ramases from the Angel of Death, seems implausible and almost silly in literal terms, because there is no possible way he can be saved from this supernatural doom. His death, however, illustrates the tragic theme of the intertwining of evil with good, the apparently wasteful destruction of good together with evil; of, in short, the mystery of evil. Moses says: "I do not know why the necessity of God/Should feed on grief; but it seems so"; and then asserts his faith in ultimate goodness: "But what does eternity bear witness to/ If not at last to hope?" Some tragic pathos is achieved by representing Phipa, Ramases' beautiful young bride-to-be, as literally rac-

21

rng the Angel of Death to Ramases' side; but the effect seems rather contrived, though it suggests symbolic relations between Love and Death which Mr. Fry explores in other plays. None of the characters except Moses, however, is really developed or attains any tragic stature.

Thor, with Angels (1948) is the most successful of these one-act miracle plays. It is the only work in which Mr. Fry's perennial theme, the conflict of the two realities, is put into specific and well-developed Christian terms; and this, together with the fact that the miracles involved were invented by Mr. Fry, is certainly one reason for its effectiveness. Though the action takes place in Kent in 596, the year of Augustine's restoration of Christianity to Britain, the play, dealing with the conflict between paganism and Christianity, is essentially a translation of the Nativity theme into British terms. Cymen, a Jutish chieftain, is the central character, and the play presents his progress from vague discontent with paganism to puzzled interest in the new dispensation to complete acceptance of Christianity once he has heard its gospel from Augustine. In a battle with the Saxons, he and his clan have taken prisoner Hoel, a British Celt, and a baptized Christian though he has half forgotten his religion. Receiving supernatural premonitions of the impending arrival of Christianity, Cymen spares Hoel's life, partly because of the dimly-apprehended message of these manifestations and partly because he suspects Hoel to be somehow their instrument. He is driven finally to overturn the pagan altars. To propitiate their angry gods for Cymen's apostasy, his clan wish to kill Hoel as a sacrifice, and, ironically, achieve their aim while Cymen is attending the council at which he hears Augustine's account of the Christian Revelation. Before his death, Hoel has fallen in love with Martina, Cymen's daughter; the only function served by this love affair is to introduce some pathos at Hoel's murder. Merlin is dug up from his charmed sleep, and wanders through the play doing some rather unnecessary prophecy and vaguely discussing a curious mixture of Druid nature-worship and Christianity. Colgrin, the steward, and his wife Anna provide some pretty elementary humor. Cymen, however, is the only character who is developed; Hoel and Martina are no more than standard young lovers, and the others are negligible.

There is an explicit parallel between the Crucifixion, completing the first Revelation of Christianity, and this second coming to equally perplexed and despairing pagans; it is made obvious by having Hoel, messenger unawares of the second coming, crucified and thrust with a spear like Christ. Mr. Fry presents admirably the contrast between the pagan and Christian attitudes, and the sense of a new dispensation, of new and hopeful answers to old questions, brought by Christianity. Thus Cymen reports the Christian message in a magnificent speech:

> I have seen our terrible gods come down
> To beg the crumbs which fall from our sins, their only
> Means of life . . . I have heard
> Word of his [Hoel's] God, and felt our lonely flesh
> Welcome to creation. The fearful silence
> Became the silence of great sympathy,
> The quiet of God and man in the mutual word.
> And never again need we sacrifice, on and on
> And on, greedy of the gods' goodwill
> But always uncertain; for sacrifice
> Can only perfectly be made by God
> And sacrifice has so been made, by God
> To God in the body of God with man,
> On a tree set up at the four crossing roads
> Of earth, heaven, time, and eternity
> Which meet upon that cross.

He asks the dead Hoel's forgiveness for the "sorrow of the world"; when Martina protests that he has not made the sorrow, he replies:

> All make all:
> For while I leave one muscle of my strength
> Undisturbed, or hug one coin of ease
> Or private peace while the huge debt of pain
> Mounts over all the earth,
> Or, fearing for myself, take half a stride
> Where I could leap; while any hour remains
> Indifferent, I have no right or reason
> To raise a cry against this blundering cruelty
> Of man.

And he prays for courage "To live by rule of God, which is forgiveness,/ Mercy, and compassion"; "God give us courage to exist in God."

In contrast to the other one-act plays, *A Phoenix too Frequent* (1946) is a comedy and does not deal with miracles nor with any religious theme. It is Mr. Fry's neatest, best-constructed, and most closely unified play, and perhaps also his funniest. Taking the old story of the Ephesian matron, traditionally (as in Petronius and

Burton) a satire on woman's lust and fickleness, Mr. Fry turns it into an affirmation of life and joy. Adding nothing to the plot as it has come down to him, he makes it support his theme by a few bold and simple strokes in characterization. Thus Dynamene's dead husband, Virilius, is made the villain ("He made the world succumb/ To his daily revolution of habit"; his was "the cautious voice which made/ Balance-sheets sound like Homer and Homer sound/ Like balance-sheets"). Tegeus, the soldier—his profession is the occasion for a good deal of topical military humor—is redeemed from misanthropy and despair of the world by admiration for Dynamene's idealism; he then persuades her, through argument and love, to give up her resolution to die; finally, she saves him from suicide through sacrificing her dead husband's body. The ironies are neat and symmetrical: her perfection of purpose revives his faith in human nature and desire to live; his love makes her give up her perfection of purpose; he converts her so completely that she volunteers to negate her former faith completely (to his shocked surprise) so that they may live and love. Thus the love-phoenix rises from its ashes; cosmic laughter affirms joy. Doto is a good comic character, in the long tradition of earthy, practical, somewhat lecherous maids (e.g., Desdemona's and Juliet's). There are no pseudo-profundities; the theme is embodied not only in the persuasions to joy and against death of both characters (at different times), but in the basic irony of the situation as Mr. Fry presents it: what is, seen from the outside, merely a bawdy and cynical demonstration of woman's fickleness, is, seen from the inside, an affirmation of joy and life:

> What appears
> Is so unlike what is. And what is madness
> To those who only observe, is often wisdom
> To those to whom it happens.

And again, as Tegeus exclaims over the revelation of love: "Can we be made of dust, as they tell us?/ What! dust with dust releasing such a light/ And such an apparition of the world/ Within one body?" The steady shift in the respective attitudes of Dynamene and Tegeus is produced wittily and plausibly, and the climax, Dynamene's falling in love and abandoning her purpose, effectively handled. The verse is restrained and light in tone, and the natural symbols—love burgeoning in the tomb, the love-phoenix rising from its ashes, the new husband living through the sacrifice of the dead

husband's body, the search for death that ends in love, and so on—
are grounded in the situation and plot. The play is limited in scope;
its structure is simple, artificial, symmetrical; in its formal opposition,
balancing, and counterpointing of attitudes and gestures it is like
ballet. Perhaps the secret of its success lies in the acceptance of these
limitations instead of striving after profundities.

The Lady's Not for Burning (1948), Mr. Fry's first three-act
comedy, and the one which established his popular reputation in both
England and this country, is excellent "theater" and a very entertaining play. It seems to me, however, to stand up least well of all
the plays under close examination, and to exemplify all Mr. Fry's
worst tendencies. The plot is, as others have pointed out, extremely
slight. In the first act, Jennet, seeking refuge from a witch-hunt,
and Thomas, seeking to be hanged, appeal to Tyson and Tappercoom
(respectively mayor and justice); by the end of the act they have
begun to fall in love. In the subplot, Richard and Nicholas are rivals
for the love of Alizon, engaged to Humphrey. Act Two begins after
Thomas and Jennet have been tortured fruitlessly; Tappercoom and
Tyson bring them together and eavesdrop on their conversation, taking Jennet's declaration of love as evidence of her allegiance to the
Devil, and therefore of witchcraft. Their sentence is that Jennet must
be burned, and (at the Chaplain's suggestion) that Thomas, to cure
his misanthropy, must join in the festivities (celebrating the approaching marriage of Alizon and Humphrey) that evening. Thomas
agrees only on condition that Jennet attend too, and this is permitted.
The third act takes place that night: Humphrey tries, unsuccessfully,
to seduce Jennet by offering freedom; Richard and Alizon elope, but
return bringing old Skipps, whom Thomas claims to have killed and
whom Jennet is supposed to have transformed into a dog. Since this
destroys the main evidence against them both, Tappercoom lets them
go, and the lovers happily depart. Thomas is presumably intended
to be deliberately theatrical, and Gielgud plays him with a fine flamboyance; the trouble is that he talks so much, and without any
rational motivation for his attitude, that he becomes extremely tire-
some. True, his desire to be hanged is his device to divert attention
from the witch-hunt; but his attitude must be taken seriously if the
movement of ideas in the play is to be coherent. He is not a prey to
custom and commonsense, a victim of material "reality," for he
converts Jennet from this point of view; and though, in Mr. Fry's

usual method of reversal, he is temporarily influenced by her attitude in the latter part of the play, he rejects it. In any case, if his attitude was ever genuine, the events of the plot do nothing to solve his problem. One can only regard him (as Jennet seems to do) as a temporarily disillusioned idealist, exaggerating his disillusion for a practical purpose. Jennet, at the beginning, "believes in the human mind," and her rational and "scientific" view of reality is changed first by the witch-hunt and then by Thomas's love and arguments, so that toward the end of the play she can refuse to save her life on Humphrey's eminently practical terms.

The basic weakness of the play is that, in terms both of plot and theme, there is no real conflict. Tappercoom and Tyson are pure caricatures. Tyson says: "The standard soul/ Must mercilessly be maintained"; "I consider it unwise/ To tempt providence with humor"; Tappercoom: "Religion/ Has made an honest woman of the supernatural/ And we won't have it kicking over the traces again." Mr. Fry simply cannot take these sensible, practical people seriously enough to make them plausible. (Nor, when he needs for thematic purposes a despairing character to be redeemed, like Tegeus or Thomas, can he make the despair or disillusion very convincing.) It is perfectly obvious that nobody is going to be hanged or burned; the problem exists purely in the realm of ideas, and when the lovers have straightened out their philosophical difficulties, the practical obstacles simply melt away. The minor characters are pretty flimsy: Richard is a male Cinderella, and his love affair with the innocent Alizon is there only to counterpoint Thomas and Jennet. Nicholas is the well-intentioned ineffective youth, contrasting with his brother Humphrey, a loutish, hard-headed, and rather likable villain; Margaret is a standard scatterbrained but desperately practical mother. The wonderful exception is the Chaplain (played magnificently in both London and New York by Eliot Makeham). He is the norm, the key to the theme, and perhaps Mr. Fry's most successful single embodiment of it. His real love is music, and he is somewhat uncomfortable in the world of dogmatic theology, but even more so in the practical world; for him, life is a perpetual miracle, and everyday reality but dimly perceived:

> I know I am not
> A practical person; legal matters and so forth
> Are Greek to me, except, of course,

That I understand Greek. And what may seem nonsensical
To men of affairs like yourselves might not seem so
To me, since everything astonishes me,
Myself most of all. When I think of myself
I can scarcely believe my senses. But there it is,
All my friends tell me I actually exist
And by an act of faith I have come to believe them.

Ironically, it is he who suggests the plan (to redeem Thomas by inviting him to join the festivities) that the two practical men have been unable to think of.

Venus Observed (1950) is Mr. Fry's latest and most ambitious comedy, and the nearest to contemporary life. All the other plays are definitely costume pieces, set in remote times: *The Firstborn* in Egypt, 1200 B.C.; *Phoenix* in Ephesus before the arrival of Christianity; *Thor* in A.D. 596; *Boy* in later medieval England; and *Lady* in 1400. In *Venus,* though the time is not specified, the whole atmosphere—the eccentric Duke, dabbling in science, the feudal retainers and mistresses—puts it back into the not-too-recent past. The historical settings are not merely pegs on which to hang costumes, but are genuinely significant; for each play embodies the spiritual climate of a historical period. Thus *Firstborn* embodies the Old Testament sense of power and mystery; *Pheonix* pagan joy in life; *Thor* the Nativity sense of Christianity's new spiritual order; *Boy* the innocent faith of medieval peasants and hagiographers; *Lady* the turbulent springtime of the Renaissance; and *Venus* the autumnal mood of our decaying civilization. Presumably Mr. Fry feels that distance in time is necessary to induce in his audiences the suspension of disbelief which his theme demands. The disadvantage is that the historical settings permit him to avoid the obligation of expressing his theme through a mature interpretation of contemporary life; they enable him to attain popular success without facing up to the real problems of verse drama in our times. For I suspect strongly that this popular success is based partly upon temporary and non-literary factors, and partly upon his faults—as witnessed by the enormous success of *Lady,* which I believe to be his worst play. The costumes and historical setting, the exuberance and color of the verse, and the hopeful theme provide a means of respectable escape from our particularly depressing present. Because of these factors, the audiences are highly conscious that they are seeing "poetic" drama; they bring to his plays not the frame of reference, the expectations, that they would normally bring to contemporary drama; but those that they would bring to a revival of Shakespeare. Thus Mr. Fry is encouraged to employ—especially in *Lady*—conventions which are not those of the contemporary stage—Elizabethan wit-combats, bombast, passages of exuberant invective and word-play—and the audiences laugh at them indulgently, as they would in Shakespeare. Thus, with this historical and self-consciously "literary" frame of reference, Mr. Fry can get by with surface effects that are theatrical rather than dramatic, can get cheap laughs from having medieval people speak like moderns. (A character in *Lady* exclaims *"Sanctus fumus!";* another exchange is: "Who the hell's that?" "The man about the gallows"; again: "I'm sorry to interrupt/ But there's a witch to see you, uncle.") This is pure stage stuff, at best momentarily amusing, at worst extremely irritating. More serious, he can, since the audience's attention is directed to these externals, get by with lyric statements of his theme instead of embodying it in an adequate structure. This trait is at its worst in *Lady*. True, this is an April afternoon and evening in about 1400, and the flamboyance and excess of the language express the mood of the budding Renaissance; but the language is full of pseudo-Elizabethan rodomontade and bombast, all the characters talking a great deal while the plot stands still. In this play particularly, much of the humor depends upon Mr. Fry's failure to make the verse functional, upon a "poetic" or bombastic passage deflated by an ironic or prosaic rejoinder. This seems to me ultimately a rather cheap effect, like the device of travestying the period by making the characters speak startlingly modern; particularly when the effect is without significance, implying no criticism of either term of the contrast.

Venus (to return from this digression) is a much better play, and certainly his best three-act comedy. Though it is, as I have said, Mr. Fry's nearest approach to contemporary life, it is removed from the level of literal reality to the plane of high fantasy not only by a certain distancing in time but primarily by the most elaborate symbolism Mr. Fry has yet employed; the play is, in fact, certainly an experiment in symbolism. The time is autumn, the mellowing season of approaching dissolution for nature, for the Duke, and for our civilization; but the constant symbol of the phoenix rising again from its ashes presages the rebirth of nature as it embodies the purification of the Duke's affections and perhaps prophesies hope for

28

civilization in its ordeal. The phoenix-symbol is suggested by the eclipse of the sun which takes place in the first act; and the time is Halloween, when ghosts (in this case, of former loves) appear and when girls see their future husbands in mirrors. The scenes are the observatory, with its telescope which is both a phallic symbol and a symbol of the Duke's detachment, and the decaying Temple of the Ancient Virtues, an obvious symbol of our moral situation. The Duke, deciding to marry again, asks his son Edgar to play Paris, choosing among the three former mistresses (vaguely paralleling Juno, Minerva, Venus) he has invited back to see the eclipse. Rosabel, Edgar's first choice, refuses to enter into the spirit of things and bitterly criticizes the Duke's heartlessness; she makes the game go sour. Meanwhile Dominic, son of Reedbeck, the Duke's agent, confronts his father with his discovery that for years he has been thieving from his employer, thereby momentarily disturbing Reedbeck's joy over the imminent arrival of his daughter Perpetua from America. When Perpetua arrives, like "Venus from the sea," both Edgar and the Duke fall in love with her immediately; but when the Duke offers her the symbolic apple, she shatters it with her little pistol, explaining that she has belonged to an association for the destruction of ugly and harmful objects. In the second act Perpetua, acting upon Dominic's suggestion that she marry the Duke so that he will not expose their father, consents to meet the Duke in the observatory that evening. In a symbolic archery match, the rivalry of Edgar and the Duke over Perpetua becomes explicit. Meanwhile Rosabel, assured that no one will be in the observatory that night, plans to burn it down to destroy the Duke's detachment ("He has to be touched by fire/ To make a human of him, and only a woman/ Who loves him can dare to do it.") The second scene presents Perpetua and the Duke in the observatory that night; she wounds his egoism by revealing, after finding that he knows about Reedbeck and about her plan, that she loves Edgar. But when it appears that they are both going to die in the fire that blazes up, they stage a passionate love scene. They are saved, however, by the butler and footman in symbolic ways that I shall explain shortly. Act Three takes place an hour later. Rosabel confesses to the Duke; Perpetua explains that she does not really love him, in spite of her profession in the flames; Reedbeck tries to confess, but the Duke refuses to hear him. The Duke forgives everybody, except Dominic, who has encouraged

Rosabel to give herself up to the police. Perpetua, now mature enough to be aware of the problem of freedom ("What is *my* freedom becomes/ Another person's compulsion. What are we to make/ Of this dilemma?"), and Edgar, now sure that he is a person in his own right and not a mere postscript to his father, are happily united. The Duke, purified by fire, plans to marry Rosabel when she is released from prison.

The central concern of the play, the realization by the Duke of the folly of his egoism and isolation, is closer to the traditional comic mode than any of the other plays. These qualities, as I have said, are symbolized by his observatory (formerly the scene of his amorous experiments). Rosabel says:

> You sit up here all night
> Looking at the stars, travelling farther and farther
> Away from living people. I hate your telescope!
> How can you know, and what, if you knew, can it mean,
> What can the darkest bruise on the human mind
> Mean, when nothing beats against you heavier
> Than a fall of rain? And out you whip
> Your impervious umbrella of satisfaction!
> How you prink across every puddle, and laugh
> To think that other men can drown.

And she comments that "What goes on in other hearts than your own" is "as remote to you as a seaside lodging-house/ To a passing whale." Hence, he confesses to Perpetua, he has been lonely in spite of his mistresses; "Saturn is alone, for all their circling round him," and observing Venus has not helped. When Perpetua rejects his love, he says: "So there's to be/ No climax and adorable close/ With ego agonistes crowned and smiling?" The symbolic flames of the burning observatory destroy his isolation ("the lost world of walls and stairs,/ Where I could cosset ghosts for their melancholy/ Charm, has let the daylight into me") through love for Perpetua, he thinks at first; but this last illusion is removed: the "babe born in the fire," the Phoenix, is not merely sexual love again, but forgiveness and selfless love. In his long final soliloquy to the drowsing Reedbeck (who counterpoints by recalling the love life of Louis XIV, another ego agonistes), he describes his reconcilement to age, his acceptance of his limitations, and his plan to marry Rosabel, for her sake, not his.

Thus the play observes Venus, and her limitations (I cannot discover any significance in the apparent pun on *Venice Preserv'd,* except ironic contrast). But the moral concepts are not as orthodox as this might suggest. Dominic, the villain, is one whose errors consist, theologically, in thinking more of the sin than of the sinner, and practically, in upholding secular justice: he tries to make Reedbeck conscious of sin (an effort strongly disapproved by all the other characters) in stealing from the Duke, suggests to Perpetua that she marry the Duke to protect her father, and encourages Rosabel to confess her arsonous exploit to the police. But even he is sorry for his actions, and says, sighing, "Ethics are very difficult." In contrast, the Duke's indulgence to human frailty has led him not only to condone Reedbeck's thefts, but to employ Bates, a former burglar, and Reddleman, a former lion tamer who lost his nerve in the war, as footman and butler respectively. It is through Bates's professional facility with ladders and Reddleman's ability to face the flames (he has regained his nerve, and sees them as symbolic lions) that he is saved from the fire. The contrast, presumably, is between Divine and Human justice, illustrating the superiority of Christian love which supersedes the Law. But the theme skates perilously close to the thin line dividing it from a merely sentimental assertion of human goodness and denial of the existence of evil such as one finds in, for example, Saroyan. Mr. Fry's attitude is, in fact, sometimes indistinguishable from Saroyan's pseudo-mystical belief in the goodness of all life and all people, and similar tendencies to formless fantasy, idiosyncrasy of style, and reliance on theatrical effects are exhibited in their extreme form in Saroyan.

Mr. Fry is better at dramatic verse than any recent writer except Eliot: his language is alive and contemporary, heightened into genuine poetry, and usually well calculated for speaking. It is infinitely superior to that of, for example, Maxwell Anderson. But it is not functional; it is frankly lyric and self-conscious, existing for its own sake, and this failure of the verse is one of the main sources of humor (it is, of course, a form of Romantic Irony). As others have pointed out, all the characters in all the plays speak very much alike; the style is self-consciously "literary," and marred by schoolboyish puns, meaningless word-play and whimsy, and allusive academic humor. *Ring Round the Moon* (1950), Mr. Fry's translation of

Anouilh's *L'Invitation au Chateau,* is in interesting contrast to most of his original work. Called "A Charade with Music," it is explicit fantasy, though no more so than *Venus.* In neatness of construction, unity of tone, deftness and restraint of language, it surpasses his own plays. Most important, it works within well-defined limitations and is not overambitious, pretending to no profound meaning; and this is a lesson Mr. Fry needs to learn. Of all Mr. Fry's plays, only *Phoenix* and perhaps *Thor* are structurally adequate. Both the three-act plays give the feeling that they are essentially one-acters padded out; this is particularly true of *Venus,* where the first act, with its modern Judgment of Paris, is a complete little play in itself, and rather thinly connected to the rest of the piece. If plot is the soul of drama, Mr. Fry's plays are of doubtful immortality.

The Chaplain in *Lady* says:

> I wish I were a thinking man, very much.
> Of course I feel a good deal, but that's no help to you.

And this I take to be the central weakness of Mr. Fry's work: a Romanticism manifested in a kind of ingenuous immaturity, in a refusal to accept limitations and restraint, and in an unwillingness to subordinate himself to his dramatic medium. This weakness appears when *Venus* or *Lady* is compared with Mr. Eliot's *Cocktail Party.* Mr. Fry's plays are, on the surface, more attractive: the language is gayer and more colorful, the action livelier, and there are the historical setting and costumes. But his verse lacks the flexibility and range, the metrical ingenuity and complex music (Mr. Fry's pattern is essentially very irregular blank verse) of Mr. Eliot's. *The Cocktail Party* stands on its own feet as drama without any special concessions and without violating contemporary stage-conventions, and this strategy seems to me far more promising for poetic drama than Mr. Fry's. (If the report is true that he is now working on a play about Henry II for Olivier, it appears that he has no intention of changing his convention.) *The Cocktail Party,* too, transcends and in a sense reverses the normal comic theme; but it is grounded firmly in contemporary life, and arrives at the transcendence and the reversal through exploring, not by-passing, the plane of everyday reality. As I have suggested, Mr. Fry is unable to take practical, commonsense reality seriously, even in order to rise above it; hence his plays are essentially fantasy, not comedy, and therefore thematically superficial in that the triumph is asserted, not earned, and structurally deficient in that there is no adequate sense of conflict. So far, Mr. Fry has not so much redeemed joy as simply affirmed it. If he can fully live up to his own statement of intentions, we may again have comedy that is both great and popular.

III

SIR EDWARD COKE: ADVOCATE OF
THE SUPREMACY OF LAW
(1552-1634)

By SAMUEL ENOCH STUMPF
(*Associate Professor of Ethics*)

IN the politically turbulent period of early seventeenth century
England, when ecclesiastical, monarchical and common law principles vied with each other for ultimate political authority, the greatest advocate of the doctrine of the supremacy of law was Sir Edward
Coke. When he was Lord Chief Justice of England, Coke was involved in an episode with King James I and the Archbishop of
Canterbury which raised poignantly the fundamental problems he
had to face in advocating this doctrine. A complaint had been received by James I from the Archbishop concerning an action taken
by the Court of Common Pleas, and on the 10th of November, 1612,
the king sent for the judges of England to discuss the issues involved
in this complaint.

The facts seem to be that the Court of High Commission (an
ecclesiastical court) had gone beyond its prescribed jurisdiction. Instead of limiting itself to the regulation of ecclesiastical matters, the
purpose for which it was specially set up, it began to deal with matters of a non-ecclesiastical nature involving persons not among the
clergy. The issue arose when the High Commission sought to arrest
a lay person on a complaint charging him with a temporal offense.
The Court of Common Pleas (a civil court), chiefly through the
instrumentality of Sir Edward Coke, stopped the Court of High
Commission in this action. As one of the most vigorous advocates
of the supremacy of the common law, Coke moved quickly to limit
the power of the High Commission, for the reasons that it was not
one of the traditional common law courts, it did not proceed according to fixed rules and its decisions were not subject to appeal. This
application of the supremacy of law whereby the Court of Common
Pleas was supreme over the Court of High Commission led the
Archbishop to propose to James I that as king he had the power to
remove the causes from the judges and decide them himself. The

Archbishop reasoned that since the king had delegated part of his power to the judges, he could take back this power whenever he wished to exercise it himself, for this was a legitimate expression of the royal prerogative. It was James's purpose in calling this Sunday morning conference to present to the judges this conception of his powers and to get their reactions to it.

Replying on behalf of the judges, Coke argued that according to the law of England all civil and criminal causes had to be tried in a court of justice in accordance with English law and custom. When James replied that law is simply a matter of reason and that he had as great a capacity to reason as the judges, Coke answered that though this was partly true, legal reasoning was a special art achieved through special training in the laws of the Realm, a training which the king did not have. To James, Coke's line of reasoning was treasonable for it would clearly place the law above the king.[1] Nevertheless, the victory lay with Coke, for it was later admitted that "the principal feather was plucked from the High Commission, and nothing remaining but stumps, and [they were no longer to] meddle with matters of importance, but with pettit crimes."[2] As a matter of fact, this court soon lost its popularity and power, and by an act of 1641 it was finally abolished, "being . . . a court by which the King's subjects sustained 'great and insufferable wrongs and oppression.'"[3]

This episode points up the dual nature of the problem of the supremacy of law as Coke understood this doctrine, for it indicates how the supreme position of law was challenged both by the subtle encroachments of the ecclesiastical courts and by the king's claim to unlimited royal prerogative. In order to establish the supremacy of law, therefore, it was necessary to limit the political authority of the Church and the king.

While Coke sought to limit the power of the church courts and of the king, his advocacy of the doctrine of the supremacy of law curiously involved him in a strong defense of the authority of the ecclesiastical courts and the Crown. But English ecclesiastical courts, it must be remembered, were frequently in conflict with other ec-

---

1. Roscoe Pound reports this incident in *The Spirit of the Common Law* (Boston: 1925), pp. 60-61. Usher gives the date of this Conference as 1608. Cf. T. F. T. Plucknett, *A Concise History of the Common Law* (3rd ed.; London: 1940), p. 49.
2. C. W. Johnson, *The Life of Sir Edward Coke* (2nd ed.; London, 1845), I, 235.
3. *Ibid.*, pp. 235-236.

clesiastical courts. Historically there were political considerations which led to the development of the doctrine that the ecclesiastical courts of the Church of England were independent of any other ecclesiastical courts. This doctrine was based upon the supporting notion that the ecclesiastical courts of the Realm derived their power from the King, who, it was held, was not subject to any other foreign powers. In his work on Ecclesiastical Law, Coke writes of "absolute" princes, a term which meant to him that the princes of England were independent or set free (*absolutus*) from Rome or any other foreign power. [4] He did not mean that the prince was absolute *within* the realm in the sense that he was not subject to its laws; Coke's famous debates with James I make this point abundantly clear. But, in order to prove England's independence of papal power by establishing the fact of the supremacy of the ecclesiastical courts of the Church of England over the courts of Rome, Coke asserted that the King is absolute and that he attains this status by heredity. This problem was political, not religious; thus, Coke says that "the Jesuits and Priests were not condemned and executed for their Priesthood and Profession, but for their treasonable and damnable Persuasions against the Crowns and dignities of Monarchs and Absolute Princes." [5] It was the opposition to the indirect power of the Pope which made the theory of Divine Right of Kings the gospel of the majority of English Protestants in the early 17th century. [6]

Coke cites the following cases, among others, which indicate how the notion of the absolute prince developed through the disputes concerning the jurisdiction of the different ecclesiastical courts. He writes first of a subject who, in the Reign of King Edward the First, brought in a Bull of Excommunication against another subject of the Realm and published it to the Lord Treasurer of England. By the ancient Common Law of England this was adjudged "Treason against the King, his Crown and Dignity; for which the offender

---

4. *England's Independency Upon Papal Power Historically and Judicially Stated,* by Sir John Davis (Attorney General of Ireland) and Sir Edward Coke (Lord Chief Justice of England). In Two *Reports,* Selected from their greater Volumes; for the convincing of our *English Romanists* and Confirming of those who are yet unperverted to the court or Church of *Rome.* With a preface written by Sir John Pettus, Knight (1674), p. 84.

5. *Ibid.*

6. *The Political Works of James I,* with an Introduction by C. H. McIlwain (Cambridge, Mass., 1918), p. xxv.

should have been drawn and hanged, but at the great instance of the Chancellor and Treasurer he was only abjured the Realm for ever." [7] In a similar case, Edward I presented his Clerk to a Benefice within the Province of York, but the Archbishop refused him on the ground that the Pope had by way of Provision conferred it upon another. Edward refused to recognize the Pope's move, whereupon the Archbishop pleaded that the Bishop of Rome had for a long time provided to that Church, as one having supreme authority in that case, and that he, the Archbishop, did not dare, nor had he the power, to put him out, which was the "Pope's Bull in Possession." "For which high contempt against the King, his Crown and Dignity in refusing to execute his Sovereign Commandment, fearing to do it against the Pope's Provision, by judgment of the Common Law the Lands of his whole Bishoprick were seized into the King's hands and lost during his life, which judgment was before any statute or Act of Parliament was made in that case." [8]

The Parliament did, however, in the Reign of Edward III, pass an act which dealt squarely with this matter. Coke writes that

> at a Parliament holden in the 25. year of King Edward the Third, (1353), it was enacted by consent of the whole parliament. That as well they that obtained Provisions from *Rome,* as they that put them in execution, should be out of the King's protection; and that a man might do with them as with the enemies of the king . . . By which law every man might kill such an offender as a common enemy against the King and his country, so hainous were such offenses holden.[9]

For these reasons it was later held, in the reign of Henry IV, that the Pope could not alter the Laws of England; Excommunication made by the Pope was of no force in England; neither was any Certificate of any Excommunication available in Law but that which was made by some Bishop of England; "for the Bishops are by the Common Laws the immediate officers and ministers of justice to the King's courts in Causes Ecclesiastical." [10]

In 1606, Robert Lalor, a priest, was indicted for having received a Bull purchased in the Court of Rome, which Bull concerned the King's Crown and Royall Dignity, containing a Commission of Authority from the Pope of Rome to Richard Brady and David Mag-

---

7. Sir John Davis and Sir Edward Coke, *op. cit.,* Coke's "Ecclesiastical Law," p. 51.
8. *Ibid.,* p. 51.
9. *Ibid.,* p. 56.
10. *Ibid.,* p. 63.

ragh to constitute a Vicar-general for the See of Rome, by the name of *See Apostolich,* in the several Dioceses of Dublin, Kildare, and Fernes within the Kingdom of Ireland. The specific charge against Lalor was that he exercised ecclesiastical jurisdiction as Vicar-general of the See of Rome, by instituting various persons to Benefices, by granting dispensations in matrimonial cases, and by doing "all other acts and things pertaining to Episcopal jurisdiction . . . against our sovereign Lord the King, his Crown and Dignity Royall, and in contempt of his Majesty." [11]

Sir John Davis writes that Lalor was indicted upon the Statute of 1392 (16 Richard II), which embodied the provisions of *Praemunire,* earlier found in the laws of Edward III. In commenting upon the reasons for the passage of this statute and similar ones which preceded it, Sir John writes that

> the causes that moved and almost enforced the English nation to make this, and other statutes of the same nature, were of the greatest importance that could possibly arise in any state. For these laws were made to uphold and maintain the Sovereignty of the King, the Liberty of the people, the Common Law, and the Commonweal, which otherwise would have been undermined and utterly ruined by the usurpation of the Bishop of *Rome.*[12]

These disputes are the historical antecedents of the issues which later arose during the time of Henry VIII. And it was out of the strife between the adherents and the opponents of Henry VIII's ecclesiastical policy that English political theory arose.[13] Later, in the time of Elizabeth, the political character of the Pope's activities was most clearly stated in the Bull, *Regnans in excelsis,* which was published February 25, 1570. Among other things, the Pope wrote on that occasion that

> We must make it known that said Elizabeth, and as many as stand on her side . . . have run into the danger of our curse: we make it also known, that we have deprived her from the right that she pretended to have in the Kingdom . . . and also from all and every her Authority, Dignity, and Privilege: we charge and forbid all and every the Nobles, Subjects and people . . . that they be not so hardy as to obey her, on her Admonitions or Laws, upon pain of the like curse upon them. . .[14]

It is clear, then, that Coke argued for the supremacy of the Eng-

---

11. Davis and Coke, *op. cit.,* Davis' section on "The Case of Praemunire," p. 5.
12. *Ibid.,* p. 6.
13. McIlwain, *op. cit.,* p. xx.
14. Davis and Coke, *op. cit.,* Coke's "Ecclesiastical Law," p. 77.

lish ecclesiastical courts because he saw the political danger of any other course. It was for precisely the same reason that, in turn, the ecclesiastical courts of the Realm were well subordinated to the Crown and their legitimate jurisdiction so carefully bounded. It could be no other way if peace was to be maintained. For religion and law both set up rules and sanctions regarding human actions. Even though these two sets of rules and sanctions deal with congruent areas in the lives of individuals, it must be remembered that they are drawn from different sources and have different motivating ends and for that reason law and religion are bound to have their own distinctive machinery for adjusting the relations between individuals. Indeed, it is *because* law and religion deal with congruent areas in the lives of individuals that the inevitability of conflict between the Church and State is always present. This explains the fact that the Canonical Law of England was subordinated to the civil law early in the history of the Realm. [15] And it was to avoid this conflict that Coke, in the Fourth Part of his *Institutes of the Laws of England,* set forth the rightful jurisdiction of the various types of ecclesiastical courts. There he made it quite clear what area the spiritual jurisdiction covers. The limits of the latter were bounded, as Coke saw the matter, by the Laws of the Realm. Furthermore, the clergy were never assembled or called together at a convocation but by the King's writ; "and they were often times commanded by the King's writ to deal with nothing that concerned the King's Laws of the Land, his Crown and Dignity, or his State, or the state of his council or Kingdom. . ." [16]

With this as a background to the relationship between the King, his law, and the Church, it is at once clear why there was such a great antagonism on the part of the crown toward the rising Presbyterians. For the latter, no less than the Papists, would seek ultimately to reduce the King and the government to the status of handmaids to the Church.[17] James was quite aware that the Presbyterians viewed life from the point of view of the duality of authority. It was in his presence as King of Scotland that Andrew Melville declared that "there are two kings and two kingdoms in Scotland, that

---

15. William Stubbs, "The Canon Law" in *Select Essays in Anglo-American Legal History* (Boston, 1907), I, 249 ff.
16. Sir Edward Coke, *The Institutes of the Laws of England* (6th ed., London, 1681), Part IV, pp. 321-322.
17. J. N. Figgis, *The Divine Right of Kings* (Cambridge, 1914), pp. 184 ff.

is, King James the head of the Commonwealth, and there is Christ Jesus the King of the Church, whose subject King James VI is, and of those Kingdom he is not a king, not a Lord, nor a head, but a member." [18] Such a doctrine was no less extreme than the theory of resistance developed by the Jesuits, so that in this connection the importance of the view that "new presbyter is but old priest writ large" can hardly be overestimated. The Works of Cartwright, says Figgis, were about as full as those of Bellarmine of claims for ecclesiastical supremacy over the civil government. Indeed, the function of the magistrate, according to Cartwright, was to persecute all "idolatry" just as Constantine persecuted in favor of orthodoxy; church government is to be the model of the civil state; the "discipline" is universal and the magistrate must maintain it as immutable; only the office bearers of the Church have liberty, and this liberty is to be used in the control of the state—for the individuals there is only the duty of obedience. [19] In addition to Cartwright there was John Knox, who declared in his *First Book of Discipline* that both rulers and ruled must be subject to the discipline, and those who disobeyed the superintendents or who profaned the Sacraments were to be punished. In short, the Presbyterian Church claimed civil supremacy.[20] Against such teachings, the theory of Divine Right was developed by the King and his supporters, and the consequent harsh treatment of the Presbyterians is understandable as a defense against a new tyranny.

Thus, the central issue of the early jurisdictional disputes between the King's courts and the courts of Rome was a question of political supremacy equally claimed by the Pope and the King. The political theory which evolved from these disputes became the weapon by which the Crown opposed the claim of the Presbyterians on grounds almost identical to those upon which the Papists were successfully resisted. But this is not to say that Coke allied himself with the King in opposition to the Puritans, as his discussion of the "absolute prince" might imply. To be sure, he had to defend the hereditary rights of the Crown against the political encroachments of foreign powers. But, when James I sought to interpret the term "absolute" by asserting an unlimited royal prerogative *within* the realm, the

18. McIlwain, *op. cit.,* pp. xxi-xxii.
19. Figgis, *op. cit.,* pp. 189-190.
20. *Ibid.,* pp. 191-194.

issue between him and Coke was joined. It was one thing to argue that England's ecclesiastical courts were independent of those of Rome because they were set up by a monarch who was independent of the Pope: but it was quite another thing to argue, as James did, that he had absolute authority in all cases within the Kingdom. It was against this point of view that Coke developed his notion of the supremacy of the law.

Coke challenged and rejected the notion of unlimited royal prerogative. His whole pattern of thought was based upon the presuppositions he regarded as embodied in Magna Charta, which instrument Coke raised to the height of greatest importance. He did not argue against the legitimate powers and authority of the Crown. Indeed, he saw his function as a judge to be simply the protection of the King and his subjects, but he felt that this was to be done on the basis of the law of the Realm. Nowhere is his acceptance of the superior power of the Crown more manifest than in his treatment of the cases of *Praemunire* which we have discussed above. But on the occasion of his election as speaker of the House of Commons in 1593, he addressed the Queen in the name of Commons at length about the critical condition of the Kingdom, then threatened by invasion, and about the designs of the Pope. However, he concluded his remarks with a claim for freedom of speech, freedom from arrest, and ready access to the person of the sovereign. [21] It was not in a belligerent attitude that Coke addressed these claims to the Queen, but rather with the feeling that certain freedoms were to be guaranteed to Englishmen under any circumstances, even when there were portents of danger to the Realm.

It becomes apparent that Coke was not opposed to the idea of the royal prerogative completely. He made this quite plain in his treatise on *Ecclesiastical Law* where he wrote that the Crown and absolute princes "hold their Kingdoms and Dominions by lawful succession, and by inherent Birth-right and decent of inheretance, (according to the fundamental laws of this Realm) immediately of Almighty God, and are not tenents of their Kingdoms (as the Jesuits would have it) at the will and pleasure of any foreign Potentate whatsoever." [22] Here Coke affirmed one of the most fundamental conceptions which buttressed the whole theory of inalienable sovereignty, namely, that

21. Johnson, *op. cit.,* Vol. 1, pp. 86 ff.
22. Davis and Coke, *op. cit.,* Coke's "Ecclesiastical Law," p. 84.

hereditary right is indefeasible.[23] This is the very idea that James himself emphasized so much and on the basis of which he claimed commensurate powers. Hereditary right complemented the Divine Right and that rendered the King unquestioned authority in the Realm.[24] This doctrine of hereditary right suggests traces of feudalism: but, as McIlwain points out, there is a significant feature of the feudal relation that is absent in the politics of James—there is no trace of the reciprocal duties of *dominus* and *homo* which were so characteristic in the medieval conception of English kingship. The latter is replaced by the Roman conception of a king *legibus solutus,* placed at a distance so far above his *subditi* that he can in no way be bound by earthly law to the performance of any duties to them.[25]

It is James's casual dismissal of "earthly law" that provides the clue to Coke's attitude toward the royal prerogative at the Sunday Morning Conference. The "fundamental law of the Realm" which Coke cited as the basis of James's hereditary right was the same law to which he referred in challenging James's power over the courts of law. Just as James derived his right to his throne "immediately of Almighty God," he likewise derived his hereditary right "according to the fundamental laws of the Realm", which meant that he was "under the law". This was Coke's historic achievement, namely, the establishment of the supremacy of common law, which led, as Pound says, to the turning of the feudal duties of the paramount lord toward his tenants into the legal duties of the king toward his subjects.[26]

There is a brief word to say about Coke's ideas of the powers of Parliament as these provide a further clue to his notion of the supremacy of law. One of his leading opinions involving the powers of parliament is found in the celebrated case of Dr. Bonham (1610). By an act of Parliament, power was given to the Royal College of Physicians to license doctors to practice. The Royal College was also given the power to punish those who practiced in violation of its rules. Dr. Bonham undertook to practice without a license and the College enjoined him. Bonham disregarded this injunction and was promptly cited for contempt and jailed. In the suit that followed, Bonham maintained that the Royal College did not rightfully have certain powers, and that it was using these powers in the wrong way.

23. Cf. Figgis, *op. cit.,* pp. 246-247.
24. McIlwain, *op. cit.,* pp. xxxiii-xxxiv.
25. *Ibid.,* pp. xlii-xliii.
26. Pound, *The Spirit of the Common Law,* p. 88.

Coke maintained that Parliament did not give the College the powers it was exercising. If Parliament did, then it had gone beyond its power because in so doing it had in effect made the College of Physicians both judge and party to its own cause. That is, since the College determined the legality of a doctor's conduct, it acted as a judge: and, since the College received the fines from the punishments handed down, it was a party to the suit. The crux of Coke's decision is found in this passage: "It appeareth in our books that in many cases the common law will control acts of Parliament and somtimes adjudge them to be utterly void; for where an act of Parliament is against common right or reason, or repugnant or impossible to be performed, the common law will control it and adjudge it to be void." [27] Thus, just as Coke sought to curb the royal prerogative, so he now sought to limit the growing powers of Parliament, and "it was with that spirit that Coke labored in the musty old *Year Books,* and from their forbidding mass of obsolescent technicalities he raises a harvest of political theory" whose fundamental thesis was the supremacy of law. [28] Coke's solution to the conflict between the Parliament and the Crown was found in the fundamental law which limited both of them.

Although we are not always sure what Coke meant by the term *law,* we do know that in Bonham's case he equated it with "common right or reason," which in many respects was a medieval conception. Yet, Coke would not agree that law was simply anybody's reason or opinion, as his dispute with James I at the Sunday Morning Conference clearly revealed. Rather, this law which Coke raised to the eminence of complete sovereignty was to be defined in quite a different way.

Coke's ideas of the supremacy of law are best understood in contrast to some of the doctrines of law prevalent during his time, particularly in contrast with the expressed views of James I.

It is not at all surprising that, in an age when there was so much controversy regarding the powers of the magistrate, the question of the rightful source, and extent, of the magistrate's power should ulti-

---

27. T. F. T. Plucknett, "Bonham's Case and Judicial Review," *Harvard Law Review,* XL (1926-1927), 34.
28. *Ibid.,* p. 30. Coke was not consistent in his views *re* the powers of Parliament: Parliament's power and jurisdiction, he said, "is so transcendent and absolute as it cannot be confined either for causes or persons within any bounds." 4 Coke's *Institutes* 36.

mately become a question of the nature of law. Certainly, this is the central issue of the *Vindiciae Contra Tyrannos*. This highly influential book, which first appeared in 1576, put great emphasis on custom as the source of law: law is said to embody principles of universal validity. The significant thing about the *Vindiciae* in this connection is that it places law prior to the king. In it, law is treated as something more majestic than the kingship, for it is the voice of God: "If God calls us on the one side to enroll us in his service, and the king on the other, is any man so void of reason that he will not say that we must leave the king, and apply ourselves to God's service: so far be it from us to believe that we are bound to obey a king, commanding anything contrary to the law of God, that contrarily, in obeying him we become rebels to God." [29] Further: "By the law of God we understand the two tables given to Moses, in the which, as in unremovable bounds, the authority of all princes ought to be fixed." [30] Having raised the question "Whether subjects are bound and ought to obey princes if they command that which is against the law of God," the author of the *Vindiciae* answers in the negative. His entire argument is based upon the authority of Scripture as well as the example of martyrs who showed that the commands of God merit obedience before any orders of any earthly prince. The king is instituted only to secure the better observance of those laws of God, and if he fails to do so, the people have a right to rebellion: if the king sins, the people should not accept this with acquiescence, "for the king loses his right, and many times his realm also, if he despises God, and if he complot with his enemies." [31] This is a lofty treatise which is most impressive when it raises high the spirit of liberty and extols the majesty of law. [32]

These ideas were gaining ground in the latter part of the sixteenth century and could have influenced James I to write in opposition to them. In 1598, five years before he came to the throne of England, James wrote *The Trew Law of Monarchies: Or The Recoproch and Mutual Duetie Betwixt a Free King, And His Natural Subjects,* [33]

---

29. *A Defense Against Tyrants,* with an Introduction and notes on authorship by Harold J. Laski (London, 1924), p. 80. Cf. Raoul Patry, *Philippe du Plessis Mornay, un huguenot homme d'Etat* (Paris, 1933).
30. *Ibid.,* p. 80.
31. *Ibid.,* p. 71.
32. Cf. J. N. Figgis, *Studies of Political Thought from Gerson to Grotius,* 1414-1625 (Cambridge, 1907), p. 136.
33. McIlwain, *op. cit.,* pp. 53-70.

in which he set down his ideas of law which represent the antithesis of what was found in the *Vindiciae*. The fundamental notion of James is that the king precedes the law: "The kings therefore in Scotland were before any estates or rankes of men within the same, before any parliaments were holden, or lawes made: and by them was the land distributed (which at first was whole theirs) states erected and decerned, and forms of gouernment deuised and established: and so it follows of necessitie, that the kings were authors and makers of the Lawes, and not the Lawes of the kings." [34] Accordingly, James saw the king as having supreme power over every person who lived in his land, "having power of life and death over every one of them: For although a just prince will not take the life of any of his subjects without a cleare law; yet the same lawes whereby he taketh them, are made by himselfe, or his predecessors; and so the power flowes always from him selfe." [35] The king being the source of law is above it: "a good king will frame all his actions to be according to the Law; yet is he not bound thereto but of his good will and for good example-giving to his subjects." [36] One of the most curious arguments which follows upon this line of reasoning is the assertion that no matter how bad the king, the people can do nothing. It was at this point that the *Vindiciae* legitimized rebellion. But James argues that since he ruled by Divine Right, only God could judge his actions. It may even be, said James, that a bad king is sent by God to punish the people.

But his main point here was that the people could not be the judges of the king's conduct, for that would make them both judge and party in their own case. James grounded this reasoning upon

the mutual paction and adstipulation (as they call it) betwixt the King and his people, at the time of his coronation. For there, say they, there is a mutual paction, and contract bound up, and sworne betwixt the King and his people: Whereupon it followeth, that if one part of the contract or Indent be broken upon the King's side, the people are no longer bound to keep their part of it, but are thereby freed of their oath. . . As to this contract alleged made at the coronation of a King . . . I confes that a King . . . willingly promiseth to his people to discharge honorably and truly the office given him by God over them: but presuming that thereafter he breaks his promise to them neuer so inexcuseable; the question is, who should be judge of the breake. . .

34. *Ibid.*, p. 62.
35. *Ibid.*, p. 63.
36. *Ibid.*, p. 63.

(A) contract cannot be thought broken by the one party, and so the other likewise to be freed therefrom, except that first a lawful triall and cognition be had by the ordinary Iudge of the breakers thereof: Or else every man may be both party Iudge in his own cause; which is absurd at once to be thought. Now in this contract (I say) betwixt the King and his people, God is doubtless the only Iudge, both because to him only the King must make account of his administration . . . likewise by the oath in the coronation, God is made Iudge and revenger of the breakers. . . Then since God is the only Iudge betwixt the two parties contractors, the cognition and revenge must only appertaine to him: It follows therefore of necessitie, that God must first sentence upon the King that breaketh, before the people can think themselves freed from their oath.[37]

Here, then, we have the fundamental clash between opposing theories of supreme authority based upon conflicting doctrines of the nature and source of law. Like the *Vindiciae,* though without the latter's heavy theological and scriptural emphasis, Coke's ideas of the supremacy of law are irreconcilable with the prevailing notions of the Monarchists, particularly with those of James. Coke was concerned with the universality of law, its stability, its freedom from passion and bias, its identity with the utterance of universal reason, as against caprice and private interest. [38]

But more precisely, what was it that Coke understood by the term law? We have already said that he equated law with "common right or reason." But "reason" had to be qualified with more exactness in order to differentiate it from mere opinion, especially James I's opinion. At the Sunday Morning Conference, Coke said to James that "causes . . . of [your] subjects are not to be decided by natural reason, but by the artificial reason and judgment of the law." [39] The particular law which Coke said was above the King was therefore no mere abstraction, but the common law of England as it was interpreted in the English courts. Gardiner feels that what Coke meant by the law was neither a collection of statutes nor the application of great principles to particular cases. Coke meant, he says, that where statutes failed him, he was to have recourse to historical precedents, or if a precedent was lacking he would simply invent a principle to justify him in deciding the way he chose.[40] This may be true but a brief glance at the fundamental source of Coke's legal thinking in-

37. *Ibid.,* p. 68.
38. Figgis, *Studies of Political Thought from Gerson to Grotius,* p. 136.
39. Pound, *op. cit.,* p. 61.
40. S. R. Gardiner, *History of England* (London, 1883), III, 6.

dicates that his opposition to the King was not at all arbitrary nor indefensible from the point of view of the law of England.

It is the Magna Charta which is of first importance to Coke. In his comments on the *Golden Passage* from this great document, Coke reveals the extent to which he is willing to go in the application of its contents. For him, Magna Charta means a limitation on the royal prerogative, even though there were many in his day who could not conceive that the King lost any prerogative which could be clearly shown to have once belonged to him.[41] Coke's comments emphasize his notion that through Magna Charta, certain rights and liberties are secured by law and one cannot be deprived of them except by rightful means. Thus: "No Man shall be Disseined: That is, put out of Seisin; or disposed of his freehold, that is, Lands or Livelihood, or of his Liberties or Free-Customs, that is of such Franchises and Freedoms, and Free-Customs as belong to him by his free Birth-Right, unless it be by lawful *Judgment,* that is a Verdict of his equals . . . or by *the law of the Land,* that is, (to speak of it once for all) by the due course and process of law."[42]

In his *Speech to the Star Chamber* in 1616 James said again that judges borrow their power from the King just as the King borrows his power from God, thus reflecting his doctrine of unlimited prerogative. Coke's rejection of this idea is found in his comment on another section of Magna Charta where he expressed his attitude toward both the supremacy of law and the function of the judge: "We Will Not Deny Nor Delay Justice: These words have been excellently expounded by the latter acts of Parliament, that by no Means common right or common law should be disturbed or delayed; no, though it be commanded under the *Great Seal or Privy Seal, Order, Writ, Letters, Message or Commandment whatsoever, either from the King or any other;* and that the justices shall proceed, as if no such writs, Letters, Orders, Messages, or Commandments, were come to them: All our judges swear to this; for it is part of their Oaths. . . . The Common Laws of the Realm should by no means be delayed, for the Law is the surest Sanctuary that man can take, and the strongest Fortress to protect the Weakest of all."[43]

41. Cf. Figgis, *Divine Right of Kings,* pp. 247-248.
42. *The Golden Passage in the Great Charter of England Called Magna Charta* with Lord Coke's Remarks and Explanations (London: Printed for use of the London Association, 1776), p. 7.
43. *Ibid.,* p. 14.

The practical consequences which followed from these convictions are easily seen. *Peacham's Case* is a prime illustration of Coke's refusal to delay justice, even at the expense of incurring the displeasure of the Crown.[44] But more significant were Coke's activities in connection with the drafting of the *Petition of Rights* in 1628, whose contents were derived mainly from Magna Charta: i.e., that no man be compelled to make or yield any gift, loan, benevolence, tax, without common consent by act of Parliament; that no freeman be imprisoned; removal of soldiers from private homes; that commissions proceeding by martial law be revoked and annulled.[45] When the King (now Charles I) replied to the Petition that there were already enough laws and that he wished the Parliament to accept his promise to observe them, Coke responded in the House of Commons by saying that then "all succeeding Kings will say 'Ye must trust me as well as ye trusted my predecessors, and trust my messages'; but messages of love never come into Parliament. Let us therefore put up a petition of right; not that I distrust the King; but that I cannot take his trust in a Parliamentary way." [46] Again, when the Lords wished to amend the Petition with the words "with due regard to leave *entire* that sovereign power wherewith your majesty is trusted . . . ", Coke immediately struck at the core of the matter and argued that this amendment

> weakens Magna Charta and all the statutes, for they are absolute, *without any saving of sovereign power*. And should we now add it, we shall weaken the foundation of law. . . Take heed what ye yield unto; Magna Charta is such a fellow, that he will have no sovereign. I wonder this sovereign was not in Magna Charta. . . If we grant this (amendment), we give a sovereign power above all laws . . . It is repugnant to our petition, a petition of right, grounded on acts of Parliament. . . Let us hold our privileges according to the law; that power that is above this is not fit for the King to have it disputed farther.[47]

Far from being mere abstractions, Coke's ideas of law were firmly rooted in the historical traditions of the laws of his country. He was greatly influenced by the medieval ideas of Bracton, but he was more deeply imbued with the many implications which he thought

---

44. Cf. Gardiner, *op. cit.,* p. 14.
45. S. R. Gardiner, *The Constitutional Documents of the Puritan Revolution,* 1625-1660 (Oxford, 1899), pp. 1-5.
46. Johnson, *op. cit.,* Vol. II, p. 236.
47. *Ibid.,* pp. 237-238.

could be derived from Magna Charta. From these sources he gained a lofty conception of law which had its highest expression in his opposition to King James I at the Sunday Morning Conference where he raised law to the status of complete sovereign and expressed this in the words of Bracton: "The King is subject not to men, but to God and the Law." [48]

48. Plucknett, *A Concise History of the Common Law,* p. 49.

IV

SHEPHERD OF HERMAS, PARABLE II

By KENDRICK GROBEL

(*Associate Professor of Biblical Theology*)

"On a walk in the country I (Hermas) had noticed an elm and a grape-vine and was reflecting about them and their fruits when the Shepherd (the angel guide from whom the book gets its name) appeared to me and said, 'What are you pondering within yourself about the elm and the grape-vine?' 'I am pondering, sir,' I said, 'that they are very well matched one to another.' 'These two trees,' said he, 'typify the servants of God.' 'I should like to know,' I said, 'what these two trees you mention typify.' 'You see,' he said, 'the elm and the grape-vine?' 'I do, sir,' I said. He said:

	(1) fruit		
(A) 'This vine		(a) but the elm is a barren	
	(2) bears		tree.
(3) But the vine			
(B)		(b) upon the elm,	
(4) unless it climb			
(C) Cannot bear much fruit		(c) lying on the ground	
(C') And bears rotten what fruit it bears		(c') not hanging on the elm.	
(4') When therefore is cast			
(B')		(b') upon the elm,	
(3') the vine			
	(2') bears		
(A') Both of itself it		(a') and of the elm.' "	
	(1') fruit		

SO begins Parable II of the Shepherd of Hermas, a second-century Christian writing once of great enough importance to be included as the last book of the Bible in the famous Codex Sinaiticus discovered by Tischendorf. It is generally dated A.D. 130-140. Both internal evidence and ecclesiastical tradition indicate Rome as the place of writing. But Martin Dibelius has shown in his remarkable commentary to the book[1] that the materials used in this longest of the works known as Apostolic Fathers had a heterogeneous pre-history. This little study is intended as a footnote to Dibelius' commentary and an homage to him.[2] It undertakes to demonstrate that this par-

---

1. *Der Hirt des Hermas,* 1923 (die apostolischen Väter, IV), supplement volume to Lietzmann's *Handbuch zum Neuen Testament.*
2. He died November 11, 1947, in his 65th year.

ticular section bears evidence of a very specific literary and geographic origin.

I

LITERARY ORIGIN

The style of the whole book is marked by dreary pedantry and wordy repetition. But here, for the parable itself, this lax style gives way to a highly disciplined one, as indicated by the letters A B C C′ B′ A′ and the numerals 1-4, both chiastically arranged. In the rest of this Parable there are other occurrences of this scheme, but none have been detected elsewhere in the book. It is scarcely conceivable that the inartistic author of the whole work is responsible for this composition; he must have taken it over already formed.

Now this is a peculiar kind of chiasm. Simple word-chiasm in the form A B, B′ A′—where the second pair of four words occurs in inverted order in relation to the first pair—probably occurs in all literatures. Higher orders of word-chiasm also occur such as this one in six members from Cicero's Somnium Scipionis:

> obruitur
> hominum
> interitu
> et oblivione
> posteritatis
> extinguitur.

But the scheme displayed at the head of this article is not word-chiasm but stichochiasm—where "sticho-" means "sense-line" (Sinnzeile). Nils W. Lund[3] has demonstrated many occurrences of this scheme in both the Old and the New Testament. One of the nicest specimens of it is Isa. 6:10:[4]

> A Make dense
> B the heart (= mind) of this people
> C and their ears make dull
> D and their eyes
> E besmear
> E′ lest they see
> D′ with their eyes
> C′ and with their ears hear
> B′ and their heart (= mind)
> A′ understand.

---

3. *Chiasmus in the New Testament,* Chapel Hill, 1942.
4. Not treated by Lund. My attention was first called to the form of the passage by Ed. König, *Stilistik, Rhetorik, Poetik in Bezug auf die biblische Literatur,* p. 147. König, however, noted only three of the chiastic pairs in the passage.

Here are five pairs in chiastic inversion around a common center, and in the middle of the series of five is one line (C and C′) where a possible further chiasm is both times avoided. Evidently the Greek translator [5] was aware of the scheme inasmuch as he preserved the word order, neither an obvious nor an easy thing to do in rendering Hebrew into Greek, even to the non-inversion in C-C′. The author of this article knows no evidence for the existence of stichochiasm outside of Hebrew and (Hebrew-influenced) Christian literature. Until such turns up the conclusion would seem to be that this parable was formed by a Jew. He might, of course, have been a Christianized Jew if there were anything specifically Christian in the section, but neither in the parable nor in its application is there anything that is not good Judaism.

The vocabulary of the application-section (not reproduced here[6]) corroborates this view: in one important respect the vocabulary is not that of "Hermas" nor that of early Christian literature. The application equates the elm with the rich man who "supports" the poor man (= the vine), who, though poor, is nevertheless rich in prayer (= the grapes) both for himself and for the charitable rich man. Thus the application has occasion to use a word for "poor" 13 times. Outside of Parable II "Hermas" mentions the "poor" at least ten times, but his word for "poor" is usually ὑστερούμενος or ἐνδεεῖς. Here, however, the word for "poor" is 12 times πένης and once πτωχός; in spite of frequent occasions to do so, the author never uses either word elsewhere. But more than that: in all Christian literature until Tatian[7] the word πένης never occurs except in recognized quotations from Hebrew or Jewish literature. For some unknown reason Christians did not use the word freely. The author of the source of this parable did. Evidently, then, he was not identical with the author of the whole book, and we have a hint that he was not a Christian.

II

GEOGRAPHICAL ORIGIN

Obviously the parable originated in a region where the elm grows. It does not grow in Palestine. Neither the Bible nor the Talmud has

---

5. i.e., of the so-called Septuagint of Isaiah.
6. The Greek text and a good translation (by the late Kirsopp Lake) can most conveniently be consulted in the Loeb Classical Library, The Apostolic Fathers, vol. II.
7. Wrote in the latter half of the second century A.D.

a name for it in the original languages, though once in Aquila's Greek translation [8] and once in King James [9] the tree creeps into a translation. It does not grow south of Palestine. Modern botanists give conflicting reports about the elm in Syria; it probably occurs sporadically on Mt. Hermon. But the Mediterranean habitat of the elm is its northern shore; the home of this parable must be sought there. Where? The vine *climbing the elm* is the key to a drastic geographical delimitation.

Why, specifically, did the author of the source choose an *elm* to support his symbolic grape-vine? Ancient agricultural writers make this answer obvious: he did not choose it but was simply observing an everyday viticultural practice of his region. The ἀγρός in which he says he was walking was not open country but a cultivated plot of ground—to be specific: an *arbustum*. This is the technical term unanimously used by Latin agronomists for the method of viticulture considered by them essential for the production of the finest Italian wines. The word means a vitiferous grove; i.e., a grove of trees planted and pruned for the sole purpose of supporting grape-vines. Detailed descriptions of the process are given by Columella and Pliny in the first century A.D. and by Palladius in the following. Significantly the species of trees selected for transplanting into arbusta were not just any available sort but fell into a definite scale of preference whose exact order Pliny gives us: [10]

> Hac ratione et arbores eliguntur: prima omnium ulmus, excepta propter nimiam frondem atinia; dein populus nigra, eadem de causa, minus densa folio. Non spernunt plerique et fraxinum ficumque, etiam oleam si non sit umbrosa ramis.[11]

Pliny goes on to list the trees used north of the Po but returns to the specific treatment of the elm as the appropriate species *par excellence:* how and when it is to be planted, pruned, transplanted, and how it is to be "wedded" [11] to the vine.

---

8. The Hatch and Redpath Concordance to the Septuagint says Symmachus' translation. This must be an error; Origen's Hexapla—and what other authority is there?—gives it as Aquila's. The passage is Isa. 41:19. The Hebrew *shiṭṭah* (acacia, locust) is the word rendered "elm."
9. Hos. 4:13 for *'elah,* terebinth.
10. *Historia naturalis* XVII 23: "Furthermore the trees are selected in the following order: *first of all the elm* except the variety called *atinia,* which has too much foliage; then the black poplar for the same reason, being less dense of leaf. Most planters do not reject either the ash or the fig or even the olive if it be not shady of branch."
11. *maritare,* a terminus technicus; cf. in our parable: "they are very well matched one to another" and "it bears fruit both of itself and of the elm."

This preference for the elm as the best arbustum-tree is confirmed by Columella and Palladius, but more strikingly still by the matter-of-fact way in which Latin literati "wed" the vine, not just to any tree, but specifically to the elm. Vergil, for instance, asks, "Under what star . . . should vines be mated with elms?" [12] The figure of speech "widow elm" [13] or "celibate elm" [14] is a commonplace. Horace says the peaceful farmer "marries the vine to widow trees" [15] and pictures the state of desolation when farming is neglected by saying,[16] "the celibate plane-tree will supplant the elms." Juvenal[17] pictures "the vine lying on the ground longing after widowed elms." The marriage of vine and elm often becomes a parable of human behavior. Seneca[18] uses it for a figure of human adultery: "This have I also seen: aged vines transplanted from their own arbustum . . . and they grasped and embraced elms not their own." [19] But the parable that most reminds one of the Hermas parable is a scene in Ovid's *Metamorphoses* [20] in which a disguised lover forlornly attempts to let this phenomenon of the farm plead his cause with his lady:

> Opposite them was an elm resplendent with luscious grapes. After he had approvingly regarded it along with its vine companion he said, "If that pruned trunk stood there without the vine, celibate, it would have nothing but its leaves to be sought after. But that vine joined together with it rests confidently upon the elm; if she (the vine) were not married, she would lie sprawling on the ground. But thou art unmoved by the vine's example, thou fleest marriage and carest not to be joined with another."

Does the recognition that Parable II is talking of an arbustum help localize it? Indeed it does: the arbustum was apparently confined to Italy—and the *elm*-arbustum to central Italy. Pliny[21] writes: "Here follows Scrofa's famous arbustum-method, strangely condemned by certain ones (Saserna and son) and even by Scrofa himself recommended only for Italy." In an earlier passage [22] Pliny has already related that the vine was allowed to sprawl "supinam in tellu-

---

12. *Georgic* I 2.
13. Or simply "mateless elm"; the expression is *vidua ulmus.*
14. *caelebs ulmus.*
15. *Carm.* IV 5, 30.
16. *Carm.* II 15, 4.
17. *Satire* 8, 18.
18. *Epistle* 86, 20.
19. *conplexae sunt non suas ulmos.*
20. 14, 663.
21. XVII 23.
22. XVII 22, 35.

rem," prone on the ground, in Africa, Egypt, Syria,[23] all of "Asia," and in many parts of Europe. Columella, born in ancient Gades [24] the son of the most distinguished planter of his province, later a resident of Italy, and a wanderer who died ih Cilicia or Syria, is a still better witness to provincial methods. He describes in detail [25] four kinds of *vineae provinciales,* none of which is an arbustum. As a matter of fact the arbustum does not belong to the genus *vinea,* is not considered a vineyard, but is always treated as *sui generis.* This world-traveler and agricultural specialist knows of the arbustum only in Italy and neighboring parts of Gaul. Polybius in his lost work *de Italia* is reported [26] to have said: διάφορον οἶνον ἐν Καπύῃ γίνεσθαι τὸν ἀναδενδρίτην καλούμενον, ᾧ μηδένα συνκρίνεσθαι.[27] His οἶνος ἀναδενδρίτης is a literal translation for the common *vinum arbustivum,* and his καλούμενον implies that that term—and therefore the thing denoted—was unfamiliar to his (Greek) readers. Without doubt the wine he refers to is the celebrated Falernian wine produced not 15 miles away from Capua, the capital of Campania, at the foot of Mt. Massicus. That Falernian wine was grown in arbusta of elm trees, we know from the demand of a petulant wife in Juvenal [28] for *ulmos Falernas* by metonymy for their produce, the famous wine. What she wanted was "champagne" —not firewood!

All this strongly indicates the probability that the author of our parable was simply moralizing upon an everyday phenomenon of which no resident of the central provinces of Italy could well be ignorant but which was rare or unknown elsewhere. The likelihood is that the parable originated there.

Summary. The characteristic remarks of "Hermas" which frame this parable and its interpretation, as we now have them, indicate that it has been edited by the author of the whole book and therefore was prior to the whole work. Literary evidence points toward Jewish authorship. Botanical data indicate the north Mediterranean littoral. Agricultural information points strongly to the central Italian provinces. We postulate a Jew of the diaspora, probably a resident of central Italy, as the originator of this parable.

---

23. Cf. the *raglith* of the Talmud.
24. Modern Cadiz.
25. *de Re Rustica* III 4.
26. By Athenaeus, *Deipnosophistes* I 31 d.
27. "Excellent is the wine in Capua that is called the arbustive; none can compare with it."
28. *Satire* VI 150.

V

THE CONSISTENCE AND QUALITIES OF
MILTON'S CHAOS

By WALTER CLYDE CURRY
(*Professor of English*)

MILTON'S chaos in *Paradise Lost* is disorderly, but it is palpable and therefore subject to processes of analysis. Upon proper consideration it is discovered to be a subsistent entity whose inherent primary qualities, such as extension, solidity or fluity, number, and motion, may as usual be grasped by perception. And these perceived primary qualities have the power of producing a variety of sensations, secondary qualities such as heat and cold, color, and sound.[1] It is heterogeneous, a mass of agglomerate materials in various stages of becoming. This chaos in all its multiplicity of detail is directly prepared by God to serve as the substrate of all generation and corruption. And underlying the consistence of chaos is that mysterious, passive matter, an efflux from Deity, which Milton calls "the chief productive stock of every subsequent good."[2] The present study considers these questions further and concerns itself also with the various differentiations to which God subjects passive matter until it becomes a chaos prepared to receive forms.

Now in Milton's account of the origin of matter he is evidently under the influence of Neoplatonic concepts of emanation. According to this philosophy, as I have shown elsewhere,[3] matter is the last and final progression of a degenerating emanation; it is a purely occult existence produced by a timeless, necessary, and eternal process. For the poet-philosopher, however, the efflux of matter from Deity occurs at a point of time[4] and involves the exercise of divine will. And having derived matter directly from God, he proceeds—

---

1. Aristotle, of course, recognized hot, cold, moist, and dry as primary qualities. But it is doubtful whether anybody before Locke distinguished clearly between primary and secondary qualities. Milton, however, includes the qualities falling under both designations in his presentation of chaos.
2. See my "Milton's Dual Concept of God as Related to Creation," *Studies in Philology,* XLVII (1950), 201-203.
3. "Milton's Chaos and Old Night," *JEGPh.,* XLVI (1947), 45 ff.
4. *De Doctrina Christiana,* edited, with the translation of Charles R. Sumner, by James Holly Hanford and Waldo Hilary Dunn, Columbia University Press, 1933, XV.22.20, and 18.25.

with apparently no consciousness of philosophical contradiction—to consider it the *first* step in the processes of an historical creation. For him it is a purely passive principle or substance, having no inherent force or power but capable of "receiving passively the exertion of divine efficacy."[5]

On gathers that the first result of God's exertion of efficacy upon passive matter is the differentiation of its indeterminate substance into individual particles called atoms. In *Paradise Lost* Milton represents graphically the embryon atoms as Satan perceives them moving in the profound void or vacuum. In their several clans some are light, some heavy, some sharp, some smooth, and in motion some are swift, some slow.[6] They "Swarm populous unnumbered as the sands of Barca or Cyrene's torrid soil" (II, 903). And that they flit about in all directions in a "void immense" cannot be doubted (II, 828). For when Satan plunges into the "hoary Deep" (II, 891)—a "void" and hyperbolical "formless Infinite" (III, 12)—he drops into a vast vacuity" (II, 932) ten thousand fathoms deep.

> and to this hour
> Down had been falling, had not, by ill chance,
> The strong rebuff of some tumultuous cloud,
> Instinct with fire and nitre, hurried him
> As many miles aloft (II, 935-939).

And all manifestations in chaos, before creation of the World, may be attributed ultimately to the qualities of these embyron atoms, moving as they do in a void and combining by chance—"Chance governs all" (II, 910)—into ever-changing agglomeration or aggregation of like to like.

Here the poet is evidently indebted in some measure to Democritus, the atomist, or to some seventeenth century popularizer of Democritean principles.[7] For Democritus[8] too postulates an infinite void or

---

5. *Ibid.,* XV.18.20.

6. *Paradise Lost,* ed. Harris Francis Fletcher, in *The Complete Poetical Works of John Milton,* New York, 1941, II, 901-2. Parenthetical references within the text are to this work and this edition.

7. On the popularity of atomism in seventeenth century philosophy and literature, see Charles T. Harrison, "Bacon, Hobbes, Boyle, and the Ancient Atomists," Harvard *Studies and Notes in Philology and Literature,* XV (1933), 191-218, and "The Ancient Atomists and English Literature of the Seventeenth Century," Harvard *Studies in Classical Philology,* XLV (1934), 1-79; F. A. Comenius, *Natural Philosophie Reformed by Divine Light or A Synopsis of Physicks,* London, 1650, pp. 28 ff. Katherine Brownell Collier, *Cosmogogonies of*

vacuum, in which an infinite number of material particles swarm about in all directions. To these atoms he attributes an unimaginable multiplicity of size and shape together with indestructibility, unchangeableness, and impenetrability. In shape some are rounded or smooth, some sharp or pointed, some provided with "hooks and eyes, balls and sockets, involuted edges, with mortice and dovetail." [9] Their motion is inherent and eternal; in combination of like to like some move more slowly than others. For example, in earthy aggregations the particles are comparatively large and of little mobility; ether is composed of smaller and rounded particles of fiery swiftness.[10] And thus watery particles occasionally meet and adhere to watery particles, airy particles adhere by chance to airy, and so on, until agglomerations of atoms, moving in vortices, and "severing themselves from the infinite vacuum, finally become a separate world or cosmos of which there are infinitely many." [11]

Resemblances of Milton's atoms to those of Democritus are evident. Differences are also apparent and significant. The poet, while postulating a void or vacuum, attributes to it merely an hyperbolical infinitude; for him only God is infinite. His atoms embody a variety of motions, but such motions are not inherently eternal; motion of all particles derives in time from an immovable Deity. He would not agree that fortuitous agglomerations of atoms might ultimately produce by chance an infinite number of worlds; for such an end the application of God's power is necessary. He would no doubt have supported the statement of his younger contemporary, the atomist Robert Boyle:

> God . . . having resolved before the creation to make such a world as this of ours, did divide (at least if he did not create it incoherent) that matter which he had provided into innumerable multitudes of variously figured corpuscles, and both connected those particles into such textures or particular bodies, and placed them in such situations

Our Fathers, New York, 1934, p. 339: in the seventeenth century "Matter was generally conceived to be a chaos of particles."

8. On Democritus, see Aristotle, *De Caelo,* trans. J. L. Stocks, Oxford, 1922, 275b20; 303a 10; 300B 9; 33a 5; *De Generatione et Corruptione,* trans. Harold H. Joachim, Oxford, 1922, 314a, 21-24; 315b 6-15, etc.; Theodor Gomperz, *Greek Thinkers,* London, 1920, I, 316-369; W. Windelband, *A History of Philosophy,* trans. James H. Tufts, New York, 1938, pp. 109-116, etc.; Cyril Bailey, *The Greek Atomists and Epicurus,* London, 1938, pp. 109-24.

9. Gomperz, *op. cit.,* I, 334.

10. *Ibid.,* I, 337.

11. *Ibid.,* I, 335.

and put them into such motions, that . . . the phenomena which he intended should appear in the universe.[12]

Having safeguarded the proper relationship between Deity and his creation, Milton levies upon Democritus—and perhaps to some extent upon Epicurus and Lucretius[13]—for such principles of atomistic philosophy as might aid in the execution of his artistic purpose.

What, then, is the origin of the four elements and how do they function in God's differentiation of prime matter into chaos? Democritus assumes, as we have seen, that the primary masses are indivisible and infinite in number and that all things are generated by their agglomeration and involution. Accordingly, air, earth, water, and fire are differentiated by the relative sizes, shapes, and motions of their respective atoms in combinations.[14] Aristotle, of course, opposes this view. He reduces all bodies to the primary constituents or "simple bodies," earth and fire, with the intermediates, water and air[15] and shows how, because of their dual qualities, they suffer a cyclic transmutation one into another.[16] But Lucretius observes that Aristotle's "simple bodies" cannot be considered "first beginnings" because they are said to undergo transmutation; there must be something which remains unchanged. "Why not rather hold," says he, "that certain particles endowed with changeless nature have perchance begotten fire, but also, by addition or subtraction of a few or by a change of motion or of order, can produce the breezes of the air, and that all things can thus be changed, the one into the other?" [17] Thus he would seem to approve the action of the Aristotelian four elements *after they have been generated out of unchangeable first beginnings, the atoms.*

Now with regard to the origin of the four elements, Milton still adheres to atomistic principles. As Satan stands in Hellmouth—

---

12. Quoted in Harrison, Harvard *Studies and Notes in Philology and Literature,* XV (1933), pp. 218 ff.

13. *Epicurus, The Extant Remains,* trans. Cyril Bailey, Oxford, 1926, *To Herodotus,* pp. 23-25, 31-37; Lucretius, *On the Nature of Things,* trans. Thomas Jackson, Oxford, 1929, pp. 11-45. Milton has no use for the uniformity of motion attributed by Epicurus to all atoms, whether single or in combination, nor for the Lucretian doctrine of the "swerve" of down-falling particles.

14. Reported by Aristotle with some perplexity, *De Caelo,* 303a 5-25.

15. *Ibid.,* 302a 11, 277b, 14, 298b 8.

16. *De Gen. et Cor.,* 331b.

17. *Op. cit.,* I, 797-803 (p. 26). Cf. II, 1112 f. (p. 73).

which casts forth smoke and ruddy flame—in sudden view there appear before his eyes secrets of the hoary Deep. And one of the secrets which he perceives is the momentary formation of elemental qualities out of embryon atoms:

> For hot, cold, moist, and dry, four champions fierce
> Strive here for mastery, and to battle bring
> Their embryon atoms; they around the flag
> Of each his faction, in their several clans,
> Light-armed or heavy, sharp, smooth, swift or slow,
> Swarm populous, unnumbered as the sands
> Of Barca or Cyrene's torrid soil . . .
> 　　　　　　　To whom these most adhere,
> He rules a moment (II, 889-907).

Here is dramatically represented the production of elemental qualities by transitory formations of atoms. Still all is confusion, conflict, and rapid alteration. In this womb of Nature there is as yet neither definite sea, nor shore, nor air, nor fire,

> But all these in their pregnant causes mixed (II, 911-13).

The "crude consistence" of primeval chaos which Satan meets later in his flight, however, would indicate that the qualities of hot, cold, moist, and dry are being properly represented in the momently changing forms of earth, water, air, and fire. Thus, as Milton says, the four elements as here conceived are "the eldest birth of Nature's womb" (V, 180-81). When stabilized and directed by God's power in creation, they behave much as do Aristotle's "simple bodies"; contrarieties in their nature are controlled and they suffer normal cyclic transmutation one into another:

> 　　　　　　in quarternion run
> Perpetual circle, multiform, and mix
> And nourish all things (V, 181-183).

But in chaos they are still unstable, uncontrolled, constantly fluctuating in atomic content and in form, energizing confusedly with "fierce extremes" (VII, 272) of heat and cold, wet and dry, in perpetual warfare. Such is the constitution of chaos. It is an actual entity representing the differentiation by God of primary matter into (1) a multitude of atoms and (2) the qualities and changing forms of the four elements. It may logically be identified with that remote secondary matter which, says Milton, the Deity has prepared for the reception of forms in creation.[18]

But let us consider further the fluctuating texture or, more properly speaking, the crude consistence and qualities of chaos. It may be perceived as an amorphous mass of momentarily agglomerated atoms and rapidly shifting elemental qualities conceived by the poet to serve a variety of epic purposes. It must furnish materials for the creation of Heaven, Hell, the Mundane Universe, and any other worlds which God may design; its consistence must be of such a nature as to permit Satan's flight through and over it and facilitate the construction of a symbolical highway, following Satan's track, from Hell to the outside shell of the World; and rebellious angels in Heaven tap its crude resources in manufacturing engines of war. One may sense its temporary solidity or fluidity or vacuity, its tremendous extension, and its wild motion. And its heterogeneous contents produce varying pressures of a palpable nature, such as noises which stun the ear and at least one color which distresses the eye.

In Satan's journey through the "illimitable ocean" of chaos, for example, momentary agglomerations of "earthy" particles packed together with only small void spaces between enable him to walk or run upon a density resembling soil, sometimes rough, sometimes steep. At other times aggregations of "watery" atoms permit him to swim and of "airy" particles to fly through straits between the dense and the rare. Sometimes he meets combinations of these earthy and watery particles in such proportions as to result in what seems to be bogs and quicksands—neither sea nor good dry land— over which he must pass, half on foot, half flying. And once a "cloud" of fiery atoms in contact with the elemental quality of nitre causes an explosion which hurls his body ten thousand miles aloft (II, 936 ff.). Sin and Death also seem to find this consistence of chaos tractable. When they start to build their broad way from Hell to the World, they discover the "illimitable ocean" to be a waste of

---

18. See *A Fuller Institution of the Art of Logic,* ed and trans. Allan H. Gilbert, New York, 1935: "In the order of nature matter follows the efficient cause, and is a sort of effect of the efficient cause; for the efficient cause prepares the matter that it may be fit for receiving the form. As the efficient cause is that which first moves, so the matter is that which is first moved" (p. 51). "Matter is commonly divided into primary and secondary; the secondary into proximate and remote" (*Id.,* p. 53). I have further discussed this question in "Milton's Scale of Nature," *Stanford Studies in Language and Literature,* ed. Hardin Craig, Stanford University, 1941, pp. 181-182.

"waters."[19] They fly out from Hell and gather whatever of "solid" or "slimy" agglomerations they can find tossed up and down as in a raging sea and crowd them to Hellmouth. There Death, with his cold and dry mace, dehydrates and petrifies the aggregated soil and so fixes it firmly; other elemental materials he binds with his Gorgonian look and with "asphaltic slime" not to move (X, 281-298). By this same process, no doubt, they overbuild disparted chaos with "bars" (X, 416), construct a bridge of "pendant rock" over the vexed Abyss, and attach it to the outside shell of the World with pins and chains of "adamant" (X, 416).

It must be observed that in the representation of this road from Hell to the World and the process of its construction, Milton appears to involve himself in artistic and logical difficulties or perhaps absurdities. The problems are painfully evident: two *allegorical* figures, Sin and Death, are depicted as building a *symbolical* road composed of such materials as "bars," "asphalt," and "rock" through an actual entity, the unformed mass of chaos, to the point where the symbolical bridge is attached to the outside shell of the created World by chains of "adamant." While Sin and Death may be imaginatively acceptable as personifications of abstract forces or powers, the materials—bars, asphalt, and adamant—in which they are said to energize are as such not native to chaos. Building materials of this nature are actualized products of God's creation of the Mundane Universe, where they may be found in abundance. In the created World of matter and form it is true that a material object—rock, asphalt, bars, a rose—can in the hands of an artist be made to symbolize spiritual or invisible or intangible realities, but the object must itself exist in accordance with the laws of its nature. That is to say, in symbolical representation a rock must be a rock situated in its normal or logical frame of reference, whatever hidden meaning may be imaginatively conceived or attached to it. But in Milton's chaos—whose consistence we have examined—it is not that the highway is, as Dr. Johnson thought, "a work too bulky for ideal

---

19. See my forthcoming "The Genesis of Milton's World," *Anglia*, LXIX, Heft 4, for a clarification of the terms *waters* (X, 285) and *fluid mass* (VII, 287) as applied to any portion of undigested chaotic matter. Comenius (*op. cit.,* p. 28) identifies Moses' "waters" and "darkness" with "a vapour or a fume . . . a Chaos of dispersed Atomes, cohering in no part thereof." I have defined Raphael's *fluid mass* as "a sort of compound containing in solution or *in potentia* all possible elements and material aspects of the visible Universe."

architects," [20] but that it is symbolically defective because the basic terms of the symbol—bars, adamant, rock—represent impossible existences in the chaos frame of reference. In chaos there are discoverable no such actualized building materials.

But perhaps the artistic situation here is not so desperate as it might at first appear. Milton is the epic poet who sometimes sacrifices logical consistency in favor of psychological effect. He evidently depends upon the knowledge of an informed reader that bars, rock, and adamant do exist *potentially* in chaos, else God could not have actualized them in the created World. Consequently, being intimately acquainted with these proximate secondary materials at hand in the Visible Universe, one willingly suspends his logical judgment for a moment and accepts bars, rock, and adamant as basic terms of the highway-symbol. This acceptance is facilitated by recognition of the powers and qualities embodied in the allegorical figures, Sin and Death. They are repulsive forces inimical to mankind. Everybody knows that death is "hungry as the grave" and cold as interstellar spaces; death is a horrible violence and a dryness which, like sorrow, "drinks our blood." Facing these mysteries, one is not surprised when Death strikes unstable materials of chaos with his cold and dry mace so that they are made solid as stone nor when his Gorgonian look reduces chaotically moving "waters" to rigidity (X, 293-297). These are such awe-inspiring images revealing profound truth about the violence and chill of death, that we are willing to grant the poet his "stable" building materials—even in chaos—for the construction of a massive road from Hell to the World. Besides, as I have recently shown,[21] the definitely limned highway serves admirably to fix directions, perspectives, and distances involved in Satan's journey from Hellmouth to Earth.[22]

---

20. Quoted in A. W. Verity, *Milton, Paradise Lost,* Cambridge, 1921, p. 597.
21. "Some Travels of Milton's Satan and the Road to Hell," *Philological Quarterly,* XXIX (1950), 225-235.
22. Evil angels would seem able actually to manipulate some aspects of the chaos-consistence. It is clear that the foundation of created Heaven of Heavens consists of several layers or grades of materials extending downward from the ethereal floor to chaos, upon which Heaven rests. Followers of Satan dig through the ethereous mould of the Heavenly landscape until they discover hidden veins of mineral and stone—not unlike those found in Earth's entrails; these are "the originals of Nature in their crude conception" (VI, 510 ff.). Further down they search for "materials dark and crude of spiritous and fiery spume" which, says Satan,

That Light which floods the heavenly regions, however, is no mere symbol. It is here, as in the World,[23] the visible manifestation of creative power exercised by the Filial Godhead. The Son, energizing in the Father, has created the Heaven of Heavens (III, 390) and all its inhabiting hosts of angels (V, 837). Satan recognizes that the ethereal and ambrosial beauties of the celestial landscape are created out of the dark materials of chaos by the tempering "Heaven's ray" and that they continue to be so sustained, shooting forth and "opening to the ambient light" (VI, 472-81). It is this same creative Light which, streaming from the battlements of Heaven, shoots a glimmering dawn far into the bosom of contiguous chaos and reduces to some extent its surface instability and disorderly becoming. For here Satan finds in his upward flight that under the creative influence of light —though he must still suffer for a time the shock of well-developed "fighting elements" (III, 1015)—Nature actually begins her farthest verge and chaos to retire (III, 1038). He wafts "on a calmer wave" for a while; and when he finally emerges fully into the precincts of light, he calmly spreads his wings in an atmosphere resembling air (III, 1041-45). Thus creative light has beaten down chaos into a sort of turbulent sea-surface [24] and has aggregated and ordered airy elements into a calm atmosphere. And this atmosphere is indeed air. God observes the Fiend coasting along the walls of Heaven "in the dun air sublime" (III, 72). Later Satan arrives on the outer shell of the World—hanging "uncertain which in ocean or in air" (III, 76)—where he walks through the "glimmering air" (III, 426) and is buffeted by storms of this "windy sea of land" (III, 440). It is evident and in no sense surprising, then, that under the sacred influence of creative Light there has been a partial "creation," i.e., a real separation out of chaotic materials of airy particles and qualities and their stabilization into air.

---

in their dark nativity the Deep
Shall yield us, pregnant with infernal flame (VI, 478 ff.).
From this passage one might reasonably conclude that, in the subtle art of making explosives, Satan's followers reveal power to command the potentials of primitive chaos.

23. For a full discussion of this conception, see my forthcoming "The Genesis of Milton's World."
24. See "Some Travels of Milton's Satan," loc. cit., pp. 232-234.

III

One of the most striking qualities of Milton's chaos is its darkness. For example, when the secrets of the hoary Deep are spread before Satan's eyes, he sees it as "a dark illimitable ocean" (II, 891); Sin and Death are said to discover building materials in the "anarchy of chaos, damp and dark" (X, 283); Satan views the bridge which they have constructed over the "dark Abyss" (X, 371); and when the King of Glory comes with his powerful Word and Spirit to create the World, it is said

> On Heavenly ground they stood, and from the shore
> They viewed the vast immeasurable Abyss,
> Outrageous as a sea, dark, wasteful, wild (VII, 210-12).

This darkness to which the eye is sensitive is also a tactile quality, i.e., it is capable of being touched or felt. At least Satan wonders who will "tempt with wandering feet/The dark . . . Abyss" and find a way "through the *palpable* [25] obscure" (II, 405-6). The poet is aware, of course, that day and night in the created World are both "unsubstantial" and that darkness is "Privation mere of light and absent day." [26] But concerning the original darkness of chaos out of which God caused the light to shine, he says, "That this darkness was far from being a mere negation or nothing, is clear from Isai. XLV.7. *I am Jehovah; I form* the light, and create darkness." [27] There can be no doubt that this primordial darkness is to be considered a positive existence created by God when he prepared passive matter for the reception of forms. It resembles in some measure the Democritean *black* and, like that one of the four primary colors, is the effect of aggregations of atoms.[28]

Occasionally, indeed, Milton raises it to the dignity of an allegorical figure, a fierce female personality informing a realm opposed to light and life. For example, the outer shell of the World divides the luminous interior from chaos and the "inroad of Darkness old" (III, 421); Adam explains to Eve how light from the celestial spheres exerts a beneficent influence.

> Lest total Darkness should by night regain
> Her old possession, and extinguish life
> In nature and all things (IV, 665-67).

25. Cf. Verity's note, *op. cit.*, p. 409.
26. *Paradise Regained*, ed. Fletcher, IV, 400.
27. *De Doctrina*, XV.17.19-21.
28. Gomperz, *op. cit.*, I, 333.

Satan conceives that he may perhaps be able to reduce the created World "To her original darkness,"

> and once more
> Erect the standard there of ancient Night (II, 984-85).

Or sometimes darkness is identified with the realm itself. Satan returns to Hell "through Darkness" (X, 394); the poet is in imagination borne "Through utter and middle Darkness" (III, 16); and Satan enquires which way lies "the nearest coast of Darkness" bordering upon the realm of light (II, 958). Here one may discern some dim reflection, perhaps, of the Manichaean conception of two territories bordering one upon the other, the Kingdom of Light and the Kingdom of Darkness, sometimes personified and so identified with their rulers.[29] Or perhaps all qualities of primordial darkness may be symbolized by that mysterious "divinity," Old Night. I have already tried to show how and in what sense this female "ruler" serves symbolically as the mother and nurse of all productive principles, the source of motion in chaos, the place in which bodies may exist and the room in which movement of bodies is possible; she is the Deep considered as extension, the Abyss which is the womb of Nature and perhaps her grave. She is sable-vested. With her consort, Chaos, she spreads her pavilion upon the wasteful Deep and erects her standard upon its dark materials.[30]

Still another quality which distinguishes Milton's chaos from most others is its greatly emphasized noise. Here the conflicting particles assail the ear and produce the sensation interpreted as sound. And the noises so sensed are tremendous and unpleasant to the point of being painful. For example, as Satan looks upon chaos, he understands that the confusion there is accompanied by "the noise of endless wars" (II, 815),

> Nor was his ear less pealed
> With noises loud and ruinous (to compare
> Great things with small) than when Bellona storms
> With all her battering engines, bent to rase
> Some capital city; or less than if this frame
> Of heaven were falling, and these elements
> In mutiny had from her axle torn
> The steadfast Earth (II, 920-927).

29. See St. Augustine, *Against the Epistle of Manichaeus Called Fundamental,* chaps. 15, 20, 21, 24, trans. Richard Stothert, *Nicene and Post-Nicene Fathers,* Buffalo, 1887, IV, with Introduction by Albert H. Newman, pp. 11-12.
30. "Milton's Chaos and Old Night," *loc. cit.,* p. 47.

As he fights his way through the dark illimitable ocean,

> At length a universal hubbub wild
> Of stunning sounds, and voices all confused,
> Borne through the hollow dark, assaults his ear
> With loudest vehemence (II, 951-954).[31]

It is not clear to me where Milton might have found precedent for the inclusion of this vivid quality in his chaos. Genesis mentions no sound in the process of creation. Du Bartas, one of his supposed sources,[32] describes the war between hot and cold, blunt and sharp particles in chaos merely as "this brawl," [33] which suggests noisy conflict. In the *Poimandres* of Hermes Trismegistus there is represented at creation a "downward tending darkness," *amorphos hyle,* which presently changes into a watery substance; "and," says the speaker, "I heard it making an indescribable sound of lamentation; for there was sent forth from it an inarticulate cry.[34] Or perhaps he is transferring the idea of auditory detail found in Biblical descriptions of "last things"—for example, in Luke 21:25, where one hears of "the sea and the waves roaring"—back to his description of "first things." [35] But the establishment of a precedent is really not necessary. Milton is unusually original in his conception of chaos. And since his imagination is largely auditory, he properly and logically associates the conflict between forces in chaos with the naturally resulting noises.

Two further properties of that space or void in which chaos exists and of which it partakes must be considered: namely, dimension and direction. Satan observes chaos as

> a dark
> Illimitable ocean, without bound
> Without dimension; where length, breadth, and highth,
> And time, and place, are lost (II, 891-894).

In order to understand such a statement as this, one must remember that Milton thinks of chaos as originally filling all space, but for him

---

31. Even allegorical and symbolical figures engage in clamorous uproar, "feel" tenfold confusion, and "hear" "unsufferable noise" (II, 967; III, 709; VI, 871; X, 478).
32. George Coffin Taylor, *Milton's Use of Du Bartas,* Cambridge, 1934.
33. Du Bartas, *His Divine Weekes and Workes,* London, 1621, p. 6.
34. *The Poimandres of Hermes Trismegistus,* ed. and trans. Walter Scott, *Hermetica,* Oxford, 1924, Libellus I, 4-5a.
35. For a detailed account of the relation between "first things" and "last things" in the Judaeo-Christian traditions, see Hermann Gunkel, *Schöpfung und Chaos in Urzeit und Endzeit,* Göttingen, 1895, *passim* but especially pp. 99-111.

the global space-continuum is only an hyperbolical infinitude existing in an infinity of Light which is God.[36] That is to say, he has in imagination expanded space to such tremendous dimension that it is immeasurable and illimitable. And the chaos which originally filled it partakes of the same quality of extension. Even that part of chaos which remains after creation of three universes—Heaven, Hell, and the World—is still thought of as being immeasurable and illimitable. But within any given portion of it—for example, that part which is visible to Satan—there can be no real dimension because its agglomerations are in a state of kaleidoscopic change and alteration. No aggregation of particles and elemental qualities is of such stability for more than an instant as to suggest that it is capable of being measured with respect to its length, breadth, and height. One may conceive of momentary dense or rare agglomerations, but they have no fixed aggregated parts which might produce measurable shapes and proportions. Interchange of aggregation and dissolution of particles is so rapid that there is produced no such thing as a "body" which can be said to occupy a definite *place* in the void. And the movements of such agglomerations are so erratic and fluctuating that they cannot be measured in terms of *time*. The imaginative poet is admirably effective and accurate, therefore, in suggesting the inconceivable confusion of chaos, where dimension—length, breadth, and height—time and place are lost.

Physicists would agree, I suppose, that direction is a quality of space. And by reason of this property when two positions are known, others may be determined in the like dimension. Mathematically speaking, there is no up and down in infinite space or indeed in the hyperbolical infinitude of Milton's void. As Epicurus says:

> Furthermore, in the infinite we must not speak of "up" and "down," as though with reference to an absolute highest and lowest—and indeed we must say that, though it is possible to proceed to infinity in the direction above our heads from wherever we take our stand, the absolute highest point will never appear to us—nor yet can that which passes beneath the point thought of to infinity be at the same time both up and down in reference to the same thing.[37]

Still Epicurus would no doubt agree with Lucretius that in infinite space atoms do fall "downward" until a "swerve" in motion causes collison and rebound in all directions. He would recognize that con-

36. See "Some Travels of Milton's Satan," *loc. cit.*, pp. 226 ff.
37. Epicurus, *op. cit.*, pp. 35 ff.

ception of space is relative as well as infinite and that we can think
of up and down "with reference to ourselves or to any point in space
of which we choose to think. The motion from our feet to our head,
however prolonged, is to us motion upward and the opposite motion
downwards." [38] It is this concept of space as relative as well as
infinite which enables Milton to give direction to movements of individuals in and over chaos. As a matter of fact, two points of reference have already been established for him by convention and authority: Heaven is "above" us, and Hell is "below." It is from this
Heaven above that the rebellious angels are cast out, and they fall
downward through chaos to Hell below. Satan ascends as in a cloudy
chair from Hellmouth into chaos, falls downward in vacuity ten
thousand fathoms, is hurled by an explosion as many miles aloft,
fights his way upward through chaos and its warring elements until
he arrives in the precincts of light off the coast of Heaven, and then
pursues a horizontal flight—in relation to the walls of Heaven—
over the turbulent sea of chaos southward to the outside shell of the
World.[39] So Milton develops that property of space called direction
in space-filling chaos.

Analysis of Milton's chaos reveals a remarkable originality of conception and clarity of execution. In his representation of chaotic materials he is attempting, Verity says, "to convey to the reader an
impression of utter confusion of the scene described: heaping image
on image, idea on idea, by which the imagination may be baffled . . .
and the mind bewildered with an insistent sense of the inconceivable."[40] This may be true, but it does not mean that Milton's thinking
and feeling are in any sense chaotic. In the bodying forth of his
grand, chaotic vision he must, as epic poet, necessarily resort to the
use of mystic symbol and allegory or other appropriate imagery. To
interpreters these may well seem bewildering or baffling; sometimes,
as Bunyan says, "metaphors make us blind." But the poet's own
imagination is evidently unclouded, his perception sensitive and
clear, and his general design carefully delineated. Selecting quite
diversified materials from a variety of philosophical and traditional

---

38. This is Cyril Bailey's commentary on *ibid.*, pp. 213-214.
39. The allegorical "individuals," Sin and Death, are represented as emerging
    upward from Hellmouth; they fly "diverse" through chaos and meet "solid" or
    slimy materials which seem to them to be "as in raging sea/ Tossed up and
    down" (X, 286-7).
40. *Op. cit.*, p. 423.

sources, he has syncretized them into a consistent chaos which is completely like no other but which is admirably adapted to his epic design. The consistence of this unique production facilitates dramatic action; its qualities, cleanly defined and related to consistence, are necessary ingredients in all subsequent creations. It is indeed "The womb of Nature, and perhaps her grave."

VI
THE DEUTERONOMIC EDITION OF JEREMIAH

By J. PHILIP HYATT
(Professor of Old Testament)

FEW questions in Old Testament criticism are as interesting and as difficult as the problem of the composition of the Book of Jeremiah. Superficially this appears to be an easy problem. In chapter 36 we have a very valuable account of the dictation by Jeremiah of many of his oracles to his scribe Baruch. The book contains biographical information concerning the prophet which seems to have been written by an eyewitness; the majority of scholars have long thought that eyewitness was Baruch. Furthermore, there are three other references to "books," in addition to those of chapter 36, which ought to be helpful, 25:13; 30:2; 51:60. Certain sections of the Book of Jeremiah seem to belong together: chapters 27–29 have striking stylistic peculiarities in common; chapters 30–31 constitute a "book of comfort"; and chapters 46–51 contain oracles directed against foreign nations.

Beneath the surface, however, there are many difficulties. Although chapters 1–24 are mostly poetry and 25–45 are mostly prose, the former contain extensive prose passages, and the latter some poetry. In chapters 1–24 the first person is usually employed by Jeremiah, and in chapters 25–45 the third person is ordinarily used in speaking about him, but there are disconcerting changes of person that are hard to explain. The book contains many duplicate passages (thirty-seven in the Massoretic text, thirty in the Septuagint, according to Workman[1]), and a number of passages appear to be parallel accounts of the same event. A chronological order apparently is sometimes employed, as mostly in chapters 1–20, but a topical order is followed in chapters 21–24, 30–31, and 46–51. Finally, the Septuagint presents many problems in the study of the composition of Jeremiah. It contains about one-eighth less material than the Massoretic Hebrew text, with numerous omissions, some additions, and some changes. Some of the passages appear in a different order in the

---

1. *The Text of Jeremiah* (Edinburgh, 1889), pp. 50-51.

Septuagint from that of the Massoretic text, especially the foreign oracles, which come after 25:13.

In view of these facts it is not surprising that Old Testament scholars have reached no consensus of opinion regarding the composition of Jeremiah, and numerous theories have been offered to explain how the book reached its present condition.

I

Every commentator on Jeremiah has had to deal with the problem of its composition, and several articles and monographs have been devoted to the subject. Without attempting to give an exhaustive history of the discussion of our problem, we shall consider a few of the views that have been advanced to explain the composition of Jeremiah, particular attention being given to those which have noted Deuteronomic elements in the book.

In 1901 Bernhard Duhm published a commentary which, although radical in many of its conclusions, showed unusual religious and literary appreciation and has greatly influenced all subsequent work on Jeremiah.[2] Duhm thought that the book consists of three types of material: Jeremiah's own words, almost exclusively poetry in Qina metre, comprising 280 Massoretic verses; Baruch's life of Jeremiah, 220 verses; and later additions, 850 verses. These later additions are from many different *Ergänzer* or *Bearbeiter,* some from as late as the early part of the first century B.C. Duhm recognized that many of the additions in the third group have much in common, in both form and substance, with the Deuteronomistic parts of the Former Prophets and may come from the same hands.

C. H. Cornill[3] thought it was possible to recover the original words of Jeremiah, including the scroll dictated in 604, and the memoirs of Baruch, but recognized that the book contains much secondary material and expansions at many points. He did not attempt to classify the secondary material. He believed that the author of the oracle against Babylon, 50:2–51:58, knew the work after the words of Jeremiah and the memoirs of Baruch had been combined, somewhat in the form that we have them now; this oracle against Babylon was composed in the postexilic period before the Chronicler.

---

2. *Das Buch Jeremia erklärt* (Kurzer Hand-Commentar z. A. T., ed. by Marti, XI), Tübingen, 1901; see especially pp. xvi-xx.
3. *Das Buch Jeremia erklärt,* Leipzig, 1905.

A. S. Peake has written one of the best commentaries on Jeremiah in English.[4] He distinguished the original utterances of Jeremiah, including those in Baruch's scroll, the series of narratives by Baruch, and supplements to these. Although not a few passages were attributed by him to the Supplementers, he did not classify them; he did recognize, however, that the Deuteronomic phraseology tends to be pronounced in additions made by the Supplementers.[5]

Paul Volz[6] recognized in the Book of Jeremiah four sources: (1) Jeremiah's own writing (for he himself made some small collections of material, e.g., 22:1–23:4 and 23:13-32); (2) Baruch's writing at Jeremiah's dictation; (3) Baruch's independent work; and (4) later additions. Many of the passages in the fourth group were added in order to make the Book of Jeremiah, like other prophetic books, useful for reading in synagogue services and usable by synagogue preachers. Volz thus speaks of *homolieartige synagogale Erweiterung* of the work of Jeremiah and Baruch. This was apparently the result of the labors of many scribes and editors.

In 1914 Sigmund Mowinckel published a monograph on the composition of Jeremiah which contains much insight but has not received as much attention as it deserves.[7] He distinguished four principal sources in Jeremiah, designated as A, B, C and D. A was a collection of Jeremianic oracles, loosely placed together by someone living in Egypt between 580 and 480 B.C. The foundation of this was Baruch's scroll. It is contained now within chapters 1–24, and is the most authentic part of the book. It is mostly poetry, and largely in the first person. B was a personal history of Jeremiah, contained within chapters 19–20, 26–45. It was written by an admirer of the prophet, but was not genuine biography or history, properly speaking. This material existed for a time in an oral stage, and was written down by someone in Egypt in the same period as A. It was not Baruch's work. This source is valuable for events in Jeremiah's life, but does not give his words in their original form. The third source, C, is the Deuteronomic source. It consists mainly of the following: 3:6-13; 7:1–8:3; 11:1-5, 9-14; 18:1-12; 21:1-10; 22:1-5; 25:1-

---

4. *Jeremiah and Lamentations* (The New-Century Bible), 2 vols., Oxford, 1910.
5. *Ibid.*, pp. 59-60.
6. *Der Prophet Jeremia übersetzt und erklärt* (Kommentar z. A. T., ed. by Sellin, X), 2d ed., Leipzig, 1928.
7. *Zur Komposition des Buches Jeremia* (Videnskapsselskapets Skrifter. II. Hist.-filos. Klasse. 1913. No. 5), Kristiana, 1914.

11a; 27; 29:1-23; 32:1-2, 6-16, 24-44; 34:1-22; 35:1-19; 39:15-18; 44:1-14; 45. This material is mostly prose, and consists largely of speeches by Jeremiah. It is characterized by a monotonous style and relatively small vocabulary. Its theme is the uninterrupted sinfulness of Judah and her punishment. It is close to Deuteronomy in form and conception of religion, and has far less value than A and B. D is the book of comfort in 30:1–31:28. Chapters 46–51 are still later, as well as some scattered portions of the book in its present form.

In a recent work, *Prophecy and Tradition,*[8] Mowinckel indicates that his view of the composition of Jeremiah has changed somewhat since he wrote his monograph in 1914. Instead of "sources" he would now speak of "traditionary circles," by which presumably he means circles in which oral tradition was preserved.

In the same year as Mowinckel's monograph, Hölscher published his *Die Profeten,* in which a section is devoted to the composition of Jeremiah.[9] He advanced the theory that our Book of Jeremiah, excluding 50:1–51:58, comes largely from a single redactor who lived in the Persian period. He made use of two *Vorlage*: an "I" source, and a "He" source, the latter being the work of Baruch. The redactor put these two sources together and edited them to a large extent, as can be seen by the number of stereotyped phrases with which the book is filled, listed by Hölscher on pp. 382-384. Many of these phrases he calls Deuteronomic, but he does not term the redactor a Deuteronomic editor.

Somewhat similar to Hölscher's view, although apparently independent, is that of H. G. May.[10] He thinks that Baruch was not the author or editor of any part of Jeremiah, but only the prophet's amanuensis. The book comes to us for the larger part from the hand of one person, whom he terms "the Biographer," a man who used many stereotyped expressions and was steeped in the Deuteronomic tradition. He employed as his materials genuine oracles of the prophet, Jeremiah's memoirs, and other materials which tradition ascribed to the prophet, and sometimes he freely composed as he went along. He lived in the period between 500 and 450 B.C., being influenced by Second Isaiah, Ezra-Nehemiah, and others. His domi-

---

8. Oslo, 1946, see especially pp. 61-65, 105-106.
9. Leipzig, 1914, pp. 379-405.
10. "Towards an Objective Approach to the Book of Jeremiah: the Biographer," *Journal of Biblical Literature,* LXI (1942), 139-155; "Jeremiah's Biographer," *Journal of Bible and Religion,* X (1942), 195-201.

nant theme was the coming restoration of the Davidic line and the union of Israel and Judah.

R. H. Pfeiffer has devoted to the composition of the Book of Jeremiah a very stimulating and important section of his *Introduction to the Old Testament*.[11] He distinguishes three types of material: words dictated or written by the prophet himself, a biography by his secretary Baruch, and miscellaneous contributions from later redactors. He is impressed by the large number of stereotyped expressions listed by Hölscher, and thinks that Baruch prepared an edition in which he combined the prophet's book with his own, and rewrote or revised many of his master's speeches in his own Deuteronomistic style.

The author of the latest full-scale commentary on Jeremiah, Wilhelm Rudolph,[12] follows the analysis of Mowinckel to a large extent, employing Mowinckel's symbols A, B, and C for the three principal sources. However, he differs from Mowinckel in a number of details. His Deuteronomic source "C" differs at several points from Mowinckel's; to it he assigns the following: 7:1–8:3; 11:1-14 (17); 16:1-13 (18); 17:19-27; 18:1-12; 21:1-10; 22:1-5; 25:1-14; 34:8-22; 35.

Of others who have written on the composition of Jeremiah, we mention briefly only two. Nathaniel Schmidt's article on Jeremiah in the *Encyclopedia Biblica* is one of the most radical treatments of the book. Not only does he relegate much of the book to late editors, but he denies that Baruch was anything more than the prophet's amanuensis. E. Podechard's article, "Le livre de Jérémie; structure et formation," *Revue Biblique,* 37 (1928), 181-197, contains some important insights, especially on the nature of chapters 26-45.

This survey should make it clear that one of the basic problems in the study of the composition of the Book of Jeremiah is the determination of the precise nature of the Deuteronomic element in the book. We cannot say, as Bishop Colenso said in the nineteenth century, that Jeremiah was both the author of Deuteronomy and editor of many of the historical books of the Old Testament.[13] There is too great a difference between the prose passages which show Deuter-

---

11. New York, 1941, pp. 500-511.
12. *Jeremia* (Handbuch z. A. T., ed. by Eissfeldt, Erste Reihe, 12), Tübingen, 1947; see especially pp. XIII-XIX.
13. *The Pentateuch and Book of Joshua Critically Examined,* Part VII (London, 1879), pp. 12, 225-227, 259-269, and Appendix 149.

onomic diction and the best poetry of Jeremiah for this to be true. Yet there are many questions relating to the Deuteronomic element in Jeremiah that are still the subject of controversy. How extensive is this element? Is it a source, either oral or written, used by an editor; or should we speak of a Deuteronomic edition of the book? If it was a source or edition, when was it made and by whom? Was Baruch the Deuteronomist? What is the value of the Deuteronomic material for recovering the life and teachings of the prophet Jeremiah?

The present writer published an article several years ago which dealt with the relationship between Jeremiah and Deuteronomy.[14] In that article I was principally concerned with the relationship of the prophet to Josiah's reforms, but gave some attention to the Deuteronomic editing of the Book of Jeremiah. My view concerning Jeremiah's relationship to the Deuteronomic reforms has remained unchanged, but I have come to a clearer opinion than was then expressed of the extent and nature of the Deuteronomic element in the Book of Jeremiah. I now believe that D was responsible for making an edition of the book in one of its early stages. The purpose of the present paper is to discuss the extent, the characteristics, the date, and the value of the Deuteronomic edition of Jeremiah.

II

The contribution to the Old Testament made by that individual whom we call the Deuteronomist, or the "school" of writers we call the Deuteronomists, was very great.[15] Since we must distinguish at least two stages in the work, designated by the symbols D_1 and D_2, it is best to think of a "school" and to speak of them in the plural; for the sake of convenience, however, we shall designate them simply by the symbol D.

D not only wrote the first and later editions of Deuteronomy, but edited in one way or another Joshua, Judges, I-II Samuel, and I-II Kings. D exhibits a remarkable uniformity of style and thought, remarkable though not of course complete.

14. "Jeremiah and Deuteronomy," *Journal of Near Eastern Studies,* I (1942), 156-173. For a recent study of the subject, see H. H. Rowley, "The Prophet Jeremiah and the Book of Deuteronomy," in *Studies in Old Testament Prophecy Presented to Professor Theodore H. Robinson,* edited by Rowley (Edinburgh, 1950), pp. 157-174.
15. The contribution is well set forth by Lindsay B. Longacre, *The Old Testament: Its Form and Purpose* (New York-Nashville, 1945), chs. I-II.

The literary style of D is distinctive and easy to recognize. It shows a tendency to use a limited number of words and phrases over and over, and the general tone is parenetic. The style sometimes has great beauty, but is frequently repetitious and monotonous. D worked with a variety of methods. Sometimes they excerpted material from their sources without change; sometimes they rewrote older material (as in Joshua) ; sometimes they were content to provide a framework for older material (as largely in Judges) ; and sometimes they composed freely, especially in speeches and prayers.

The ideas of D are likewise distinctive and very pervasive. Their most important ideas were the following. Yahweh alone is to be worshiped by Israel, and that with a pure worship cleansed of pagan elements, with legitimate sacrifice only in the Jerusalem temple. Idolatry, the worship of foreign deities, is one of the greatest of sins. D had great interest in working out a theology of history, with special emphasis on the doctrine of divine retribution: Yahweh always punishes the wicked and rewards the righteous. A high social morality is demanded, with social justice for all, and with humanitarianism directed toward the unfortunate members of society.

The presence of Deuteronomic words and phrases in the Book of Jeremiah has frequently been pointed out. In order that we may have a sound basis for our discussion of the work of D, we shall list the more important D words and phrases appearing in Jeremiah, those which are of special significance in identifying D passages.[16]

(1) The following are brief D phrases which occur in Jeremiah: *a mighty hand and outstretched arm; provoke me* (or, *Yahweh*) *to anger,* especially in the infinitive *l'hak'isēnî* and the like ; *the stranger, the fatherless, and the widow; serve* (or, *go after*) *other gods; make his name dwell there; gods* (or, *people,* or *land*) *which thou knowest not; the land* (or, *place*) *which I gave to you and your fathers; when I brought them from the land of Egypt; house of bondage; hearken to his voice; do that which is right* (or, *evil*) *in the eyes of Yahweh; (all) that he commanded you; the evil that he pronounced against you; a taunt, a reproach, a desolation, a proverb, a curse, a hissing,* etc., in a series, in various forms ; *with all the heart and all the soul;*

---

16. For further details and scriptural references, cf. the lists given by Hölscher, *op. cit.,* pp. 382-384; May, *Journal of Biblical Literature,* LXI (1942), pp. 154-155; and S. R. Driver, *Deuteronomy* (International Critical Commentary), pp. lxxviii-lxxxiv. My lists are not exhaustive.

the work of the hands (i.e., idols) ; *sent unto you all his servants the prophets.*

(2) Longer phrases which show very close relationships to Deuteronomy, especially chapter 28, are the following: *the dead bodies of this people shall be food for the birds of the sky and the beasts of the earth, with none to frighten them away* (Jer. 7:33; 16:4; 19:7; Deut. 28:26) ; *behold, I will bring evil on this place, so that whoever hears it, his ears shall tingle* (Jer. 19:3; II Kings 21:12) ; *I will rejoice over them to do them good* (Jer. 32:41; Deut. 28:63) ; *I will cause them to eat the flesh of their sons and the flesh of their daughters . . . in the siege and in the distress with which their enemies shall distress them"* (Jer. 19:9; Deut. 28:53) ; *I will make them a terror to all the kingdoms of the earth* (Jer. 15:4; 24:9; 29:18; cf. Deut. 28:25) ; *to a land which you have not known, neither you nor your fathers, and there you shall serve other gods night and day* (Jer. 16:3; Deut. 28:36) ; *why has Yahweh done thus to this great city?* (Jer. 22:8; cf. 16:10; Deut. 29:24; I Kings 9:8) ; *you shall seek me and find me when you seek me with your whole heart* (Jer. 29:13; Deut. 4:29) ; *you shall walk in all the way I command you, in order that it may be well with you* (Jer. 7:23; Deut. 5:30) ; *to fear me all the days, for their good* (Jer. 32:39; Deut. 4:10; 6:24) ; *when I brought them from the land of Egypt, from the iron furnace* (Jer. 11:4; Deut. 4:20).

(3) In addition to these, a number of stereotyped phrases occur in Jeremiah, often in association with the above, and are therefore to be considered as characteristic of D in Jeremiah although they do not appear (or appear only very rarely) in D writing elsewhere: *amend your ways and your doings; into the hand of those who seek their life; they did not hearken, and did not incline their ear; this house which is called by my name; for I am with thee to save thee and deliver thee; king, princes, priests, and prophets; walk in my law which I have given them; men of Judah and inhabitants of Jerusalem; his life shall be given* (or, *I will give*) *to him for a prey; sword, famine, and pestilence; turn now, each from his evil way; voice of joy and voice of gladness, voice of the bride and voice of the bridegroom;* and the contrasting ideas in the verbs, *build and plant, pull down and uproot.*

In identifying the D elements of Jeremiah, we must not employ the criterion of diction in a mechanical way, and we must use other criteria along with those of diction. Some of the phrases listed above may occur sporadically in genuine passages, but when several of them occur in a given passage, it is doubtless the work of D. Some of the phrases may in fact have been borrowed in the first place from genuine portions of Jeremiah. In addition to diction, we must use the criteria of style and of ideas, and we must give consideration to the motive of D in adding, or editing, a given passage.

III

The work of D in the Book of Jeremiah, as I conceive it, may be set forth as follows, beginning with the first chapter and working through to the end of the book.

In chapter 1, D has added vss. 15-16, 18-19 to the account of the call of Jeremiah and his two visions, which were in Baruch's scroll. Vss. 15-16 are the counterpart of 25:1-13a, also written by D, as we shall see below. Vs. 16 in particular shows D phraseology. Here it is predicted that the nations will come to surround Jerusalem and the cities of Judah to witness the judgment which God will pass on them; in chapter 25 they are the agents of the judgment. Vs. 15 may have originally read, not "all the families of the kingdoms of the north," but "a kingdom of the north" as was originally the case in 25:9. In 25:9 the Septuagint reads πατριὰν ἀπὸ βορρᾶ; in 1:15 it reads πάσας τὰς βασιλείας ἀπὸ βορρᾶ τῆς γῆς. Chapter 25 has been expanded and its general purport changed, as we shall show later; after the change was made there, a corresponding change was made in 1:15-16. Both were prophecies after the capture of Jerusalem by the Babylonians in 587 B.C. 1:18-19 borrows from 15:20, but is a prosaic piling up of figures and listing of the various classes in Judah, very characteristic of D. It is D's judgment on the life of Jeremiah written after his death. These verses have been appended to vs. 17, which originally stood in Baruch's scroll immediately after vs. 14.

In chapter 3, vss. 6-18 are widely considered secondary in whole or in part. Vs. 19 is a good continuation of vs. 5, but not of vs. 18. 3:6-14 is by D. It has little D diction, but does emphasize the sin of worship on the high places which D abhorred, and vs. 8 recalls the law of Deut. 24:1-4. D has derived the idea that Judah is worse than Israel from Ezekiel; see Ezek. 16:44-63; 23. D has incorporated a genuine oracle of the prophet, vss. 12b-14a, in the latter part of the section, but has misunderstood the meaning of the word "return," tak-

79

ing it to mean return from exile rather than repentance. 3:15-18 is also secondary, but from another editor, living during the exile or in the postexilic period; the ideas are similar to those found in Isa. 2:2-4; Micah 4:1-4; Ezek. 34; 37:16-28; Zech. 8:1-8, and elsewhere; to 3:17, cf. Jer. 14:21; 17:12 (also secondary).

5:18-19 is D's explanation of the exile in a form and in words very similar to those of Jer. 9:12-16; 16:10-13; 22:8-9; Deut. 29:22-28; and I Kings 9:8-9. Anyone who will compare all of these passages should be readily convinced that they are all from the same pen. They are designed to give a ready explanation for the desolation of Judah in 587 B.C., written after Nebuchadnezzar's invasion and his capture of Jerusalem.

7:1–8:3 is the first long section contributed by D to the Book of Jeremiah. The whole section is filled with D phraseology, and is in D's characteristic prose style. It contains several verses that are duplicates of, or clearly parallel to, other D passages: 7:16=11:14 (cf. 14:11-12); to 7:24 cf. 11:8; to 7:30-33 cf. 32:34-35; 19:6-7; to 7:34 cf. 16:9; 25:10. D has collected here various teachings of Jeremiah dealing with cultic places and practices. Mowinckel has appropriately compared the collection with Matthew's Sermon on the Mount. The teachings were not all given at one place and one time, but they constitute some of the most important of Jeremiah's messages. We do not have here the actual words of the prophet, since D style pervades the whole section, but we do have for the most part the substance of his teachings, for they agree in the main with his sayings elsewhere. The "temple sermon" probably extends only through 7:15. 7:21-26 may have been spoken on the same occasion, but more probably it was not. The parallel account of the "temple sermon" in 26:4-6 contains only the substance of 7:2-15, and the prophet's words reach their climax in 7:14-15; it is unlikely that the religious leaders would have allowed him to continue had he wished to do so. 7:29 is poetry, and may be a direct quotation from the prophet's sayings.

8:19b is a D gloss which breaks into the context. The poem places in the mouth of the people the question in 19a and the statement in 20. Vs. 19b is clearly a prosaic gloss in which Yahweh speaks rather than the people. The idea and phraseology are Deuteronomic.

9:12-16 is by D, comparable to 5:18-19. See the discussion above of that passage.

11:1-17 is another long contribution by D. This passage has been much discussed by critics and is very important for the study of the relationship between Jeremiah and Deuteronomy. The whole section is of D origin, though verses 15-16 have been taken unchanged from a collection of Jeremiah's own words, from either Baruch's scroll or some other collection. For detailed proof of this view, see my remarks in *Journal of Near Eastern Studies,* I (1942), 168-170. D wrote this section for a twofold purpose: (1) to show that Jeremiah was one of a line of prophets who had called on Israel to obey "the words of this covenant," as the Deuteronomists understood them (that is, the decalogue in Deut. 4:13; 9:9, 11, 15; the Deuteronomic code itself in Deut. 29:1, 9, 21—but between these two there was no contradiction in their minds); and (2) to say that because the people had not obeyed the covenant the evils pronounced for disobedience (as in Deut. 28:15-68) had come upon them. This section is therefore prophecy after the event. It is largely a free composition of the Deuteronomic editor, and we cannot recover a Jeremianic kernel with any certainty. D's incorporation of a genuine poem by the prophet (vss. 15-16) may be compared with his method in 1:15-19, where vs. 17 is a genuine saying, and with 7:1–8:3, where 7:29 is a genuine saying.

In 13:1-11, the parable of the waist-cloth, D has appended verse 11, thus making an unnecessary application of a single detail of the parable; cf. Deut. 26:19, and the use of the verb "cleave" in Deut. 10:20; 11:22; 13:4; Jos. 22:5; 23:8; II Kings 18:6.

14:1–15:4, which purports to be a word of Yahweh concerning the drouth, offers many puzzles to the interpreter. Several of the verses have to do with other subjects than drouth, some of them suggesting invasion or the like (see especially vss. 12, 13, 18). The heading in 14:1 is very late, being similar to the headings in 46:1; 47:1 and 49:34, all undeniably late. Within this congeries, 14:11-12 and 15:1-4 may be of D origin. 14:11 is closely parallel to 7:16 and 11:14, both in D sections; and D phraseology is very evident in 15:4. The emphasis on the sin of Manasseh is such as we find in II Kings 21:11-15; 23:26-27; 24:3-4. 14:13-18 is very likely genuine, but the editor who put the whole section together lived later than D.

In chapter 16, vss. 1-13, 18 are from D, as correctly pointed out by Rudolph. In vss. 1-13 D has revised a genuine account of Jeremiah's celibacy; his terminology is especially evident in vss. 4, 9, and 10-13. On 10-13, see the remarks above on 5:18-19. The whole is written from the standpoint of one who lived after the events of 587. It is not hypercritical for us to doubt that D gives the correct reason for Jeremiah's celibacy; the true reason may be that his complete and wholehearted devotion to his prophetic mission left no room for devotion to a wife and family. 16:14-15 is virtually a duplicate of 23:7-8, the original position of the passage; the verses have been inserted here (after D) in order to soften to some degree the preceding prediction of exile. If we then consider the whole section, 16:1-13, 16-18, we see that D has included a genuine poem of Jeremiah's (vss. 16-17) along with material of his own composition. The method of D here is thus similar to that which he employed in 11:1-17, where D included a genuine poem (11:15-16) with material of his own composition.

17:2b-3a is a gloss by D. Jeremiah says in vss. 1-2a that the sins of the people are written in two places: in their hearts and in the cultus. The prophet means that the cultus itself is a source of sin to the people, but D here adds a series of specific objects used in the cultus which are intended to convey the idea that it is not the cultus *per se* which is wrong, but a false variety of it. The gloss consists of the words "their altars and their Asherim by the green trees on the high hills, the mountains in the open country."

17:19-27, on Sabbath observance, is in the style and diction of D, as recognized by Rudolph. Its phraseology should be compared with that of other Deuteronomic passages, particularly Jer. 7:2, 24, 26; 11:8; 22:2, 4, 5. Nearly all critical scholars consider the passage secondary, and non-Jeremianic in its extreme emphasis on the importance of the proper observance of the Sabbath. It is not necessary to date it in the time of Nehemiah, as some scholars have done, comparing Neh. 13:15-22. It is possible, and even probable, that such interest in the Sabbath arose during the exilic period. Similar interest may be seen in Isa. 56:2-6; 58:13-14. The date of these passages has been the subject of much debate; W. S. McCullough has recently presented strong arguments for dating Isa. 56-66 in the period between 587 and 562.[17]

In chapter 18, D has added his own interpretation of the parable of the potter, vss. 7-12. The most obvious and simple meaning of the parable in vss. 1-6 is that Yahweh has good plans for Israel

---

17. *Journal of Biblical Literature*, LXVII (1948), 27-36.

and wishes to make her a good nation; if he does not succeed at first, as a potter spoils a vessel, he will remold her according to his designs. The initiative and the plans are God's; ultimately, the parable said, God will make of Israel what he wishes. The interpretation given in vss. 7-12 changes the underlying thought and makes the fate of the people depend upon what *they* do, not God. In addition to the fact that vss. 7-12 contain D phraseology is the fact that it sets forth D's fundamental doctrine of divine retribution. We may suppose that D found the parable in one of his sources and left it intact up to vs. 7; then he simply added vss. 7-12 or substituted them for the application made in his source.

In 19:1–20:6 we have an account of a symbolic action and speech by Jeremiah which led to his being placed in stocks by Pashhur. As the text now stands, two things have been combined in this section: (1) an account of the symbolic action in which the prophet broke an earthen flask, his address to the people in the temple court, and his imprisonment (19:1-2a, 10–11a, 14–15; 20:1-6), and (2) a "sermon" on Topheth (19:2b-9, 11b-13). The first of these is authentic and probably came from Baruch's memoirs; D has inserted into this his own long speech about Topheth, and has slightly revised the account of the arrest and punishment of Jeremiah. D phraseology is especially evident in vss. 3 (cf. II Kings 21:12), 7 (cf. Deut. 28:26), and 9 (cf. Deut. 28:53). D inserted the sermon on Topheth at this point because of the similarity in Hebrew between "the earthen flask" and "the potsherd gate"; he has played on the name Topheth, and in vss. 7-9 on the word *baqbūq* ("flask"). The abominations committed at Topheth in the valley of Hinnom are referred to by D also in Jer. 7:31ff.; 32:35.

21:1-12 is D's version of the incident reported in 37:3-10 (which stood in Baruch's memoirs). The relationship of these two sections to each other has been variously conceived by critics. Some believe that both refer to the same event, and combine parts of both to secure one complete account. Others accept them as accounts of two separate missions from Zedekiah. It would be dogmatic to deny that Zedekiah could have sent two separate missions to Jeremiah, one at the beginning of the Babylonian siege of Jerusalem (21:1-12) and the other during the interval when Egyptian help was coming to the city and the Babylonians temporarily lifted their siege (37:3-10). It is more likely, however, that 21:1-12 is simply D's rewriting of the incident which is more accurately reported in chapter 37, for the following reasons: Zephaniah the son of Maaseiah appears as an envoy in both; the time of the mission in chapter 21 is vague; D phraseology and ideas pervade 21:1-12; and the account is artificially constructed, in that vss. 3-7 are addressed to Zedekiah through the envoys, whereas vss. 8-10 are addressed to the people (although the conference presumably was secret), and verses 11-12 are directed to the royal house in general and consist of general admonitions based on 22:3 and 4:4.

22:1-5 is D's introduction to the group of oracles about the kings of Judah in 22:1–23:6. Since D furnishes the introduction, it was probably he who collected most of these oracles as we now have them (23:1-6 are probably later than D). They were not in Baruch's scroll, because they include oracles against kings who lived later than 604. In addition to the fact that 22:1-5 has D diction and ideas, we should observe that the admonitions are directed to the royal house in general rather than to a specific king, that they are conventional in tone, and that the promises attached are greater and more materialistic than Jeremiah usually made.

Within the group of oracles against Judaean kings, 22:8-9 was written by D (see the remarks on 5:18-19 above), and 22:24-27 may be his work. The latter has some D phrases, and is to be considered as prophecy after the event.

Chapter 24 must be assigned wholly to D. The difficulties in this chapter have been noted by critics, but most accept it as genuine, a few bracketing certain verses as secondary. Duhm declared it to be the work of an editor; May assigns it unequivocally to the Biographer. The attitude expressed here about the exiles accords well with the attitude of later times which saw in the Jews who had gone into Babylonian exile and later returned the true Israelites, and with the view of those who considered the exiled Jehoiachin as the legitimate king and opposed the claims of Zedekiah. It does not accord with Jeremiah's ideas expressed elsewhere, and is filled with D phraseology, most noticeably in verses 6, 7, 9 and 10. It is difficult to believe that Jeremiah thought God's favor depended on whether one were exiled or not, rather than upon repentance and obedience. In chapter 5 he expressed the opinion that all classes in Jerusalem were sinful. The viewpoint of chapter 24 is not consonant with Jeremiah's viewpoint in the letter to the exiles in chapter 29, nor with his general attitude toward Zedekiah. That king was friendly to the prophet and apparently wished to follow his counsel, but was weak and unwilling to risk the disfavor of the pro-Egyptian party among his officials. The view of this chapter does not accord with Jeremiah's decision at the fall of Jerusalem in 587 to remain in Palestine. We do not need, however, to date chapter 24 in the time of Ezra-Nehemiah. The mention of the exiles in Egypt suggests that the Egyptian exile chronicled in Jer. 43-44 was of recent occurrence, and the general tenor suggests that opposition to Zedekiah was of vivid memory. It is noteworthy that D frequently displays a friendly attitude toward Babylonia and her rulers. Whether D freely composed this chapter or rewrote some material which he found, we do not know; but in its present form it is his product and not Jeremiah's.

Chapter 25 is one of the most interesting and important portions of the Book of Jeremiah for the study of D. Here we must assign verses 1-13a *in their original form* to D. He wrote the section to form the conclusion to what he believed was Baruch's scroll of 604 (as shown by the reference to the fourth year of Jehoiakim in 25:1). We must recall that he had written 1:15-16 at the beginning of the book. The words "this book" in vs. 13 refer backward, not forward, and this section originally concluded with those words. Compare the "book" of 51:60, which refers back to the oracles against Babylon. The differences between the Massoretic text and the Septuagint in 25:1-13 are very striking: the Septuagint omits the references to Babylon and Nebuchadnezzar, having in verse 9 πατριὰν ἀπὸ βορρᾶ; vs. 12 is much shorter than in the Hebrew; and the Septuagint uses first person instead of third person in vss. 4-5. The Septuagint represents a more nearly original form of this passage than the Massoretic text, but not quite the original, since some changes were made in the Septuagint *Vorlage* in the same direction as the present Hebrew text. Skinner has printed a translation of what he believes to have been the original text.[18] He is certainly correct in the main. In its original form, as it came from the pen of D, 25:1-13a was directed against Judah and Jerusalem, not against Babylonia and other nations; this is clearly pointed out at the outset in vs. 2, and is implied in the nature of the sins for which punishment is promised.

---

18. *Prophecy and Religion* (Cambridge, 1922), pp. 240-241. Skinner accepts the conjecture that these verses were the conclusion (rather than the introduction, as some scholars have thought) of the volume of prophecies dictated by Jeremiah to Baruch.

There is only a vague reference to the coming of a "family from the north," such as D believed possible in 604. This section was edited at a later time, after D, in order to make it serve as an introduction to the oracles against the foreign nations, probably by the editor of 25:13b-38. In the Septuagint the oracles against the foreign nations stand after 25:13; this was probably their original position, though it is possible that 25:13a-38 once stood just before the foreign oracles, even in the Hebrew text.

There is no doubt that D phraseology and ideas pervade 25:1-13a in their original form. D has not, however, worked over 13b-38; vs. 18, which has some D phrases, either is misplaced or is imitation of D phraseology. The foreign oracles show no trace of D redaction. We must conclude, then, that when the oracles against foreign nations were collected, 25:13b-38 was written (probably with the inclusion of some authentic sayings of the prophet) as their introduction, and 25:1-13a was revised to make it apply to the foreign nations rather than to Judah.

Chapter 26 is D's report of the temple sermon of Jeremiah and his subsequent arrest and trial. His rewriting is confined almost entirely to the summary of the sermon in vss. 4-6, which is filled with D phrases. Since D had given what he considered a full report in chapter 7, he was satisfied with only a brief résumé here; the account of subsequent events bears few marks of D redaction (see vss. 13, 19). For the whole chapter, D used as source a part of Baruch's memoirs.

Chapter 27 is D's version of a symbolic action and message of the prophet. It is not, however, merely a parallel to chapter 28, as Mowinckel thought. D has here taken from Baruch's memoirs an account of the action and words of Jeremiah and expanded them; his diction is especially evident in vss. 5, 8, and 13. The account as we now have it is repetitious, being addressed in turn to the foreign envoys, to Zedekiah, and to the priests and all the people; there is careless interchange of first and third persons.

Chapter 29, containing Jeremiah's letter to the exiles, was originally in Baruch's memoirs, but has been revised somewhat by D. His ideas and phraseology are evident in vss. 10-20, especially in vss. 16-20, which have been considered by most critics as secondary. For evidence of D phraseology, the following comparisons should be made: cf. vs. 13 with Deut. 4:29 and I Kings 8:48; cf. vs. 14 with Deut. 30:3, 5; and cf. vs. 18 with Deut. 28:25. Within vss.

10-14 there may be some of the prophet's own words and ideas (particularly verse 11), but the passage has been revised to such an extent that we cannot recover his words with precision.

Chapter 32 is an excellent example of the method of D. He found in Baruch's memoirs (32:1, 6-15) a straightforward account of Jeremiah's purchase of a field at Anathoth with a simple "word of the Lord" appended as explanation of the significance of the act (vs. 15). To this D has added a long section, vss. 16-44, repeating some of the genuine material in vss. 43-44. (32:2-5 is probably from a later editor.) Nearly all critics see in this chapter some secondary material after vs. 16; even Condamin admits that vss. 17-23 and 28-35 are secondary. Mowinckel assigns vss. 1-2, 6-16 and 24-44 to his "C," but D phraseology is as evident in vss. 17-23 as in other parts of the long section. Vss. 17-44 are an excellent summary of D's theology of history, including his interpretation of the Babylonian exile and his hope for the future. His hope for the future is expressed in positive terms, but it is more general than is found in later eschatological passages which have been included in the Book of Jeremiah.

In chapter 33, vss. 1-13 may be D's revision of some incident which is now obscurely preserved in vss. 4-5, where the text is difficult to understand. D phrascology is not strong, but may be present in such verses as 9 and 11. On the other hand, the whole passage may be much later than D, with some imitation of D terminology. Vss. 14-26 are not in the Septuagint and are probably later than D.

In chapter 34, D has rewritten vss. 8-22, the account of the release of Hebrew slaves during the Babylonian siege of Jerusalem. Not only is D phraseology abundant, but the release is confused with the sabbatical release of slaves according to the law of Deut. 15. In the nature of the case it must have been a release by special proclamation, since the sabbatical release of so many slaves could not have fallen at one time. D's hand is particularly evident in vss. 13-15 and 17. It may be that D has not preserved the real motive for the prophet's condemnation of the people's release of their slaves and then taking them back when danger seemed past. He may well have condemned them for their hypocrisy; the release of slaves during the siege would have been to the economic advantage of the owners, relieving them of the burden of feeding and caring for them when food was scarce. Mowinckel assigns the entire chapter to "C," but there is no trace of D in vss. 1-7.

In chapter 35, D has rewritten and expanded the speech of Jeremiah in vss. 12-19 and slightly retouched the early part. In addition to the strong diction of D in vss. 13, 15, 17, note the recurrence of the words *miṣwāh* and *miṣwōth* so frequently employed by D, and the idea of retribution which was so often emphasized by D. The original oracle of the prophet may be preserved in vss. 18-19.

In chapter 36, vss. 28-31 are D's rewriting of the word of Yahweh to Jeremiah concerning the dictation of a second scroll. Duhm pointed out a number of artificial elements in this section: Jehoiakim is addressed as if Jeremiah were not at the time in hiding with Baruch; the king is condemned for burning the first scroll as if that were the worst thing he had done; and the prediction that Jehoiakim would have no descendant overlooks the fact that his son Jehoiachin did rule. The whole has the tone of one of D's freely composed speeches. 36:27-28, 32 gives all the authentic information we need about the writing of the second scroll.

37:1-2 may be a historical note by D, giving a general estimate of Zedekiah and his reign of the type familiar in the Books of Kings. D has not touched the rest of the chapter, but 21:1-12, as noted above, is his version of the incident of 37:3-10.

In chapter 38, vss. 2 and 23 are from D. The former has the diction and the ideas of D; the genuine verse is 3. Vs. 23 is a prosaic explanation of the preceding verse.

Chapters 39-40 present a number of difficulties, as all commentators have recognized, but an easy and simple solution is possible. The two stories of the treatment of the prophet by Babylonian officials in 39:14 and 40:1-6 cannot be harmonized. In chapter 39, only vss. 3 and 14 are original, but they give all the information needed concerning the release of Jeremiah: he was released from prison by the officials named in vs. 3 (Nebuzaradan not being among them, for he did not appear in Jerusalem until a month later, according to Jer. 52:12), and he was then placed in the custody of Gedaliah. 39:1-2, 4-13, 15-18; 40:1-6 is all from D. 39:1-2, 4-10 is a shortened account of the events narrated in Jer. 52:4-16 (=II Kings 25:1-12). The latter is Deuteronomic, but the material in Jer. 39 is from the D editor of Jeremiah, who used the same sources as the editor of II Kings 25. 39:11-13; 40:1-6 is a legendary account of the treatment of the prophet; this account tends to elevate the standing of the prophet and to justify the actions of Nebuchadnezzar and Nebuzaradan. It is hard to see how anyone can believe that Nebuzaradan spoke the words reported in 40:2-3, where he is made to expound the Deuteronomic doctrine of retribution. 39:15-18 is also by D. His diction occurs here, and the story is told because D could not allow Ebed-melech to go unrewarded.

40:7–42:6 has been untouched by D, but his revision is clearly evident in 42:7-22. The section is repetitious and burdensome, and has many conventional D phrases. The kernel of the prophet's answer to those who wished to go to Egypt is contained in vss. 9-14, but even that shows traces of D revision.

Chapter 44 has been rewritten by D. It probably rests upon authentic words of Jeremiah, preserved in Baruch's memoirs, but the phrasing is D's and the theme is a favorite of his. It is not worthwhile to attempt to recover the prophet's original words, since the whole section has been worked over by D.

Chapter 45 has caused critics much labor in interpretation. Its subject matter seems insignificant, and the date given in vs. 1 seems to most commentators open to question. Erbt saw in the chapter the last words of Jeremiah before he sent Baruch to the Gola in Babylonia to be his witness.[19] I believe Mowinckel is right in assigning the chapter to D; he does not give strong reasons for his opinion, but seems to reach his decision by a process of eliminating the chapter from other sources. The chapter does have some familiar D phrases, particularly in vss. 4 and 5b. This is D's final word in the Book of Jeremiah, a word in which he pays tribute to Baruch, whose memoirs and collection of Jeremiah's sayings he had used. By D's doctrine of retribution, the faithful Baruch must have his reward. But he says that Baruch must not seek too great things for himself: such great things as attempting to influence Jeremiah to stay in Palestine (43:3).

IV

The date of D's work on Jeremiah can be fixed within fairly close limits. The following data bear upon this question:

(1) The fall of Jerusalem, the period of Gedaliah's governorship, and the flight to Egypt are chronicled in the latter part of the book.

---

19. *Jeremia und seine Zeit* (Göttingen, 1902), pp. 83-86.

Jerusalem fell in 587, but we do not know how long the governorship of Gedaliah lasted. The impression given by chapters 40–41 is that it lasted for a very brief time. However, if the third deportation, of which the date is given in Jeremiah 52:30, was connected with the punishment inflicted on Judah for the murder of Gedaliah, the governorship may have lasted for about five years, to 582.

(2) 44:30 predicts that Hophra, the Egyptian Pharaoh, will be given into the hands of his enemies, as Zedekiah had been given into the hand of Nebuchadnezzar. Hophra was overthrown by Amasis about the year 570 B.C. The passage in Jeremiah is probably prophecy after the event; it has been written by D, or at least left standing by him.

(3) 22:26 is a prediction of the death in exile of Jehoiachin. This is probably from D, and again prophecy after the event. Jehoiachin was taken out of prison and given preferential treatment by Amel-Marduk, as we know from Jer. 52:31-33 and from cuneiform sources. This was in the first year (not the accession year) of Amel-Marduk, 561-60. It is not known how long after this Jehoiachin died.

(4) Chapter 24, as we have seen, seems to come from a time when the exile in Egypt had occurred and opposition to the legitimacy of Zedekiah's rule was active, or at least of vivid memory.

(5) Very instructive for the dating of D—particularly the determination of his *terminus ad quem*—is a comparison of the Massoretic text and the Septuagint in chapters 25 and 27. In both cases it seems very probable that the Septuagint is nearer to the original text than the Hebrew; it is much easier in both cases to account for the addition to the Septuagint *Vorlage* than to account for the intentional omission by the Septuagint translators. In chapter 25 the Septuagint omits the references to Babylon and Nebuchadnezzar, and has a much shorter text in vs. 12, not referring to the punishment of the king of Babylon and the Chaldeans. In chapter 27, the Septuagint omits vs. 7, which says that the "time" of Nebuchadnezzar is coming, when his kingdom will be overthrown; and the Septuagint has a shorter version of vss. 20-22 in which there is no reference to the return from exile of the vessels taken by the Babylonians from Jerusalem. In their original form, then, both of these passages came from the time of the exile, not after the exile was over, when Babylon had been overthrown and Jews had returned to Palestine.

(6) In general accord with this is the fact that the prophecies of return from exile in D are vague and general. This is best and most clearly seen in 32:36 ff. If D is responsible for the figure "seventy years" in 25:12; 29:10 (and that is open to question), even that is no indication that he knew how long the Chaldean kingdom or the Jewish exile lasted. It is a vague number—probably two generations or "the days of one king" as in Isa. 23:15.

(7) The attitude of D towards the Babylonians and Nebuchadnezzar is in general friendly. For example, he speaks of Nebuchadnezzar as the servant of Yahweh (27:6; cf. 25:9) and justifies the actions of Nebuchadnezzar and Nebuzaradan in 39:11ff; 40:1ff. The hatred of Babylon shown in the oracles against Babylon (chs. 50–51) is absent.

(8) The D editor of Jeremiah has his closest affinities, both in style and in substance, with the exilic D editor of Deuteronomy, Kings, Joshua, and other books edited by the D school. There are very close affinities with the exilic portions of Deuteronomy 28.[20] The similarity extends to long phrases, especially those in which the sufferings endured by Jerusalem in the time of the Babylonian siege are described. For the "predictions" of the taking of Jerusalem and the exile, one should compare also the following: I Kings 8:46-53; 9:1-9; II Kings 17:19-20; 21:7-15; 22:14-20; 23:26-27.

In the light of these data we must conclude that the D editor of Jeremiah lived during the time of the Babylonian exile; a date around 550 B.C. cannot be far wrong. Not only is there no evidence in his work of the end of the exile, but there is also no evidence of the influence of II Isaiah and early postexilic writers. II Isaiah's influence can be best seen in Jer. 10:1-16; 16:19-20; 30:10-11; 31:7-14, 35-37, but these passages show no trace of D diction and were not in his edition.

V

We may now give a summary statement describing the Deuteronomic edition of Jeremiah—its purpose, leading themes, sources, methods, and values.

The primary purpose which led D to make an edition of Jeremiah was to show how Jeremiah, the outstanding prophet at the time of Judah's decline and downfall, was in general agreement with the

20. See the list of Driver, *op. cit.*, p. xciii.

ideas and purposes of the Deuteronomic school. In actuality Jeremiah probably never gave active support to the Deuteronomic reforms, if indeed he was prophesying in 621 and the immediately following years; at some points he was more likely an active antagonist of those reforms. Yet, to the Deuteronomic school it was unthinkable that Jeremiah should have been out of harmony with them. Hence, his book was edited to show that he was generally in agreement with their ideas and at one time was an ardent evangelist for the Josianic reforms (11:1-17).

In his edition of Jeremiah the outstanding theme of D is that all of history is under the control of Yahweh. He had led Israel out of Egypt and into the land of Canaan. But there they fell into the worship of false gods. Nevertheless Yahweh gave them many opportunities to repent, sending them many prophets, among whom Jeremiah was one. But Israel persisted in its idolatry, and Yahweh gave them into the hand of Nebuchadnezzar, who destroyed Jerusalem and exiled many Jews. But Yahweh's ultimate plans for Israel are good rather than evil, and so he will ultimately restore them to their land. Writing about 550, his hopes for the future are positive, but expressed in vague terms.

In his edition of Jeremiah D seems to have a special fondness for the use of symbolic actions, and for composing "sermons" and prayers. One must recall that Deuteronomy itself consists of several long speeches by Moses and that in Kings and elsewhere the Deuteronomists were given to the free composition of speeches and prayers. D used the same methods in compiling his edition of Jeremiah as were used elsewhere. Sometimes he excerpted original material from his sources without change; at other times he revised or rewrote his sources; and at still other times he composed freely. Particularly instructive examples of passages in which D incorporates original materials unchanged within sections composed or revised by him are the following: 1:15-19 (17 being genuine); 7:1–8:3 (7:29 being a direct quotation); 11:1-17 (15-16 being genuine); and 16:1-13, 16-18 (16-17 being authentic).

In making his edition of Jeremiah, D employed at least three sources: (1) Baruch's scroll written at Jeremiah's dictation in 604; (2) a collection (or collections) of genuine oracles of the prophet, made by Baruch and/or others; and (3) Baruch's memoirs.

It is not possible to recover each of these sources in our present book with complete confidence. However, some tentative conclusions may be reached by careful consideration of the probable date and background of the individual passages and oracles, and by attention to literary form. The present writer has attempted to separate these various sources, and his conclusions will be given below; it is not possible within the scope of this paper to give the detailed evidence for these conclusions.

Baruch's scroll consisted of the messages spoken by Jeremiah from the beginning of his career to the time of dictation, 604. It must have consisted primarily, if not exclusively, of oracles of condemnation and threat, as the account of its dictation in chapter 36 implies. The materials in the scroll incorporated in our present book by D are probably contained within the first six chapters, consisting at least of the following: 1:4-14, 17; 2; 3:1-5, 12b-14a, 19-25; 4; 5:1-17, 20-30; 6.

D also had at his disposal a collection, or collections, of genuine oracles of Jeremiah which had been made by Baruch or others. In this group we must place all genuine oracles uttered after the dictation of Baruch's scroll, and those which are not oracles of condemnation and threat. It is entirely possible that a few passages which we list in this group were in Baruch's scroll, but most of them can definitely be excluded from it because they are later than 604, or they are lamentations, confessions of the prophet, or lyrical poems. In this group there is evidence for the collection of some of the oracles by subject matter, as in 23:9-33. To this second group we assign the following: 8:4–9:26 (9:10-11, 17-22 suggest the invasion in 602 by bands of Chaldeans and others described in II Kings 24:2); 10:17-22 (probably 598); 10:23-24; 11:15-16; 11:18–12:6 (a confession); 12:7-13 (probably 602); 13:1-11 (probably late Jehoiakim); 13:12-14 (probably reflects the civil strife in Zedekiah's reign); 13:15-19 (597); 13:20-27 (between 605 and 598); 14:2-6, 13-18; 15:5-9 (a lamentation); 15:10-21 (confession); 16:16-17; 17:1-2a, 3b-4, 9-10, 14-18 (partly confession); 18:1-6, 13-23; 20:7-18 (confession); 21:13-14; 22:6-7, 10-12, 13-23, 28-30; 23:9-33.

Baruch's memoirs do not really constitute a biography; they do not cover a sufficient portion of Jeremiah's life to be that. Baruch was concerned largely to record Jeremiah's conflicts with priests and false prophets, and to record the last days of Jeremiah, from the time of the Babylonian invasion to the flight into Egypt. Volz properly calls the latter a *Leidensgeschichte,* comparing it in fullness of detail with the passion narratives of the gospels. Baruch's memoirs consisted of materials now found within the following, in some cases revised at length by D: 19:1-2a, 10-11a, 14-15; 20:1-6; 26–29; 32:1, 6-15; 34–36; 37:3-21; 38; 39:3, 14; 40:7–42:13; 43; and 44. Our discussion above should make it clear that we do not consider Baruch to be the Deuteronomist, as suggested by Pfeiffer. It is possible at a number of points to see clearly the difference between Baruch's work and that of D; perhaps the best examples are the difference between 32:6-15 (Baruch) and 32:16-44 (D); and between 37:3-10 (Baruch) and 21:1-12 (D). Also, we must deny that Baruch was only the amanuensis of the prophet, as maintained by May and Schmidt. Not only is Baruch the most likely candidate for the authorship of those portions of the book which seem to come from an eyewitness (which we call Baruch's memoirs); there is evidence within the Book of Jeremiah that Baruch was more than a professional amanuensis. In 36:19 he is advised by the officials to hide with Jeremiah after the reading of the scroll. This would hardly have been necessary if he were only a hired agent of the prophet, not his disciple and associate. In 43:3 Baruch is accused of unduly influencing the prophet in the decision about flight to Egypt. Whether he sought to exert such influence or not, it is significant that he was accused of doing so. We should, therefore, consider Baruch as more than Jeremiah's hired scribe; he was his disciple and companion.

Our present Book of Jeremiah was not complete when the Deuteronomic edition was completed. A number of passages, and collections of material, were added to D's edition before the book reached its present form. These consisted of eschatological predictions which show the influence of later prophets, brief poems from "Wisdom" teachers, oracles against foreign nations, and the like. The following passages are post-Deuteronomic additions to the Book of Jeremiah: 1:1-3; 3:15-18; 10:1-16 (showing II Isaiah's influence); 10:25 (= Ps. 79:6-7); 12:14-17; 14:7-9, 19-22; 16:14-15 (=23:7-8); 16:19-21; 17:5-8, 11-13; 23:1-8, 34-40 (the latter a very late "rabbinic" play on the word *massā'*) and 33:14-26 (or all of 33). Chapters 30–31 in their present form were collected later than D, for some passages show the influence of II Isaiah (30:10-11; 31:7-14, 35-37) and possibly of Nehemiah's time (31:38-40). It is entirely possible that these two chapters include genuine poems of the prophet, such as 30:12-15; 31:2-6, 15-20. The oracles against foreign nations now preserved in chapters 46–51 were collected later than D; yet, some of them may be authentic, such as the first oracle against Egypt. Chapter 52 was taken from II Kings 24:18–25:21, 27-30. Jer. 52: 28-30 is missing both in II Kings and in the Septuagint of Jeremiah, but seems to be a reliable list.

A final word may be said about the value of the Deuteronomic edition for the student of Jeremiah's life and thought. We can only make a few general remarks and give a few examples, for a complete evaluation of D would require minute consideration of every passage.

The value of D's work in Jeremiah varies as it does in other books edited by the Deuteronomists. Where he incorporates older material from his sources, that material may be quite authentic. Material from the sources listed above as (1) and (2) is generally the most authentic and most valuable in the book. Baruch's memoirs are usually reliable for the narration of events, but he did not attempt to give Jeremiah's own words; he reports Jeremiah's sayings in his own style. The least valuable of D's work consists of the freely composed speeches found in his edition. Sometimes he retains ideas of the prophet, or his own ideas agree with those of the prophet, but at other times his ideas vary from those of Jeremiah.

As examples of the varying value of D's work we may compare chapters 7 and 26 on the one hand with chapter 24 on the other. Chapter 7 is D's work, but in the main it preserves Jeremiah's thoughts, though not in his own words. In chapter 26, D has rewritten only the temple sermon, the rest being left virtually intact. Chapter 24, on the other hand, is not true to the thoughts of Jeremiah, as we have seen, but gives only the idea of D and others like him.

Our final statement regarding D's edition of Jeremiah must be an expression of gratitude. He has preserved for us the larger portion of our present Book of Jeremiah, and without his work much of this material might well have sunk into oblivion.[21]

---

21. Much of the research on this paper was carried on with the assistance of a Carnegie summer grant in 1947 made by the Nashville University Center Research Council. It is a pleasure to acknowledge the valuable aid afforded by this grant.

VII

THOMAS LODGE'S USE OF AGRIPPA'S CHAPTER ON ALCHEMY

By EDGAR HILL DUNCAN

(Associate Professor of English)

I

THREE notable diatribes against alchemy and its practitioners seem to be the chief sources for ideas and information about the "cozening science" used by popular writers in the last decades of Elizabeth's reign. The three were Chaucer's *Canon's Yeoman's Tale,* two of Erasmus' dialogues in the *Colloquia Familiaria: Alcumistica* and πτωχολογια (especially the former), and Henry Cornelius Agrippa's chapter on alchemy in the *De Incertitudine et Vanitate Scientiarum et Artium* (1530). Reginald Scot, for example, finds in Chaucer's tale all of the material for the first two chapters of the fourteenth book of *The Discoverie of Witchcraft* (1584) : "Of the art of Alcumystrie, of their woords of art and devises to bleare mens eies, and to procure credit to their profession."[1] His lists of the terms, materials, and instruments used by the alchemists are made, by putting them into some kind of order, from Chaucer's Yeoman's confused account. There are three acknowledged quotations from the Prologue to the Tale in these two chapters, and another in chapter III. Chapter V, which comprises in length almost a third of the whole fourteenth book, consists of an elaborate retelling of Erasmus' *Alcumistica,* the story of how the monk Balbinus was gulled by a brother monk, who pretended to know the art of transmutation. Another of Erasmus' colloquies, the *Convivium Fabulosam,* is retold in the final chapter. The comic underplot of Lyly's *Gallathea,* 1585, involves the conflict between an alchemist and his servant, the alchemy in the scenes being principally derived, as R. W. Bond has shown,[2] from Scot with an independent use of Chaucer.

Robert Greene's brief passing digs at alchemical trickery in three

---

1. Edited with an introduction by the Rev. Montague Summers. London: John Rodkin, 1930. The fourteenth book occupies pp. 204-216.
2. Introduction to *Gallathea,* in his edition of the *Complete Works of John Lyly* (Oxford, 1902), II, 423.

pamphlets published in 1592,[3] if indeed they are based on more than his personal knowledge of contemporary London life, would seem to reflect a casual acquaintance, at least, with Agrippa. Agrippa's book had been translated into English in 1569, with a second edition in 1575, by James Sanford under the title *Of the Vanitie and Uncertaintie of Artes and Sciences*.[4] It seems likely that Tom Nashe knew the translation, for in a pamphlet of 1593[5] he uses a phrase, "the dust of wisedome called Alcumie," which is reminiscent of Sanford's rendering of Agrippa's *de luto stultitiae (sapientiae dicere debui)*[6]: "of the dyst of foolishness, (of wisdome I should say)." In his mock recantation *Lenten Stuffe* (1599) Nashe pretends, incidentally, to have become a convert to the alchemists' faith, aided by his famous red herring, for, he says:

> *Cornelius Agrippa* maketh mention of some philosophers that held the skinne of the sheep that bare the golden fleece, to be nothing but a book of Alcumy written upon it, so if wee should examine matters to the proofe, wee shoulde finde the redde Herrings skinne to be little lesse: the accidens of Alcumy I will sweare it is . . .[7]

With Greene and Nashe remarks humorously derogatory of alchemy are brief and merely incidental to the chief subjects of their satiric pens. In *A Fig for Momus*, 1595, Lodge undertook something more elaborate—a formal verse epistle which he entitled "The Anatomie of Alchymie." It consists of 112 iambic pentameter lines riming alternately except for the couplets at lines 101-2 and 111-12. The substance is taken, with some rather skillful adaptation of prose to rimed verse, from Agrippa's chapter on alchemy. How closely Lodge often follows his source may be observed by a comparison of the following lines with the pertinent passage in Agrippa, which

---

3. *The Blacke Bookes Messenger, A Quippe for an Upstart Courtier, and A Groatsworth of Wit. . . .* For the passages, cf. Robert Greene, *Works* (Ed. A. B. Grosart, Edinburgh: Constable, 1881-6), XI, 25, 227; XII, 107 f.

4. All of the quotations below are from the edition of 1575: *Imprinted at London, by Henrie Bynneman, dwelling in Knightryder streete, at the signe of the Mermayde, Anno. 1575.* Chapter 90, "Of Alcumie," occupies ff. 157r-159v.

5. *Strange News of the Interception of Certain Letters, Works* (Ed. A. B. Grosart, London: Aylesbury, 1883-4), II, 176.

6. Citations of Agrippa's Latin original are from the Cologne edition of 1575: *Henrici Cornelii Agrippae ab Nettesheym, De Incertitudine et vanitate scientiarum declamatio invectiva . . . Coloniae, apud Theodorum Baumium, sub signo arboris. Anno. 1575: Cap. XC: De Alchemistica.*

7. Nashe, *Works,* V, 300. Sanford's translation of Agrippa runs: "Yet there are some whiche thinke that the skinne of the golden fleece was a booke of *Alcumie* written upon a skin after the manner of the aunciensts, wherein was conteyned the knowledge to make golde." *Op. cit.,* f. 158v.

I give both in the Latin and in Sanford's translation. The immediate subject is the deliberate mystification and obfuscation indulged in by writers of alchemical treatises.

> But let us marke their misteries and spel
> Their vaine *Aenigmata* and *Problemes* darke.
> First aske they where the flying Eagle dwels,
> Next of the dancing fooles, craft coyning clarke,
> Then of the Lyon greene, and flying Hart.
> Next of the Dragon, swallowing his tayle,
> Then of the swelling toade, they prattle art,
> Next of more blacke, then blacke, they chuse to rayle,
> Then of the crowes-head, tell they waighty things,
> And straight of *Hermes* seale, they fighting speake,
> Some of their *Lutum sapientiae* sings,
> Thus on these toies, their bitter iests they breake.[8]

. . . verum nimis longum foret, narrare omnia huius artis stulta mysteria, ac inania aenigmata, de leone viridi, de ceruo fugitivo, de aquila volante, de stulto saltante, de dracone cauda[m] suam vorante, de bufone inflato, de capite corui, deq[ue] illo nigro nigrius nigro, de sigillo Hermetis, de luto stultitiae (sapientiae dicere debui) ac simili-b[us] nugis innumeris.

But it should be overlong to recount all of the foolish mysteries and vayne riddles of this Arte, of the greene Lion, of the fugitive Harte, of the fleing Egle, of the dauncing foole, of the Dragon deuouring his tayle, of the swollen toade, of the Crowes heade, and of that blacke, which is blacker than blacke, of the seale of Hermes, of the dyst of foolishnesse, (of wisdome I should say) and of infinite like trifles.

Lodge's adaptation of his source material is not always so direct as in these lines. In constructing the opening passage, for example, he drew from several places in Agrippa. Excluding the epistolary salutation, the passage reads:

> . . . that hidden lore,
> Ycleped Alchymie these latter times: . . .
> This fruite of foolish innovation
> Is first condemn'd by deepest-red devines,
> Not as an art, but as the seale of shift,
> The persecution of natures power . . . (3-4, 7-10)

The ideas of the "hidden lore" and of "innovation" were suggested by Agrippa's "I coulde saye moreover very many things of this Arte, (yet not verie much against me,) if I had not sworne, (as they are wont to doe who receyve orders) to keepe silence. And this silence

---

8. *The Complete Works of Thomas Lodge* (Glasgow: Printed for the Hunterian Club, 1883), III, 69. Lines 73-84.

is so constantly, and religiously observed for the auncient Philosophers and wryters, that any where there is founde no Philosopher
and faithful writer of approued authoritie that in any place hath
with one worde made mencion of this Art: which thing hath induced
many to beleeve that all the bookes of that Arte were but of late
yeares inuented. . ." Earlier in his discussion Agrippa had remarked
that disappointed practitioners often descended to "naughtie Artes"
and that "therefore this Arte was not onely banished by the ciuill
lawes from the *Romaine* publicke weale, but also by the Canon de-
crees, was forbidden in all the Christian Churches." Hence Lodge's
line 8. The "persecution of natures power" is a phrase from Agrippa's
opening sentence, which Sanford translates "Alcumie . . . whether it
ought to be termed an Arte . . . *or a pursuite of nature . . .*"; Lodge's
indebtedness is more immediately evident when we see the Latin:
sive naturae persecutio dici debeat. The grouping *de sigillo Hermetis,
de luto stultitiae,* quoted above, which is found in still another part
of Agrippa's chapter is probably the source of "the seale of shift"
of line 9.

At times Lodge fails to transmit the whole effective weight of the
argument of his source, as may be seen in his adaptation of Agrippa's opening sentence. In that sentence Agrippa cleverly makes use of
a truism of alchemical theory, that art imitates nature,[9] turning it
against those who argue for the theoretical possibility of transmutation:

> . . . the vanitie whereof is easely perceyued in this, that it promiseth the
> thinges which nature in nowise can abide, nor attaine, whereas notwith-
> standing no Arte can surmounte nature, but doth imitate, and folowe
> it aloofe of, and the force of nature is farre stronger than of Arte.

This bit of cogent reasoning becomes with Lodge the much more
generalized and less pointed:

> For if with iealous eies we iustly prie
> Into the scope, and issue of the same
> Nature, (the mistres of Philosophie)
> Is lost herein, and wanteth power, and name. (13-16)

For the construction of the first thirty lines of his Epistle, Lodge
draws bits from various places in Agrippa's chapter shaping them,

9. E.g.: "In these works," says Arnold of Villa Nova, "it is necessary to imitate
nature, whoever wishes to make a more perfect medicine of the imperfect."
Rosarium Philosophorum, Cap. I. *Bibliotheca Chemica Curiosa* (ed. J. J. Man-
get, Geneva, 1702), I, 662.

though but loosely, into a definition of alchemy and a statement of the ironic contrast between the aims of alchemists and the pathetic foolishness of their actual accomplishment. Two lines in this part appear to be indebted to another source:

> These silly idiots plie the fire so fast;
> That sodainly they blow up man and house . . . (26-27)

which may be a reminiscence of Chaucer's Yeoman's account of how, because of the mismanagement of the fire,

> The pot tobreketh, and farewell, al is go!
> Thise metals been of so greet violence,
> Oure walles mowe nat make hem resistance,
> But if they weren wrought of lym and stoon;
> They percen so, and throgh the wal they goon.[10]

In the remainder of the poem, lines 31-112, Lodge makes a more systematic appropriation of Agrippa, following Agrippa's order of presentation and using most of the material in the latter three fourths of Agrippa's chapter.

There is an important difference from Agrippa, however, in the point of view which Lodge adopts. Agrippa writes as an initiate, though a frustrated one, as one who has worked in the art and knows some of its secrets, at least, from the inside. In fact in an earlier treatise which was written in 1510 though not published until 1531, *De Occulta Philosophia*, he recounts his alchemical experimentings, stating that he had learned to separate a spirit from gold and silver which is supposed to have the power to convert into gold or silver any other metal upon which it is properly projected, but adding that he was never able to produce more gold in this manner "than the weight of that was out of which we extracted the spirit." [11] Lodge, on the other hand, while he borrows Agrippa's subject matter, does not borrow his point of view; he is instead the rank outsider. His skillful manipulation of this change may be noted in his adaptation of the following passage:

> Finally, of y^t onely blessed thing alone, besides which there is no other thing, yet to be found in every place, the subiect of the most holy stone of the Philosophers, I meane, y^t is to say, I have almost rashly uttered the name of the thing whereby I should be a sacrilege and forsworne,

---

10. Chaucer, *Works* (Ed. F. N. Robinson, New York: Houghton Mifflin Co., 1933), *CYT*, 11. 907-11.
11. *Three Books of Occult Philosophy* (Translated by J. F[riske], London, 1651), pp. 32-33.

yet I will speak it with circumlocution, but somwhat more obscure, that none but yong beginners in the Arte, and they which be trained up in the mysteries thereof, may understand it. It is a thing, which hath substance, and not overmuch fierie, nor altogither earthly, nor symplie watrie, nor a moste sharpe, nor a most blunte qualitie, but indifferent, and light in touching, and after a sort tender, or at least not harde, not unpleasant, but after a sorte sweete in taste, soote in smell, delectable to the sight, pleasant and iocunde to the hering, large to the imagination: I may say no more, and yet there be things greater than these.

The circumlocutory ironies of Agrippa's first sentence take their rise from the frustration (now humorously regarded but none the less real) of the adept or partial adept. For this sentence, Lodge substitutes a quatrain developed from the point of view of the convinced disbeliever, convinced not by experience but because he is rational. I will, he says, though no adept in the art, by the aid of reason and nature construct a *dream* which will be the *fact* of alchemy. He then proceeds to construct his dream, using with admirable economy the details in Agrippa's next sentence and pointing up the irony of the alchemist's situation with an ironic couplet, which he underlines for emphasis:

> Yet unto artists will I sing a saw,
> Perhaps may smell of art, though I have none,
> Wherein by reasons light and natures law,
> The dreame of beeing, which they build upon,
> There is a thing in substance full compleate,
> Not wholely earthly, not inflam'd too much,
> Not simply watrie, though it water eate,
> Not sharpest, nor yet dullest in the touch,
> A qualitie light felt, and apt in curing,
> And somewhat soft, at leastwise not too hard,
> Not bitter, but in tast some sweet procuring:
> Sweet-smelling, much delighting mans regard
>   *It feedes the eare, it amplifies the thought,*
>   *Except to those that know it, it is nought.* (89-102)

Of the 112 lines of Lodge's Epistle all but nineteen have their immediate source in Agrippa's chapter. Two of the nineteen may, as we have seen, derive from Chaucer. The others contain no alchemical matter. While he likely knew and may mainly have relied on Sanford's translation, rather than a Latin text, the evidence hardly admits of definite proof that he did so, since Sanford's translation is completely faithful and literal, and since the exigencies of verse would prevent Lodge from borrowing verbatim any extensive turns of phrase. On the other hand it seems quite certain that, if he did not work wholly from the Latin, he did have a Latin text by him as he composed. For instance in the first passage quoted above he uses (line 83) the Latin phrase *Lutum sapientiae* rather than Sanford's "dyst . . . of wisdome." Again, line 74, "Their vaine Aenigmata and Problemes darke," seems to show immediate use of the Latin: *stulta mysteria, inania aenigmata.* Sanford translated the final clause of Agrippa's *credulorum hominum aures verbis ditant, pecunia inanes ut reddant lòculos* as "to the end y^t they may empty their purses." Lodge uses an alternative meaning for *loculos,* and his lines based on this sentence read:

> They by their words enritch believing sots,
> Whereas in deede they emptie all their chists. (33-34)

The latter half of the first line of Lodge's climactic couplet (line 101) which we have just examined, "it amplifies the thought," appears to be his own independent rendering of Agrippa's *cogitatu latam,* though without the bolstering of the second line it is a less felicitous expression than Sanford's "large to the imagination."

II

In view of the easy-going ethics of the Elizabethans with regard to the borrowing of handy source material perhaps no comment is necessary on Lodge's cavalier appropriation of Agrippa on alchemy. Yet Lodge does register a demurrer concerning the poems in *A Fig for Momus* which, it seems to me, is justified, at least in the case of "The Anatomie of Alchymie." In the preface "To the Gentlemen Readers" he writes that he has so entitled his book not in contempt of the learned but "in despight of the detractor," [12] and continues:

> This cause (gentlemen) hath drawne me to use this title, and under this title I have thought good to include *Satyres, Eclogues,* and *Epistles:* . . . because I would write in that forme, wherin no man might chalenge me with servile imitation, (wherewith heretofore I have been unjustlie taxed.) . . .

12. It is not impossible that Lodge got a suggestion for the title of the book, and perhaps for the tone of part of the preface, from a copy of Agrippa's work. At any rate in an edition of *De Incertitudine* . . . published in Antwerp in 1534 there is a prefatory poem addressed *Ad Lectorem* in which Agrippa is compared with various ancient worthies, mythical and historical, from Pluto to Aristotle, the first line of which is: *Inter Diuos nullos non capit Momus.* The poem is not in the edition of 1575 which I have used, nor was it translated by Sanford. The O. E. D. records three usages of Momus as the god of ridicule in books in English prior to the year in which Lodge's was published.

. . . For my *Epistles,* they are in that kind, wherein no Englishman of our time hath publiquely written, which if they please, may draw on more, if displease, have their priviledge by authoritee. Briefly, I have so written, as I have read: so read, as I can judge.

His claim of being the first in his generation to publish in the genre of the metrical epistle seems to be a just one. And I believe that he can be absolved, within the canons of Elizabethan poetic criticism, of any blame of "servile imitation" as far as the subject matter of the letter on alchemy is concerned.

While Lodge nowhere makes any specific indication of his indebtedness to Agrippa, he does include in his preface the disarming sentence just quoted as to the bookish nature of his material. In defense of his method of "borrowing" he could have cited Sidney's *Apology for Poetry,* printed also in 1595:

So then the best of the Historian is subject to the Poet; for whatsoeuer action, or faction, whatsouer counsell, pollicy . . . the Historian is bound to recite, that may the Poet (if he list) with his imitation make his own; beautifying it both for further teaching, and more delighting, as it pleaseth him: hauing all, from *Dante* his heauen to hys hell, vnder the authoritie of his penne. Which if I be asked what Poets haue done so . . . I might well name some . . .[13]

As a recent commentator on this passage has observed, it "admits no limitations: everything that has been written lies ready for the poet." [14]

But if the poet's imitation is not to be "servile" he must, as Sidney writes, "make [what he borrows] his own." And Lodge took some pains to do just that. He adapted the material to the genre of the epistle by placing it within the framework of a graceful salutation and a complimentary closing. He omitted parts of Agrippa's account, notably a section on the incidental benefits of alchemical experimenting (that it had been responsible for the discovery of the properties of various substances and of ways of working with and combining metals) as being antithetic to his purpose of satire. He made some additions. For instance, Agrippa had cited "the obscure names, and used by no other, of Giber, Morienus, Gilgilis and others of that sorte," which he found frequently quoted as authorities in alchemical treatises, as evidence "that all the bookes of that Arte were but of late years inuented." Lodge retained only the first

13. *Elizabethan Critical Essays* (Edited by Gregory Smith, Oxford, 1904), I. 169.
14. Harold Ogden White, *Plagiarism and Imitation During the English Renaissance* (Cambridge, 1935), p. 61.

name on Agrippa's list, made his own substitutions for the others, and adapted his list to his point of view of rationally exposing a supposed art that is in reality a futility and fraud:

> For why? *Philosophie* nere knew this art,
> But some vaine upstarts, (sonnes of subtletie,
> As *Giberis,* and witles Salesart,
> *Bacon,* and *Hermes* father of this fraud,
> Began the same in termes, and words obscure,
> (To studious of deceit and foolish laud,)
> Hoping by toyes to make their craft endure. (67-73)

We have already seen how his point of view dictated his borrowing for the climactic passage, lines 89-102.

A poet can make a borrowed subject matter his own, says Sidney, by "beautifying it . . . as it pleaseth him." Lodge "beautified" by using alliteration extensively:

> The favorites of this too fond conceite . . .
> Robb'd, and bereft of rent, and olde receite,
> Are like a crased clocke, that cannot chime:
> Olde, clothles . . .   (45, 47-9)

> Plagu'd with the palsie . . .
> By tempring of quick-silver quickly caught. (51-2)[15]

He elevated Agrippa's *natura* to the dignity of a personification, "Nature, (the mistres of Philosophie)." He indulged the Elizabethan love of mythological allusion with comparison of alchemists' promises to the "enchanting noates" of the Sirens "along the shores of Cicely." On the hint of a mediocre pun from Agrippa, *ex alcumistis cacochimici,* he pictured for his Elizabethan readers the "cousening artists" as resembling "Cacus creeping from his den." Without the help of Agrippa he gave them the apt and well-turned metaphor "Danaes golden shower/Doth ravish wits."

That Lodge was a rank plagiarist according to modern standards no one will deny. Recent studies of the sources of his prose pamphlets by Miss Walker and Mr. Ringler make the point quite clear.[16] Much of his verse is also imitative in a way which neither

---

15. Agrippa: *Argenti vivi contrectatione paralytici.* Sanford: "paraliticke thorowe the continuall handling of quicksiluer."

16. Alice Walker, "The Reading of an Elizabethan: Some Sources of the Prose Pamphlets of Thomas Lodge," *RES,* VIII (1932), 264-81; William Ringler, "The Source of Lodge's *Reply to Gosson," RES,* XV (1939), 164-71.

modern nor Elizabethan critical standards would altogether condone. Another poem in the *Fig for Momus* volume, the sixth
Epistle, "In praise of his Mistris dogge" has been characterized as
"nothing more than a stringing together of extracts from Bouchet's
serée 'Du Chien.' " [17] In view of these facts it is pleasant and
perhaps not without value to retrace his use of Agrippa's chapter
in writing his "Anatomie of Alchymie" and to concur with him
that as far as that Epistle is concerned "no man might challenge
[him] with servile imitation."

17. Walker, *RES*, VIII, 276.

VIII

REVELATION IN THE SHORT STORY:
A NOTE ON METHODOLOGY

By WALTER SULLIVAN

(Instructor in English)

IN 1842 Edgar Allan Poe reviewed Hawthorne's *Twice Told Tales* for *Graham's Magazine,* and while he was on the subject, he attempted seriously to define the short prose narrative. The definition was at least historically important: it gave reasonable proof that the short story form is a *genre, per se;* thus it not only avoided the assumption that the "brief tale" owes its brevity to some fortuitous circumstance, but consequently it discredited the critical practice of judging the short story by the same standards that are applied to longer works of prose fiction. Poe, however, was in many ways a limited man and in most ways a thoroughly contrary one. His statement was laudably ambitious, but at the same time it was characteristically overbearing. He subordinated the aesthetic importance of the novel (which he could not write) to that of the short story. Ultimately, he could not see beyond the limited ramifications of his cherished shibboleth—perusal at a single sitting.

Poe's definition of the short story, then, was not completely satisfactory, but it remained the best one available for over a hundred years. Subsequent artists discovered new prose techniques. Subsequent critics were perceptive enough to recognize the significance of each new development in the art of the short story; indeed, they created a technical vocabulary not dreamed of in Poe's critical philosophy. But in the end, most people who even tentatively took into consideration the differences between the novel and the story were inclined either to speak vaguely about varying degrees of complexity, or else to content themselves with the fact that a story was simply not as long as a novel. The difference, as it were, could be measured physically. It was only in 1950 that Mark Schorer publicly made the first authentic distinction between the two major forms of prose fiction.

In *The Story, A Critical Anthology* Mr. Schorer points out that the "short story is an art of moral revelation, the novel an art of moral evolution." He goes on to say, "In both story and novel there is change, but the first is a change of view that we are briefly shown, the other a change of conduct that more leisurely we trace." If one reduces this definition to a lower level of abstraction, it might be put this way: a short story is a form of prose fiction which exploits a dramatic situation in order to bring about the significant development of one or more characters from a particular state of innocence to a particular kind of knowledge. It should be noted that, unlike Aristotle's definition of tragedy, this statement concerning the short story makes no attempt to explore the nature of the reader's experience. That is, Mr. Schorer is certainly not suggesting that the short story is didactic, and it is not precisely his duty as a critic to describe what happens to the perceptive man in the presence of artistic beauty. He has simply devised a critical definition that strikes the heart of the matter. Every first-rate short story writer does, at his best, exactly what Mr. Schorer describes. A change of view is the *sine qua non* of the story, the fundamental methodological concept to which more superficial technical accomplishments are, in a sense, epiphenomenal. A study of the short story form should begin with an examination of the general methods that have been used successfully to achieve moral revelation.

In practically all short stories, revelation is the result of a series of closely related dramatic incidents, and the complete force of the change of view is almost never realized until the end of the story. But depending on where the change of view occurs in the narrative sequence, revelation may be termed either *logical* or *anticipated*. Joyce's *Araby* is a splendid example of the former method. This is the story of a young man (the unnamed narrative I) idealistically in love with the sister of one of his playmates.

> Her image accompanied me even in places the most hostile to romance. On Saturday evenings when my aunt went marketing I had to go to carry some of the parcels. We walked through the flaring streets, jostled by drunken men and bargaining women, amid the curses of labourers, the shrill litanies of shop-boys who stood on guard by the barrels of pigs' cheeks, the nasal chanting of street-singers, who sang a *come-all-you* about O'Donovan Rossa, or a ballad about the troubles in our native land. These noises converged in a single sensation of life for me: I imagined that I bore my chalice safely through a throng of foes. Her name sprang to my lips at moments in strange prayers and praises which I myself did not understand. My eyes were often full of

tears (I could not tell why) and at times a flood from my heart seemed to pour itself out into my bosom. I thought little of the future. I did not know whether I would ever speak to her or not or, if I spoke to her, how I could tell her of my confused adoration. But my body was like a harp and her words and gestures were like fingers running upon the wires.

What should be noted here, aside from the sheer beauty of the prose, is the boy's romanticism, his naiveté—in a word, his innocence. Because his uncle lingers at the pub, the young man is late in arriving at Araby, but he is not too late. The bazaar is still open; the wares are still for sale. The young female attendant breaks off her conversation with the English gentlemen to offer, not uncivilly, to help him. But the boy is no longer child enough to sustain his romantic infatuation. He leaves empty handed.

> Gazing up into the darkness I saw myself as a creature driven and derided by vanity; and my eyes burned with anguish and anger.

These are the final lines of the story, and in them the change of view is made complete. What is more important, the initial state of innocence does not begin to give way to knowledge until the last two hundred words of the narrative. Incidents which develop the youth's lack of understanding lead toward the ultimate scene of enlightenment.

This method of simple chronological movement, *i.e.*, logical development, from one state of experience to another may be contrasted with that employed by Robert Penn Warren in *When the Light Gets Green*. Here again, one sees a story from the first person point of view of a child. The little boy watches the life of his grandfather become more and more meaningless as a new age chokes out the vitality of the old way and smothers the old traditions. What is revealed to the boy is the inexorable, destructive power of time, and the emotion attendant to the revelation appears in the second paragraph. Note the final sentences.

> He turned his face to the green wavy glass, first one side and then the other in quarter profile, and lifted the long shears, which trembled a little, to cut the beard. His face being turned like that, with his good nose and pointed grey beard, he looked like General Robert E. Lee without any white horse to ride. My grandfather had been a soldier too, but now he wore blue jean pants and when he leaned over like that toward the mirror I couldn't help but notice how small his hips and backsides were. Only they weren't just small, they were shrunken. I noticed how the blue jeans hung loose from his suspenders and loose

off his legs and down around his shoes. And in the morning when I
noticed all this about his legs and backsides, I felt a tight feeling in my
stomach like when you walk behind a woman and see the high heel of
her shoe is worn and twisted and jerks her ankle every time she takes
a step.

From this point Mr. Warren proceeds to develop the stern significance of the revelation until all implications inherent in the original
change of view are brought into focus. The old man—and of course
with him the period he represents—later sickens and dies. "It's time
to die. Nobody loves me," Grandfather says. Indeed, the boy suddenly
realizes this is true, but the point is that he arrived at this revelation
and reacted emotionally to it at the beginning of the narrative. The
fundamental nature of the change of view is not altered; only the
boy's attitude toward what has been revealed to him is modified by
a more complete understanding.[1]

To turn from a question of where revelation occurs to one of how
the change of view comes about, it is necessary to examine the
relationship of the perceptive consciousness to the story's design of
action. Another dichotomy is readily established; depending on the
relative position of the character who attains moral knowledge to the
main line of the plot, moral revelation is either *intra-concatinate* or
extra-concatinate. Hemingway's *The Short Happy Life of Francis
Macomber* furnishes an excellent example of the first method.

The change of view in *Macomber* is on a rather grand scale. The
young playboy-sportsman learns something about the nature of fear.
" 'You know I don't think I'd ever be afraid of anything again,'
Macomber said to Wilson. 'Something happened in me after we
first saw the buff and started after him. Like a dam bursting. It
was pure excitement.' " What happens to him is that he comes to an
understanding that will, one is led to believe, not only make him a
better hunting companion, but change a great many other aspects of
his character as well. Both Hemingway's manly metaphysics and the
short story form as described by Mr. Schorer demand that death
occur before any further alteration of conduct has time to develop.
What makes this story intra-concatinate is the fact that the dramatic
action of the story, the narrated sequence of events, centers around,

---

1. The method of anticipated revelation should not be confused with the mere
device of foreshadowing. Adumbration in prose fiction is concerned primarily
with furnishing some clue to a future event in the action of the piece. That is,
foreshadowing is used to integrate plot—which functions to reveal, but which
is not the moral revelation.

and is at all times directly concerned with, Macomber. The character's participation forces his own change of view.

In an extra-concatinate story such as *That Evening Sun,* moral revelation comes about in a different way. Faulkner's piece provides an account of the marital infidelity and ultimate murder of a Negro woman named Nancy. It is not very astounding that a writer of Faulkner's genius was able to mold this old, and from a writer's point of view rather dangerous, material—adultery, miscegenation, violent death—into an excellent story. At least part of the success of the narrative is a result of the extra-concatinate method. The story is Quentin Compson's story, not Nancy's. It is his presence, along with that of Caddy and Jason, which gives the story its power and it is to him that the moral revelation comes. What Nancy knows at the end of the piece, she was aware of in the beginning and her conduct is not the reader's chief concern. At the end of the story, Quentin asks, "Who will do our washing now, Father?" and here with the consummation of the change of view the story ends. Revelation is achieved in the character at the fringe of the action, one who, strictly speaking, does not have a direct interest in the chain of events.

It is not necessary to point out that stories are not always rigidly intra- or extra-concatinate, and it would doubtless be difficult to determine exactly at what point some stories cease or begin to employ logical or anticipated revelation. For example, in Caroline Gordon's *The Last Day in the Field* Aleck Maury reaches the exact point of revelation at the very end of the story, when the last bird is killed, the last day is ended. But from the beginning of the story, the old sportsman has been flirting with revelation. He looks at the elderberry bushes which still resist the autumn and says, " 'Ah-h, it'll get you yet!' . . . thinking how frost creeps higher and higher out of the ground each night of fall." Or consider Andrew Lytle's story, *Jericho, Jericho, Jericho.* It is easy enough to discover where the old lady comes to knowledge, but exactly how the change of view is wrought is a different matter. Certainly revelation is not entirely the result of her own past life (action in which she directly participates) but rather a conclusion forced upon her by the juxtaposition of what she has done with the action which takes place around her bedside.

The problems raised by these stories are not causes for alarm, but neither are they invitations to invent still further methodological terminology. Unless one is naming the parts of a rifle or a cyclotron, there is a point beyond which mere tagging ceases to be an honest effort toward clarification and becomes a clever performance. In the end, one is forced manfully to admit either that Housman correctly assessed the number of critics nature allows us; or that the artist not only says something that the critic may perhaps feel but never repeat, the writer also knows something about his craft that the critic can never know.

Even though it is difficult in some cases precisely to distinguish between various methods of revelation, it is none the less apparent that many literary failures may be attributed in part at least to faulty revelatory methodology. One can easily imagine what would happen if Quentin Compson were plunged into the middle of the action in *That Evening Sun,* or if Macomber watched the hunt from the sidelines. Indeed, William Faulkner's extra-concatinate story, *Hair,* is unsuccessful simply because it does employ this method. The dramatic aspects of the story are underdeveloped and the change of view is both slight and insignificant.

There is one more point to be considered. Because it is an art of moral revelation and not one of moral evolution, the short story did not properly begin to exist as a fully developed art form until the final years of the nineteenth century. Short narratives were written earlier, and when one examines, for instance, the work of Poe, Hawthorne, and Simms, he finds some excellent pieces of literature, some of which are constructed within the limits of the *genre* as it is known today. Hawthorne's *Rappaccini's Daughter* is an example. The story is perhaps one of Hawthorne's best, and it does not collapse under the weight of its allegory as some of his other short works seem to do. One need not dwell on the fact that young Giovanni suffers a rather unpleasant change of view. He finds the poison in the flower and learns something of the nature of evil. But the revelation here is double as is often the case in the successfully executed, complex story. Beatrice passes from innocence to knowledge.

"I see it! I see it!" shrieked Beatrice. "It is my father's fatal science! No, no, Giovanni; it was not I! Never, Never! I dreamed only to love thee and be with thee a little time, and so to let thee pass away, leaving but thine image in my heart. For, Giovanni, believe it, though my body be nourished with poison, my spirit is God's creature, and craves love as its daily food. But my father,—he has united us in this fearful sympathy. Yes; spurn me, tread upon me, kill me! Oh, what is death after such words as thine? But it was not I. Not for a world of bliss would I have done it."

Nobody ever had a more complete or more moral revelation than this.

There can be no doubt that the prose literature of the eighteen hundreds includes many short works of fiction that will not qualify as short stories under this paper's definition. But to point out a tale by de Maupassant or Defoe or Petronius as a refutation of Mr. Schorer's definition is somewhat like citing the satyr dance to disprove a particular theory of tragedy. The specific aesthetic instances out of which a *genre* develops are not necessarily examples of artistic achievement within that *genre*. A tale may be ever so fine and still not be a short story.

Allen Tate speaks of "the best short story before Henry James," and he is quite correct in pointing to the work of James as not only an historical but a qualitative dividing line. Because he was the first English language writer to explore intelligently and successfully the potentialities of the limited point of view technique, he was also the first writer in English completely to understand the short story form. The evolution of the short story as an art of moral revelation became possible only after a method was found to allow the artist to develop significant dramatic tensions in areas of human experience heretofore relatively neglected. Physical action was necessarily subordinated to mental reaction for the story is a change of view, not a change of conduct.

Many successful short story artists continue to employ, in one degree or another, the omniscient author technique, but no writer, proficient or otherwise, works outside the broad influence of James and the later stream of consciousness technicians who followed him. In 1914 *Dubliners* was finally published and the development of the short story *genre* was complete.

IX

THE FRIENDSHIP MOTIF IN MIDDLE ENGLISH LITERATURE

By ROB ROY PURDY

(*Associate Professor of English*)

THE theme of friendship in the Middle Ages has been grossly misunderstood by scholars. Laurens J. Mills, in an otherwise admirable study,[1] finds in the Middle Ages a "rarity of treatment of the theme in its purity and for its own sake." He ascribes several causes to the lack of popularity in England: the lack of general education, influence of the church, the feudal system, the influence of the Teutonic theme of sworn brotherhood. It seems surprising, however, in view of the known influence of the Neoplatonists on mediaeval thinking, that the classical theme of friendship should not crop up in various forms. It is our purpose here to examine references to friendship in Middle English literature, with a view toward showing parallels with the great system of Neoplatonic thought.

Plato did not evolve a distinctive theory of friendship as such. There are, however, numerous references to friendship in his works, and by synthesizing these references with corollary statements in the Neoplatonists we can approximate the background of ideas in this respect on which the mediaevalist may have drawn.

Basic to the Platonic concept of friendship is the insistence that the emotion—if we may call it that—is in some way connected with the Platonic idea of good. Thus in the *Republic,* after a long argument between Socrates and Polemarchus, it is concluded "that he is a friend who is, as well as seems, good; and that he who seems only, and is not good, only seems to be and is not a friend." [2] The *Phaedrus* goes even further, and states that the idea of friendship among the good is an ordinance of Fate:

> Fate which has ordained that there shall be no friendship among the evil has also ordained that there shall ever be friendship among the good.[3]

---

1. *One Soul in Bodies Twain,* Bloomington, 1937, p. 16 f.
2. *Republic,* I, 334-335, in *The Dialogues of Plato,* trans. Jowett, New York, 1937, I, 599.
3. *Phaedrus,* 255, in *ibid.,* pp. 258-59.

Later developments of the theory followed the same line of thought; we notice an emphasis on virtue in friendship in Aristotle,[4] in Cicero,[5] and in the Christianizing of the theme given by the later Church Fathers.

But a more immediate development was a series of related friendship ideas that grew out of this fundamental theory of virtue. Since friendship exists only among the virtuous, it follows that among friends there is one common quality, virtue. Then, argues the classical philosopher, friends are alike in virtue; that is to say, they are alike in essential spiritual qualities. A logical outgrowth of this idea is the application of the old principle of similarity, of like being attracted to like. Plato has many references on this point:

> The poets . . . are to us in a manner the fathers and authors of wisdom, and they speak of friends in no light or trivial manner, but God himself, as they say, makes them and draws them to one another; and this they express, if I am not mistaken, in the following words:—'God is ever drawing like towards like, and making them acquainted.' [6]
> The good are like one another, and friends to one another.[7]
> Those who say that the like is friendly to the like mean to intimate, if I rightly apprehend them, that the good only is the friend of the good, and of him only; but that the evil never attains to any real friendship either with good or evil.[8]
> The old proverb says that 'birds of a feather flock together' . . . and similarity begets friendship.[9]
> To me every man appears to be most the friend of him who is most like to him—like to like, as the ancient sages say.[10]
> The friendship which arises from contraries is horrible and coarse, and has often no tie of communion; but that which arises from likeness is gentle, and has a tie of communion which lasts through life.[11]

There are striking similarities in Aristotle:

> Some define it as a matter of similarity; they say that we love those who are like ourselves: whence the proverbs 'Like finds his like,' 'Birds of a feather flock together,' and so on.[12]

> Does friendship exist among the like, as is thought and said? For 'Jackdaw sits by jackdaw,' as the proverb has it.

---

4. *The Nicomachean Ethics*, i, 3, trans. Rackham, Loeb Classical Library, Cambridge, 1926, pp. 461, 519.
5. *De Amicitia*, 5. 18, trans. Falconer, Loeb Classical Library, Cambridge, 1922, p. 127; 18. 65, p. 177; etc.
6. *Lysis*, 213-14, in *The Dialogues of Plato, ed. cit.*, I, 42.
7. *Ibid.*
8. *Ibid.*
9. *Phaedrus*, 240, in *The Dialogues of Plato, ed. cit.*, I, 245.
10. *Gorgias*, 510, in *ibid.*, 571.
11. *Laws*, 8, 837, in *ibid.*, II, 586.
12. *The Nicomachean Ethics*, 8. 1, *ed cit.*, p. 453.

'Unto the like God ever brings the like.' [13]

Among later writers Plutarch gives the best expression of this point:

Real friendship has always its origin from likeness.[14]

Friendship generally takes its rise from a conformity of tempers and dispositions.[15]

Closely related to the principle of similarity is the idea of equality or harmony among friends. Here again, Plato is careful to emphasize, the equality is one of virtue, and not gifts or honors:

for servants and masters never can be friends, nor good and bad, merely because they are declared to have equal privileges . . . The old saying, that 'equality makes friendship,' is happy and also true; but there is obscurity and confusion as to what sort of equality is meant. For there are two equalities which are called by the same name, but are in reality in many ways almost the opposite of one another; one of them may be introduced without difficulty, by any state or any legislator in the distribution of honours: this is the rule of measure, weight, and number, which regulates and apportions them. But there is another equality, of a better and higher kind, which is not so easily recognized . . . For it gives to the greater more, and to the inferior less and in proportion to the nature of each; and, above all, greater honour always to the greater virtue, and to the less less; and to either in proportion to their respective measure of virtue and education.[16]

Mills seems to misinterpret this aspect of the classical ideal of friendship. He does not cite the above passage from Plato, but he quotes from Aristotle to show the necessity of equality among friends, and interprets the idea as meaning social and economic equality.[17] But even Aristotle suggests that the equality can be one of virtue: "For even those who are friends through virtue are mutually friends by a sort of equality of virtue." [18] And Cicero stresses the point that friendship puts inferior and superior on an equal basis: "It is of the utmost importance in friendship that superior and inferior should

---

13. *Magna Moralia.* 1208[b] 7-10, ed. Ross, Oxford 1908, Vol. 9.

14. *Moralia,* ed. Goodwin, Boston, 1898, I, 472.

15. *Ibid.,* II, 106.

16. *Laws,* VI, 757, in *The Dialogues of Plato, ed. cit.,* II, 519.

17. *Op. cit.,* p. 7 and note, Mills's interpretation is used to back up his thesis that mediaeval society did not offer situations conducive to the development of the classical ideal of friendship: "Aristotle's emphasis upon equality carries with it the corollary that numerous friendships could exist only in a democratic society. It is, to anticipate, the decidedly feudal nature of the Middle Ages that contributed to the lack of friendship worship in that period. On the other hand, the feeling of democracy in England, combined with other conditions, aided in the spread of friendship theory in the sixteenth century."

18. *Ethica Eudemia,* 1238[b] 15-18, trans. Ross, Oxford, 1908, Vol. 9.

stand on an equality." [19] It would seem then, that equality may exist either as a condition or as a result of friendship.[20]

If equality did not come as a result of friendship, it would be difficult to explain the numerous classical references to communal ownership of property among friends. Plato made much of the concept: in the *Laws* there is a reference to "the ancient saying, that 'Friends have all things in common' "; [21] in *Lysis* Socrates finds it unnecessary to ask which is the richer of Lysis and Menexemus; for they are friends, and "friends have all things in common, so that one of you can be no richer than the other, if you say truly that you are friends"; [22] and at the end of the *Phaedrus,* when Socrates has made his closing prayer, Phaedrus says, "Ask the same for me, for friends should have all things in common." [23] The idea seemed to meet the approval of Plato's followers. Aristotle paraphrases the "ancient saying" somewhat:

> The proverb says 'Friends' goods are common property,' and this is correct, since community is the essence of friendship.[24]

Plutarch seems to be acquainted with the idea: "All things ought to be in common amongst friends"; [25] and Terence makes reference to the "old saying":

> It's an old saying that friends have all things in common.[26]

In its most complete and most attractively artistic form, the classical friendship motif developed one aspect of a myth told by Aristophanes in the *Symposium.* The story is told of how the god created man. Because man in his original state was proud and insolent, Zeus had the body separated into two parts; ever since that time the two halves have wandered about longing for each other. But this longing was something other than desire for sexual intercourse—it was a desire to become one with the beloved:

19. *De Amicitia,* 19. 69., *ed. cit.*
20. *Cf.* L. Dugas, *l'Amitie antique,* 2nd ed., Paris, 1914, p. 187: "L'egalite est donc toujours la loi en amitie; ou elle la fonde, ou elle la derive."
21. *Laws,* V, 539, in *The Dialogues of Plato. ed. cit.,* II, 506; *cf. Republic,* V, 449, in *ibid.,* I, 710.
22. *Lysis,* 207, in *ibid.,* I, 35.
23. *Phaedrus,* 279, in *ibid.,* 282.
24. *The Nicomachean Ethics,* 8. 8, *ed. cit.,* p. 484.
25. *Moralia, ed. cit.,* II, 136.
26. *The Brothers,* trans. Sargeaunt, Loeb Classical Library, Cambridge, 1931, II, 273.

there is not a man of them who when he heard the proposal (to melt the two into one) would deny or would not acknowledge that this meeting and melting into one another, this becoming one instead of two, was the very expression of his ancient need.[27]

Plato's followers were quick to see in this concept of the divided soul a statement to explain the nature of the relationship between friends. Friends were actually two parts of one soul, and because of the natural affinity of like for like, these two souls could not be happy on earth until they had united again. Accordingly, they would seek out each other and become inseparable friends. Echoes of this idea appear in Aristotle, Cicero, and Plutarch.

Aristotle:

> All the proverbs agree with this; for example, 'Friends have one soul between them,' 'Friends' goods are common property,' 'Friendship is equality,' 'The knee is nearer than the shin.' [28]

> According to the proverb—when we wish to describe a very great friend, we say 'My soul and his are one.' [29]

> We say about friendship such things as that friendship is equality, and true friends a single soul.[30]

Cicero:

> By the law of his nature, is this the case with man who loves both himself and uses his reason to seek out another whose soul he may so mingle with his own as almost to make one out of two.[31]

> The effect of friendship is to make, as it were, one soul out of many.[32]

Plutarch:

> Single friendship by kind discourses and good offices cements, unites, and condenses as it were two parties.[33]

> Two friends, though severed in body, yet have their souls joined and as it were melted together, and neither desire to be two nor believe themselves to be separate persons.[34]

---

27. *Symposium*, 192, in *The Dialogues of Plato, ed. cit.*, I, 318. The concept of the split soul as developed in the *Symposium* is perhaps basic to all later developments of friendship theory, since there were originally according to Plato three sexes—male, female, and the union of the two—the concept of the split soul could be used to explain the love of man for man, woman for woman, man for woman. Thus in some late uses of the theory, especially in the Renaissance, the friendship theme was directly related to the theme of sexual love.
28. *The Nicomachean Ethics*, 8. 8, *ed. cit.*, p. 484.
29. *Magna Moralia*, 1211ª 32-34, *ed. cit.*
30. *Ethica Eudemia*, 1240ᵇ 1-3, *ed. cit.*
31. *De Amicitia*, 21. 81, *ed. cit.*, p. 189.
32. *Ibid.*, 25. 92, p. 199.
33. *Moralia, ed. cit.*, I, 469.
34. *Ibid.*, IV, 301.

Closely related to this is the idea that a friend is another self. Aristotle:

> A friend is another self.[35]

> One could see the nature and attributes of the friend, . . . such as to be a second self, at least, if you make a very great friend, as the saying has it, 'Here is another Heracles, a dear other self.' [36]

Cicero:

> He who looks upon a true friend, looks, as it were, upon a sort of image of himself.[37]

Plato:

> One with you in friendship . . . your second self.[38]

Plutarch:

> We usually esteem a friend another self.[39]

The classical concept of friendship and its relationship to virtue cannot be fully stated without taking notice of the corollary idea that among the wicked and evil-minded friendship cannot exist. In the *Phaedrus,* we remember, Plato says that "Fate . . . has ordained that there shall be no friendship among the evil";[40] in *Lysis* he emphasizes the same thought: "The good only is the friend of the good, and of him only; but the evil never attains to any real friendship, whether with good or evil." [41] The reference goes on to explain why:

> The bad, as is often said of them, are never at unity with one another or with themselves; for they are passionate and restless, and anything which is at variance and enmity with itself is not likely to be in union or harmony with any other thing.[42]

Cicero follows Plato in denying friendship among the wicked, but specifies flattery as the worst possible foe to friendship, as a vice of fickle and wicked men:

> Nothing is to be considered a greater bane of friendship than fawning, cajolery, or flattery; . . . a vice peculiar to fickle and falsehearted men . . . Hypocrisy is not only wicked under all circumstances, because it pollutes truth and takes away the power to discern it, but it is also es-

---

35. *The Nicomachean Ethics,* 9. 4, *ed. cit.,* p. 535.
36. *Magna Moralia,* 1213ᵃ 18-19, *ed. cit.*
37. *De Amicitia,* 7. 25, *ed. cit.* p. 133.
38. *Parmenides,* 128, in *The Dialogues of Plato, ed. cit.,* II, 89.
39. *Moralia, ed cit.,* I, 465.
40. *Phaedrus,* 255, in *The Dialogues of Plato, ed. cit.,* I, 462.
41. *Lysis,* 214, in *ibid.,* p. 63.
42. *Idem.*

pecially inimical to friendship, since it utterly destroys sincerity, without which the word friendship can have no meaning.[43]

This survey of various classical ideas shows that the tradition which the mediaevalist fell heir to was a virtual system of ideas in the friendship motif. Basic to the whole concept was the idea that friendship was founded upon virtue; from this central point there developed corollary ideas that equality and similarity characterize true friendship, that friends have but one soul, that a true friend is but a second self, and that friendship could not exist among those who lacked virtue. This was the heritage, which, combined with the Christian influences of the Church Fathers, developed into the multitude of literary allusions which we find in Middle English literature.

II

In his discussion of the influence of the Church upon the classical friendship tradition, Mills makes a rather provocative statement:

> As a result of the influence and tendencies of the church, the real renaissance of friendship thought had to await until more favorable times. It is doubtful, however, whether the classical theories of friendship could have been appreciated in a feudal society.[44]

After making this strong prediction, the author seems peculiarly blind to classical influence which he himself cites. It is difficult to conceive of a complete blackout of the friendship tradition in a period rich with other Platonic concepts, despite the strong Christianizing influences of the Fathers. Rather, one would expect to find in regard to this concept—as in many others—that the Fathers used and adapted to Christian thinking much of the Platonic idea without covering up or destroying its ancient pagan birthright.[45]

---

43. *De Amicitia,* 25. 91 *f., ed. cit.,* p. 199.
44. *Op. cit.,* p. 18.
45. *Cf.* E. K. Rand's refutation of the view that the mediaeval church held the classes subservient to theological ends: "It has also been maintained by some that the Christian programme is not really humanistic, since the ancient arts have in it a subordinate and merely relative value; they have become handmaids of the Church. 'It is this mental position of the arts,' an eminent scholar remarks [Eduard Norden, *Die antike Kunstprosa,* 2nd ed., II, 680] 'that betokens the fundamental difference between the Middle Ages and Humanism.' But surely Cicero, the prince of humanists, did not set the arts among the absolutes. For him they led the way either to the active life of the statesman or to the contemplative life of the philosopher—ideals between which he wavered at various moments in his career. In precisely the same way, the liberal doctors of the Church cultivated the ancient studies, both for their own value and for their indispensable connection with the new philosophy that Christianity had brought in." (*Founders of the Middle Ages,* 2nd ed., Cambridge, 1929, pp. 65-66.)

We would expect the Platonic idea of virtue in friendship to find ready acceptance among the Fathers, but sometimes we find even the phraseology of the classical writers used to express corollary ideas of the Platonic concept. Thus, Augustine, in attempting to describe his feelings at the death of a very dear friend, calls upon the language of the Platonic tradition:

> I wondered yet more that myself, who was to him a second self, could live, he being dead. Well said one of his friends, 'Thou half of my soul:' for I felt that my soul and his soul were 'one soul in two bodies:' and therefore was my life a horror to me, because I would not live halved.[46]

One of the most complete discussions of friendship among the churchmen is that of the twelfth-century *De spirituali amicitia* of St. Ailred.[47] The work, based on Cicero's *De amicitia,* is an interesting example of the way in which classical ideas can combine with the Christian tradition with no loss to either philosophy. Book I defines friendship as "rerum humanarum et divinarum, cum benevolentia et charitate consensio," [48] and goes on to show that "Amicitia igitur ipsa virtus est, qua talis dilectionis ac dulcedinis foedere ipsi animi copulantur, et efficiuntur unum de pluribus." [49] After quotations from Augustine, Jerome, and various books of the Bible, he concludes that "Deus amicitia est." [50] Thus we can point out specific Platonic touches in his identification of friendship with the highest virtue and goodness, God, and in his insistence upon virtue and goodness as the basis of friendship.

Book II has as its subject "De fructu amicitiae et excellentia ejus." Here "Aelredus" explains that friendship with man leads to friendship with God, and that real friendship can exist only among the good. There are also discussions of the benefits which follow friendships, as well as the troubles and difficulties which friendship may bring us.

Book III shows us that the foundation of all friendship is love, and "fundamentum illus Dei amor est." [51] Opposed to this are the vices of the wicked, which prevent friendship: *convicia, improperium, secretorum revelatio, superbia,* and *plaga dolosa.* One should aid his

---

46. *The Confessions of St. Augustine,* IV, par. 11, trans. E. B. Pusey, New York, 1909, p. 58.
47. In Migne, *Patrologia Latina,* Paris, 1855 CXCV, Cols. 659-702.
48. *Ibid.,* Col. 662.
49. *Ibid.,* Col. 663.
50. *Ibid.,* Col. 670.
51. *Ibid.,* Col. 679.

friend willingly and unasked: "Haec lex in amicitia sanciatur, ut ab amicix honesta petamus, et pro omicis honesta faciamus, nec exspectemus ut regemur; cunctatio sempter absit." [52] Real friendship results in a sharing of goods, and the bond is much more spiritual if both participants renounce all worldly goods.[53] The true friendship is with God: "Haec est vera et aeterna amicitia, quae hic inchoatur, ibi perficitur; quae hic paucorum est, ubi pauci boni; ubi omnium, ubi omnes boni." [54] But one can come to Christ through love of others, and thus is the world made one through spiritual friendship: "cum haec amicitia, ad quam hic paucos admittimus, transfundetur in omnes, et ab omnibus refundetur in Deum, cum Deus fuerit omnia in omnibus." [55]

We can see in this sketchy summary that much has been adapted, and little changed, of the classical friendship motif. Plato has the virtue in one friend attract the like virtue in another, and virtue, or good, is synonymous with God. Ailred has love of friends lead us to love of Christ, because again, the virtue we see in our friend is synonymous with the greater love which unites the world. The difference here is one of terminology, not of concept. Mills admits the influence of the classical tradition on the *De spirituali amicitia,* but he dismisses the work with the statement, "it seems to have had no effect on medieval literature, whatever the clergy may have thought of it." [56]

But Ailred's work is in no sense an isolated example. John of Salisbury's *Polycraticus* cites Cicero as an authority for his discussion of flattery as a vice against friendship: "Adulator enim omnis uirtutis inimicus est." [57] And in another passage he agrees with Cicero in insisting upon virtue as a prerequisite to friendship:

Si tamen inter malos caritas aut amicitia esse potest, hoc etenim quaesitum est. Sed tandem placuit eam nisi in bonis esse non posse. Magna utique inter molles et malos concordia sed ea tantum a caritate discedit, quantum lux distat a tenebris. Et licet interdum mali, sicut et boni, idem uelle uel idem nolle possint, amicitiae tamen titulum non assequuntur. Vnde et Crispo, historicorum inter Latinos Potissimo, sed et ipsi

52. *Ibid.,* Col. 694.
53. *Ibid.,* Col. 694.
54. *Ibid.,* Col. 690.
55. *Ibid.,* Col. 702.
56. *Op. cit.,* p. 24.
57. *Ioannis Saresberiensis episcopi Carnotensis policratici sive De nugis curialium et vestigiis philosophorum libri VIII,* ed. Clemens O. I. Webb, Oxford, 1919, I, 177.

Ciceroni placuit in malis factionem esse quod in uiris bonis uera amicitia est.[58]

And in his views on friendship, John of Salisbury follows Ailred in stressing ethical principles that harmonize with the concepts of mediaeval Christianity.[59]

We can observe a like moralizing, but a definite classical influence, in the *Versus Hugonis Sotovaginae:*

> Philosophus quidam quaesitus quid sit amicus,
>   Pauca prius meditans, sic ait, "Alter ego."
> Alterutri sed nemo potest modo dicere vere,
>   "Sum velut alter tu, tu velut alter ego."
> Hoc in amore decet sapientem quemque tenere,
>   Ne sit suspectus vel simulatus amor.
> Ingenui magis est odisse palam vel amare,
>   Quam ficto vultu quid velit occulere.
> Lex in amicitia sit, amicos poscere honesta,
>   Propter eos prorsus turpe nihil gerere.
> Non amor est, alter cum verum audire recusat,
>   Alter mentiri cuneta paratur ei.
> Aures qui claudit cum vere objurgat amicus,
>   Desperanda salue illius est penitus.
> Unus de multis sit consiliator amicis,
>   Cujus nota fides et sapientia sit.[60]

"A certain philosopher questioned what a friend may be;
After meditating a little, he spoke thus: "Another I."
But no one is able to say truly in any manner what-
        soever,
"I am another you, you are another I."
It is meet to hold him wise in love
Whose love is neither suspected nor simulated.
Better it is to hate or to love openly
Than with feigned countenance to hide what is felt.
Let the law in friendship be to demand of friends
        honest things,
And against them to do nothing knowingly of evil.
It is not love when the other refused to hear the
        truth
Or to falsify things attributed to him.
He who closes his ears when a friend swears truly,

---

58. *Ibid.,* I, 211. "If, however, there is able to be among the wicked, esteem or friendship, this indeed has been questioned. For it pleases it that this is not able to be except among the good. Surely great concord among the weak and the wicked is as far removed from friendship as light is removed from darkness. And although the wicked, like the good, are able to wish for friendship or not desire it, nevertheless they do not achieve the glory of friendship. Whence, to Crispo, chief among Latin historians, and to Cicero himself, it was the opinion that what among the evil was simply a company of persons associated together was among good men true friendship."

59. See Haskins, *The Renaissance of the Twelfth Century,* Cambridge, 1928.

60. *The Anglo-Latin Satirical Poems,* Vol. II, ed. Wright, London, 1872, in *Rerum britannicarum medii aevi scriptores; chronicles and memorials of Great Britain and Ireland during the middle ages* (Rolls Series, no. 59) p. 219.

His safety is fully to be despaired of.
One of many friends may be a counsellor
Who is noted for faith and wisdom.

A work close to the Middle English period in point of language
as well as in time is the eleventh-century Anglo-Saxon version of
Defensor's *Liber Scintillarum*.[61] This work gives summaries of discussions of the Church Fathers on the vices and virtues, and various
other subjects. The section "be freondscipe/ be feondscipe" gives
a general discussion of friendship, with classical and Christian influences side by side. Thus Solomon is quoted as insisting upon
fidelity between friends, and deprecating all treachery:

se đe forsyhđ freond his waedligende on heortan ys frynd weligra
manega inntingan đinne asmea mid frynd đinum / digle utlendiscum
ne onwreoh đu.[62]

Jesus son of Sirach discusses fidelity in friendship, urges us to avoid
the false friends, and urges us to fear God as necessary for true
friendship:

se đe ondraet drihten emne he haefđ freondsype godne forđi aefter him
byđ freondscype his [63]

Jerome sees in friendship a holy unifying principle:

On freondum sođlice na đincg byđ soht ac willa halig lufu ungeđyld
naefđ leas hlisa rađe byđ ofsett đa đe sođ lufu gesamnađ eorđena
langness na ascyrađ.[64]

Several statements attributed to Isadore reflect classical views:

freondscype gewis mid nanre strengđe byđ utalocen on manum timan
byđ adilegud . . . se sođ ys freondscype se naht secđ of đingum freondes-
butan sylfe welwyllednysse gewislice đaet sylfwylles he lufige lufi-
gende.[65]

He warns against false friends:

---

61. Ed. Rhodes, EETS. ES., 93 (London, 1889). The Latin original belongs to the
eighth century.
62. *Ibid.*, p. 193. The Latin reads: "Qui despicit amicum suum. indigen corde est
Amici diuitium multi; Causam tuam tracta cum amico tuo. et secretum ex-
traneo ne reueles."
63. *Ibid.*, p. 193 f. "Qui timet dominum aeque habebit amicitiam bonam. quoniam
secundum illum crit amicitia illius."
64. *Ibid.*, p. 196 f. "In amicis enim non res queritur sed voluntas; Sanctuns amor
impatient am non habet falsus rumor cita obprimitur; Quos caritas iungit ter-
rarum longitudo non separat."
65. *Ibid.*, p. 197 f. "Amicitia certa nulla ui excluditur. nullo tempere aboletur . . .
Illa vera est amicitia. quae hihil querit ex rebus amici. nisi solam beniuolen-
tiam sciliest ut gratis amet amantem;"

oft ður̄h hiwunge freondscype byð gegaderud ðaet se ðe na mihte open-
lice beswican he beswice facenlice.[66]

Here again true friendship is related to love of God:

daenne soðlice freond byð gelufud gif na for hyne ac for gode byð lufud
se ðe soðlice unmetlice freond lufað for hyne ma hyne naes for gode
lufað.[67]

III

It is not difficult to refute Mills's contention that the Christianized
form of friendship as exemplified in Ailred and Defensor "had no
effect on mediaeval literature, no matter what the clergy thought of
it." For the mediaeval belief that the soul of man was but part of
God's essence and could be led to God through friendship appeared
frequently along with the corollary idea (also in the Platonists) that
falsity to this friendship was falsity to God, and therefore a sin.

Thus the *Avenbite* explains the nature of true friendship by the
analogy of a hand or foot helping the other parts of the body: in like
manner we should be willing to lay down our soul for our friend, or
as Christ did for us:

Huanne ðe on uot slyt: ðe oðer him helpð. An haste huanne me wyle
smite ðet heaued: ðe hand hire deð be-uore. Ine ðisen we onderstondeð /
wolwelde / and clene louerede. ðeruore zayð god in his spell. 'ðet more
louerede ne may by: ðanne zette his zaule uor his urend.' dise urendrede
ous sscwcde Icsu crist ðe zoðe urend ðet uor ous layde his zaule and
his body to ðe dyaðe ... yet god layde his zaule uor ous: and we ssolle
legge oure zaules nor oure broðen / ðet is uor oure mixte, yet we
byeð a riʒt leme of ðe bodie / huerof his ðet heaued.[68]

"The Mirror of St. Edmund" explains that God made man in the
likeness of the Trinity so that there might be a spiritual brotherhood
among men, and that we should love this spiritual brotherhood more
than the fleshly brotherhood:

and ðis broðerhede mare suld we lufe, and mare dere halde ðan ðe
broðerhede of ðe flesche, in als mekill als ðe saule es mars nobyll ðan de
flesche, and in als mekill als Godde oure fadir of heuen es mare nobill
and mare for to lufe ðan oure fleschly fadir.[69]

---

66. *Ibid.*, p. 197. "Sepe per simulationem amicitia colligitur: ut qui non potuit
aperte decipere decipiat fraudulenter."
67. *Ibid.* "Tunc vere amicus amatur si non pro. se. sed pro deo amatur; Qui enim
intemperanter amicum amat pro se magis illum non pro deo amat."
68. Dan Michel's *Avenbite of Inwyt,* ed. Morris, EETS. OS., 23 (London, 1866),
p. 149.
69. In *Religious Pieces,* ed. Perry, EETS. OS., 26 (London, 1867), p. 34.

And, the author is careful to explain, whatever goodness or fairness we have within us in common with other men, we have it of our Father in heaven:

> whate-sa-euer we hafe in body or in saule, of gudnes or of fairenes, we hafe it of oure fadyr of heuen, Godde, ðat es till vs fadir, and euenly till all his creaturs.[70]

The language here bears some resemblance to Ailred's statement that virtue and goodness, the basis for friendship, originate in God.

The "Dominica V. Quadragesimae" seems to be in the tradition when it sees in our relationship to God an equality which should make "nan mon to beoran nið ne onde to nane cristene monne." [71] Also we read, a man cannot love God unless he first love his brother, and this love is not to be with words alone, but with deeds: "naut one mid worde ne mid tunge, ac ec mid worke and mid soðfest-nesse." [72]

In "þe Wohunge of Ure Lauerd" a man leaves all his fleshly friends because he can find a universal friendship in Jesus Christ: "for i ðe ane mai ich alle frend finden." [73] And in a similar vein is the litany in *The Romans of Partenay* where mercy and grace and pity are taken for granted by the Partenay family because of the "frendlyhed" of the deity.[74]

Thus friendship among men is but a part of that greater friendship of man for God; hence, falsity in friendship is much to be despised by Christian and Platonist alike. In the religious literature, as well as in the secular, the height of opprobrium seems to be that of a man who plays false to friendship. Thus in "The Maccabees" the wicked alderman Nicanor is sent to destroy the Jews, but he is made more wicked in the sight of the reader by going up to Judas with the words, "Ne com ic for nanum gefeohte ac for freondscipe to eow." [75] But Judas discovers the deceit in time, and in the end Nicanor is slain and Judas is victorious. Further on in the same work we learn

70. *Ibid.*
71. In *Old English Homilies and Homiletic Treatises,* ed. Morris, EETS. OS., 34 (London, 1868), p. 125.
72. *Ibid. Cf.* Gregory's words in the *Liber Scintillarum:* "ðaenne to soðan getrywe we synd gif ðaet we mid wordum behatað mid weorcum we gefyllað." *Op. cit.,* p. 197.
73. *Old English Homilies, ed. cit.,* p. 275.
74. Ed. Skeat, EETS. OS., 22 (London, 1866), p. 220.
75. Aelfric's *Lives of Saints,* ed. Skeat, EETS. OS., 76, 114 (London, 1881, 1900), II, 106.

how seriously the Christian writers regarded war between friends. Of the four kinds of war, the fourth which is war between friends is the worst, for it is "very miserable and endless sorrow":

and paet feorpe gefeoht ðe betwux freondum bið. is swiðe earmlic and endeless sorh.[76]

In *Vices and Virtues* those who simulate friendship are placed in the same class as those who tax their fellow Christians, and those who turn right into wrong:

Wa ȝeu ðe beplaitið ȝeuer emcristen, and waended ðat rihte te w(r)ohȝe, and ðat wohȝe te rihte, and ðe nimeð mede for ȝeuer swikele spache(s), ðe speked an aniðer half, swilche ȝie here beire friend waere.[77]

And in the A-text of *Piers Plowman* the character Envy reaches a sufficiently heinous state of villainy by describing the method he used to revile his neighbor: he would fawn upon him in the market-place, and pretend to be his friend, but behind his back he would think murderous thought, and say things to break up his home.[78] In this manner Envy is placed in his proper place among the vices.

There are some references to friendship in the religious literature which seem to be purely classical in terminology. In the "Lyf of S. Cycyle" Tiburcius and Urban cause considerable amazement when they desire to go to their death together, rather than make heathen sacrifices:

> O purpyl flowrys of youth delycous,
> O brothirly affeccyoun, in oon knyt
> Indyssolubylly, how ben may yt
> At ye to deth as gladly go
> As to a feste?[79]

The relationship between the two youths is not developed in detail, but the language in this passage is in the Platonic tradition of one soul in two bodies.

In the "Vita S. Martini Episcopi" there is an interesting illustration of the classical concept of equality among friends as a result of,

76. *Ibid.*, p. 114.
77. *The Book of Vices and Virtues,* Part I, ed. Holthausen, EETS. OS., 89 (London, 1888), p. 81.
78. *The Vision of William Langland concerning Piers Plowman,* Part I, ed. Skeat, EETS., OS., 28 (London, 1898), p. 56.
79. Bokenham's *Legendys of Hooly Wummen,* ed. Serjeantson, EETS. OS., 206 (London, 1938), p. 217.

and not a condition for, friendship. When Martin was fifteen years old, we read, he was sent into military service along with one of his slaves. But the slave became his friend, so Martin served him, and they ate together as equals.

> ðe ða he fiftyne wintre waes. betaeht to ðam gewinne mid anum his ðeowant ðe his gesiðe waes. ðam he sylf ðenode. swiðor ðonne he him. and samod hi gereordeden swa swa gelican.[80]

The same idea from a different point of view appears in "The Proverbs of Alfred." True happiness consists in removing the barriers of social and economic position and living on a common plane of friendship:

> And luue ðyne nexte.
> He is at ðe neode god.
> At chepynge. and at chyreche.
> freond ðu ðe iwurche.
> wyð pouere and wið riche.
> wið alle monne ilyche.
> ðanne myht ðu sikerliche.
> sely sytte.[81]

Even as late as the fourteenth century there are direct quotations from the classicists on friendship. The *Speculum Christiani* has little to say on the subject, but it does quote Seneca on the necessity of maintaining the virtuous quality in friendship:

> Vices of frende owe to be broken. I loue hym not, bot that I offend hym aȝeyns them. Whether I schal profyte or not, I wot not. I haue leuere frenschip or lucly hape fayle me than feyth.[82]

But the most complete fusion of mediaeval Christian and Platonic concepts in the religious literature appears in the work of Richard Rolle. His "Fire of Love" uses much of the *De Amicitia*,[83] but there is much that is mediaeval also. For instance, he explains that friendship is the knitting of two souls, but the two souls should be man's soul and God:

> Frenshyp is knytynge of two wyllis to lyke ðinges concentynge & to vnlyke dissentyng, and ðis frenschyp may be betwyx guyd & be-twix euyll, bot ðe dyuers desyrs. & moste ðis aght to be betwix god and mans

80. Aelfric's *Lives*, Vol. II, *ed. cit.*, p. 223.
81. *An Old English Miscellany*, ed. Morris, EETS. OS., 49 (London, 1872), p. 124.
82. Ed. Holmstedt, EETS. OS., 182 (London, 1933), p. 184.
83. John P. Schneider, *The Prose Style of Richard Rolle of Hampole with Special Reference to Its Euphuistic Tendencies*, Baltimore, 1906, points out parallel *passages* in *De Amicitia* and the *Fire of Love*.

saule, ðe qwhilk his wyll to godis wyll is bun to conferme in all ðinge, so ðat qwhat god wyll it wyll, & ðat god wyll not nor it wyll.[84]

There is an interesting explanation of the concept of divided souls:

> In mennys desyrs qwer is tru frenschyp/ god forbede ðat bodily son-dyrans make partynge of sawlis, bot rather ðe knot vnlousyd of drawynge frenschyp sal comforth heuynes of bodily sondyrynge, ðat ðe freynd with his freynd sall ðink he is, qwhils he seys stedfanes of wills vnlowsyd. It is certan trw frenschyp qwhen a freynd behauys hym to his frende als to hymself / qwhen he ðinkis his freynd hym-self in anodyr body, & his freynd he lufis for hym-self, not for profett þat he trowys of hym to haue.[85]

If friendship is a virtue, as some say, and exists perfectly only when the participants are equal in virtue, what is the result when one of the friends strays from virtue? Rolle has a very practical answer: Friendship, as a virtue, calls back the erring Friend:

> In frendys sothely is it noȝt necessary ðe tone be chawngyd for chaun-gynge of ðat toðer, bot frensshyp, sene it is vertew, inpossibyll it is ðat it be voydyd in any man with-out his chayngyng/ Qwherfore it is not brokyn for errore of ðe tone, bot, ande it be trew frenschyp, more bisy it sall be to call hym agayn ðat erryd.[86]

The discussion continues with a statement of the stability of friendship in time of adversity, and the ability of a friend to draw a friend to good.[87] But the true friendship, he asserts again, is found in God, for no man can do without His friendship.

Mills's deprecatory attitude toward the vitality of the friendship theme in mediaeval England applied to the secular literature as well as the religious. Here again we believe a careful scrutiny will show his position hardly justifiable; the friendship theme is so frequently illustrated in Middle English literature that one might argue for a continuity of the tradition from classical times to the Renaissance. It is true, as Mills points out, that many of the man-to-man relationships in English literature are those of sworn-brotherhood, but it is also true that in many of these, the classical influence seems to be still apparent.

One of the better-known friendship stories in Middle English is that of *Amis and Amiloun,* a story which Mills refers to "as funda-

---

84. Englisht by Richard Misyn, ed. Harvey, EETS. OS., 106 (London, 1896), p. 90 f.
85. *Ibid.*
86. *Ibid.,* p. 92.
87. *Ibid.,* p. 93.

mentally that of two sworn-brothers." [88] The contention is based, apparently, on an account of a troth between the two youths in which they pledged to help each other whenever there was need. [89] But the boys were close friends before the oath, and there are other evidences that the relationship is one of the divided soul. For instance, the two sons were born on the same day, and when they grew up they looked so much alike no one in the court could tell them apart:

> In al ðe court was ðer no wiȝt,
> Erl, baron, swain no kniȝt,
> Neither lef no loðe,
> So lyche were ðai boð of siȝt
> And of on waxing, ypliȝt,
> I tel ȝow for soðe,
> In al ðing ðey were so liche,
> ðer was neiðer pouer no riche,
> Who so beheld hem boðe,
> Fader ne moder ðat couðe sain,
> ðat knew ðe hendi children tvain,
> But by coloure of her cloðe. [90]

The friends eventually separate, but no complications arise until a false steward asks Amis to give him the place in his affections once held by Amiloun. But Amis remains true to his friend, and the steward plots revenge. The opportunity comes when he spies upon Amis and the daughter of the Duke, and reports that Amis has dishonored the maiden. Since he cannot truthfully swear his innocence, he goes to Amiloun, who substitutes in the combat for Amis, and wins the fight. So Amis wins the daughter in marriage.

But because of the deception in the combat, Amiloun had contracted leprosy. Driven from his home, he comes to Amis, who cuts the throats of his children to obtain blood that will cleanse his friend of the disease. The children are later miraculously restored to life, and Amiloun regains his lost estates. So the story ends happily, but the friendship does not end. Significantly, the two friends die on the same day, and we can suggest that the divided soul becomes one again unto eternity:

> Boð on oo day were ðey dede
> And in oo graue were ðet leide,

---

88. *Op. cit.,* p. 39.
89. *Amis and Amiloun,* ed. Leach, EETS. OS., 203 (London, 1937), p. 7.
90. *Ibid.,* p. 4.

> ꝺe knyȝtes boꝺ twoo;
> And for her trewꝺ and her godhede
> ꝺe blisse of heuyn ꝺey haue to mede,
> ꝺat lasteꝺ euer moo.[91]

We must not overlook another aspect of the story of *Amis and Amiloun* that suggests classical influence. The steward feigns friendship, or at least an interest in friendship, and the close relationship which ensues gives him an opportunity to practice treachery. An almost identical situation appears in *Guy of Warwick*. Morgadour comes to Guy and feigns friendship:

> . . . my frende dere,
> With herte y loue the in good manere.
> Moche y desire thy loue to haue,
> And therof hertly y the craue:
> And in-to the Chambre lete vs goo,
> Amonges the maydens some sportes to doo
> Before thy lemman, Clarice the free,
> Themperours doughter of bright blee,
> Whiles the Emperour is to wode goo,
> To chace the herte and the Roo.[92]

In Clarice's bower Guy wins at chess. Morgadour becomes angry, and informs the Emperor that Guy has dishonored his daughter. Guy successfully defends himself on this occasion, but Morgadour repeatedly attempts to do him injury until Guy is forced to kill him.

In Gower's *Confessio Amantis* the treachery is that in which a friend proves false because of the love of a woman. Amphitrion deceives Geta and wins his lady-love for himself:

> Of Geta and Amphitrion,
> That whilom weren bothe as on
> Of frendschipe and of compaignie,
> I rede how that Supplantarie
> In love, as it betidde tho,
> Be guilded hath on of hem two.[93]

The treachery in this passage Mills assigns loosely to "feudal relationships." But falsity in friendship was a commonplace from classical times, as we have pointed out, and in this particular passage the reference to the two friends that "weren bothe as on" is quite close to the Platonic tradition.

---

91. *Ibid.,* p. 100.
92. Ed. Zupitza, EETS. ES., 48 (London, 1887), pp. 183-185.
93. *The English Works of John Gower,* ed. Macaulay, EETS. Es., 82 (London, 1900), II, ll. 2477 ff.

Lydgate makes use of the story of Atreus and Thyestes to illustrate the mediaeval attitude toward deceit in friendship. In several pages of mournful verse, Thyestes seems to be lamenting not the wrong done to him by Atreus, but the treacherous nature of a wrong done under guise of fraternal friendship:

> But as a brother sholde his brother triste,
> I trusted hym off herte, will & thought;
> Bi apparence non othir cause I wiste,
> For in his persone I supposid nouht
> That euer he koude so fals a thyng ha wrouht.
> But who may soner a-nother man deceyue,
> Than hein whom no malice men conceyue? (ll. 3893-99)[94]

The treachery follows the familiar pattern: Atreus accuses Thyestes of corrupting his wife's virtue, and Thyestes is exiled as a result. But afterwards Atreus professes repentance, and the two make up their differences:

> On outher part forgete & set a-side,
> That nothyng afftir sholde our loue deuyde;
> But of oon will and oon entencioun
> Leede al our liff withoute dyuysioun. (ll. 3945-48)[95]

But the relationship is doomed to fail because it lacks virtue and sincerity:

> There is no damage in comparisoun,
> That may be likned, bi no raesemblaunce,
> To feyned trouthe and symulacioun,
> Whan fraude is hid with a fair contenaunce,
> Pretendyng trouthe outward bi disseyuance,
> And vndirnethe, off most fals entent,
> Off doubilnesse darith the serpent. (ll. 3956-62)[96]

Yet Atreus appears to be true; he receives Thyestes gladly, and gives him half his kingdom. This is the scene just before Thyestes is served the dismembered bodies of his children at the banquet:

> First how freendlie he dede me embrace
> Off hertli gladnesse withynne his armis tweyne,
> And how for icie the teris on his face
> Ful entierli gan doun distill & rayne,
> That, for my part, I koude me nat restreyne,
> But that I muste off frenshipe fraternall
> Weepe as dede he in his estat roiall. (ll. 3984-90)[97]

---

94. Lydgate's *Fall of Princes*, Part I, ed. Bergen, Washington, 1925, p. 108.
95. *Ibid.*, p. 109.
96. *Ibid.*, p. 109 f.
97. *Ibid.*, p. 110.

In moralizing on the episode, Lydgate points òut that there is no damage more perilous "Than in frenshepes whan there is straungenesse A maner parti,"

> And whan on trouthe tweyne hertis assure,
> Vndepartid off verray parfitnesse,
> It were a cicious froward cursidnesse,
> Ther loue so knet, to losne it or onbynde,
> Hatful to God and contrari onto kynde. (ll. 4231-35)[98]

Lydgate has a short account of the friendship of Thesus and Pirithous. When Thesus is captured by Cerberus, Pirithous rescues him, with the help of Hercules. The friendship was apparently sincere and in the proper classical tradition; the two were so equal in feats of arms that both were given the name Hercules to signify their equal prowess:

> Thei were in armys brethre bothe tweyne,
> Louede as brethre bothe in werre and pes,
> That nouther koude onto other feyne,
> Ther liff to iuparte & putte hemsilff in pres.
> And bother as brethre wer callid Hercules,
> To signefie, poetis can weel tell,
> This name in conquest all other doth excell.
>   (ll. 4369-75)[99]

Quite in keeping with the skeptical mediaeval attitude toward fidelity in friendship is the poem "Scilicet vt fulvum spectatur in ignibus aurum, Tempore sic durc est inspicienda fides."[100] A rich young man had great possessions and a great store of friends, but he wonders how true his friends are:

> as who's so mad
> To think that friendship doth not wealth pursue,
> Though for the moste part fained & vntrue? (ll. 2-4)

So he kills a calf, places it in a sack, and tells his friends that he has killed a man:

> 'My friendes,' quoth he, 'your loves I now must trie,
> For friendes are truly prov'de in misery;
> Vnlesse your succours doe my life defend,
> I am in danger of a shamefull end.
> Knowe, in my rage I have slain a man this day,

---

98. *Ibid.*, p. 117.
99. *Ibid.*, p. 121.
100. In *The Times' Whistle,* ed. Cowper, EETS. OS., 48 (London, 1917), pp. 120-122.

> And knowe not where his body to conveigh
> And hide it from the searchers inquisition,
> My house being subject to no mean suspition.
> Healp me, good Sirs, in my distressed state,
> Since thus to you my griefs I doe dilate.' (11.13-22)

Of course, his friends all turn against him, but he finally does find one, an old friend whose friendship had been "prov'de in divers hard assaies," who vows secrecy and promises to help. So, having found a true friend, the rich young man tells him the trick, and

> Resolved straight a knot with him to tie
> Of never-dying friendship to their end,
> Thus each to other was a perfect friend,
> Meanwhile the other from him he removde,
> Whose fained love sufficientlie was prov'de.
> (ll. 58-62)

It is important to point out that the false friends did not refuse to shield the murderer out of a sense of virtue; theirs was a more practical outlook:

> '. . . While your estate was good,
> And your selfe free from danger of the lawe,
> The fatnesse of your purse had power to drawe
> Our wealth-pursuing loves; but you must knowe,
> Our friendships with your fortunes ebbe or flowe.'
> (ll. 28-32)

But not all mediaeval episodes on friendship end in deceit; there are some examples that look on the positive side. There is the rather unusual relationship of Launcelot and Galehot,[101] who became friends while fighting each other on the battlefield. Galehot notices and admires Launcelot's prowess, even though he is fighting for Galehot's enemy, Artus. The two knights engage in combat and Launcelot is unhorsed, but Galehot offers his own horse to the man he already loves. After the battle, Galehot asks Launcelot to be his guest, and Launcelot agrees on condition that Galehot do whatever he asks. Galehot honors Launcelot in every possible way, gives him a luxurious bed, and rests by his side to try to soothe his restless sleep.

The next morning Launcelot makes his request: Galehot, after conquering his enemy, is to place himself unconditionally at Artus'

---

101. "Le Livre de Lancelot del Lac," Part I, in *The Vulgate Version of The Arthurian Romances*, Vol. III, ed. Sommer, Washington, 1910, pp. 242 ff.

disposal. It is significant that Galehot agrees because he knows his friend could not possibly ask anything dishonorable:

> Sire fait il ia ne mait diex se vous naures le don Quar ie ne poroie riens faire por vous ou ie peusse honte auoir.[102]

So through the virtuous quality of friendship peace is brought about between Galehot and Artus.

In the *Romans of Partenay* there is also an accidental meeting of warriors who become friends. In this story the warrior Uriens, setting out upon adventure, chances to land upon the island of Cyprus, where he breaks the siege of the Saracens against the King of Cyprus. But the King was sorely wounded, and calls upon Uriens, "off frendlyhed," to visit him. Then, in true classical tradition, the King announces that he wants nothing of his friend, but begs Uriens to accept everything he owns, his kingdom and his daughter. Uriens gallantly accepts, not as payment for his assistance, but as a favor to his friend.[103]

The long and beautiful friendship of Reynawde and Mawgis[104] places great emphasis upon the virtuous qualities of the two participants. They go through a long series of adventures, always protecting each other in time of need, always respecting the fidelity of their friendship. The relationship seems to be completely in the classical tradition; for example, when Mawgis steals three horses laden with gold from Charlemagne, he gives half of the loot to Reynawde.[105] When Mawgis departs secretly after delivering Charlemagne into the hands of Reynawde, the latter is so broken up that he nearly loses his mind:

> Thenne beganne Reynawde for to wepe full tendrely for his cosin that was this goon/ and all wepynge, he came agayne to the barons/ and sayd to theim how Mawgys was goon awaye wythoute his knowledge, whereof he was soo wrothe and soo sori that he wente almoste oute of his mynde.[106]

When Reynawde's brother Richard is wounded, Mawgis is so upset at Reynawde's weeping that he agrees to cure Richard with magic:

---

102. *Ibid.,* p. 247.
103. *Ed. cit.,* pp. 26 f.
104. *The Foure Sonnes of Aymon,* ed. Richardson, EETS. OS., 44, 45 (London, 1885).
105. *Ibid.,* p. 130.
106. *Ibid.,* p. 406.

fayr cosin, take hede what I shall say, & leve this sorrow; ye know wel that ye be all my cosins/ and therfore we ought to parforce ourselfe for to socour thone theother whan it is nede.[107]

Reynawde consents to do anything his cousin may command:

For ye wote well that dyde never ony thyng that was agenst your wyll; nor there is no man in the worlde for whom I wolde doo so moche as I wold for you.[108]

When he is not with Reynawde, Mawgis goes into a hermitage to practice his devotions, as a virtuous knight should. But he comes out of his solitude to assist Reynawde at the siege of Jerusalem, and renews his vows of friendship:

for I have delibered that I shall be noo hermyte as longe as we ben togyder, but I shall helpe you wythe all my power. But one thynge I telle you, That never whyle I live, I shall cast noo charme more, for I have promysed it god, and all the sayntes, to whom I pray to kepe me therfro/ but I telle you that I love you so hertly, that if I sholde be dampned/ yet shold I com out of my hermytage for to socour you yf ye had nede.[109]

Thus friendship assumes a role above that of religion, because in a virtuous relationship there can be no wrong. Reynawde's good qualities are emphasized in his declining years: after the death of his wife he refuses to marry again and devotes his time to raising three virtuous sons. At his death his body is miraculously borne up to heaven.

There is a long passage in the *Mirour de l'omne* in which Gower praises friendship in a manner quite in accord with the classical view. This passage, a 50-line summary of the friendship tradition,[110] has the familiar evaluation of friendship as better than worldly goods,

> Ly sage en son escript diffine
> Qe l'orr et l'argent que l'en fine
> Riens valt en comparacious
> A l'amiste q'est pure et fine;

a statement that a friend is a second self ("Mon bon amy est l'autre je"), a suggestion of the divine relationship ("Sicomme la chose q'est divine"), and above all, a reference to Love as a unifying principle:

> Sique d'amour le benefice
> Du guerre exteignt toute malice
> Et nous fait vivre en unite.

---

107. *Ibid.*, p. 276.
108. *Ibid.*, p. 277.
109. *Ibid.*, p. 403 f.
110. *The Complete Works of John Gower*, ed. Macaulay, Oxford, 1899-1900, I, 159, ll. 13693 ff.

This bit of philosophic speculation alone could be sufficient to remove the passage from the category of feudalistic influence.

Mills finds in Chaucer a synthesis of the courtly love tradition, classical friendship, and sworn brotherhood.[111] This is not the place for an analysis of the use of courtly love material in the Middle Ages. But it might be to the point to suggest that courtly love and Platonic ideas on friendship are more closely related than is generally recognized. They cannot be categorically divided, then, for it is difficult to tell where one ends and the other begins.

As an example of the court-of-love position as held by Chaucer, Mills cites passages from the *Romaunt de la Rose*. In the example he quotes [112] Love appears to the Lover (the poet) in a dream and offers him three consolations: Swete-Thought, Swete-Speche, Swete-Loking; also a bit of advice:

> Therfore I rede thee that thou gett
> A felowe that can well concele,
> And kepe thi counsell, and well hele,
> To whom go shewe hooly thine herte,
> Both wele and woo, joye and smerte;
> To gete comfort to hym thou goo,
> And pryvyly, bitweene yow twoo,
> Yee shall speke of that goodly thyng
> That hath thyn herte in hir kepyng;
> Of hir beaute, and hir semblaunce,
> And of hir goodly countenance.
> Of all thy stat thou shalt hym sey,
> And aske hym counseill how thou may
> Do ony thyng that may hir plese;
> For it to thee shall do gret ese,
> That he may wite thou trust hym soo,
> Bothe of thi wele and of thi woo.
> And if his herte to love be sett,

---

111. For an example, in Thomas Usk's *The Testament of Love,* we find Platonic echoes in the advice Lady Love is giving the prisoner: 'O my nory, wenest thou that my maner be, to foryete my friends or my servaunts? nay,' quod she, 'it is my ful entente to visyte and comforte all my friendshippes and allyes, as wel in tyme of perturbacion as of moost propertee of bliss.' (Book I, Chap. II.) 'Good contemplacion,' quod she, 'of wel-doing in virtue in tyme coming, bothe in pleasaunce of me and of thy Margarit-peerle. Hastely thyn hert in ful blisse with her shal be esed.' (Book II, Chap. X.) Cited in Mills, *op. cit.,* pp. 52 ff., from W. W. Skeat, *Chaucerian and Other Pieces.* Here we have an application of friendship theories in the relationship of Lady Love and the Lover, and a use of the idea of virtue among friends applied to the relationship of the Lover and his Lady.

112. *Ibid.*

His companye is myche the bett.
For resoun wole, he shewe to thee
All uttirly his pryvyte;
And what she is he loveth so,
To thee pleynly he shal undo,
Withoute drede of only shame,
Bothe tell hir renoun and hir name.
Thanne shall he forther, fer and ner,
And namely to thi lady der,
In syker wise; ye, every other
Shall helpen as his owne brother,
In trouthe, withoute doublenesse,
And kepen cloos in sikernesse.
For it is a noble thyng, in fay,
To have a man thou darst say
Thy pryve counsell every deel;
For that wole conforte thee right well,
And thou shalt holde thee well apayed,
Whanne such a freend thou hast assayed.[113]

Now there is no doubt that this is in what is known as the court-of-love tradition; it cannot be readily conceded, however, that the passage has been divorced from the Platonic tradition. Since a friend is another self, it would follow that friendship would place some value on the necessity of confidence between friends,[114] though the use of the friend to help attain the desired one is no doubt in the courtly tradition.

In the second part of the *Romaunt de la Rose* there is a passage of a hundred lines or more in which Reason makes an extended analysis of friendship.[115] The passage shows the influence of the Platonic concept in reference to the unity of souls (Of wille knit bitwixe two), the communal ownership of property (Whan wille and goodis ben in comune), the suggestion of a divine unifying principle (Grounded by goddis ordinaunce, Hool, withoute discordaunce), the necessity for virtue (For no man may be amiable, But yf he be so ferme and stable, That for tune change him not), for equality (If bothe the hertis Love hath fered, Joy and woo they shull depart, And take evenly ech his part).

Chaucer's *Troilus and Criseyde,* like the *Romaunt de la Rose,* is in the court-of-love tradition, but here, again, the friendship motif

---

113. *The Complete Works of Geoffrey Chaucer,* ed. Robinson, Cambridge, 1933, p. 692, ll. 2856-92.
114. *Cf.* Dugas, "Ils confirment leur amitie par ce qui devrait la detruire," *op. cit.,* p. 244; *cf. De amicitia,* Chap. VII.
115. *The Complete Works of Geoffrey Chaucer, ed. cit.,* ll. 521-5304.

is very much in evidence. Mills sets up the thesis that Chaucer is in this poem presenting classical theories of friendship, but by inversion; that is, Chaucer has one friend play false to another thus giving the basis for the tragedy.[116] This point of view, however, is effectively combatted by Professor Slaughter, who shows that Pandarus' actions in the poem are those of a perfect and faithful friend.[117] Slaughter sum up his position as follows:

> Pandarus fits the pattern, and is completely justified. He and Troilus trust each other, not for reward, but for love of friendship; and keep their confidences secret. Pandarus must be esteemed as a perfect and faithful friend if he is regarded as being always within the charmed circle of courtly love, for his action conforms entirely with the notion of Guillaume de Lorris in the first part of *The Romaunt of the Rose*.[118]

In *The Knight's Tale* the relationship between the two chief characters, Palamon and Arcite, is presented by Chaucer as a friendship pact that comes into conflict with love. There is no evidence, however, that the friendship here depicted is in the Platonic tradition:

> "It nere," quod he, "to thee no greet honour
> For to be fals, ne for to be traitour
> To me, that an thy cosyn and thy brother
> Ysworn ful depe, and ech of us till oother,
> That nevere for to dyen in the peyne,
> Til that the deeth departe shal us tweyne,
> Neither of us in love to hyndred oothre,
> Ne in noon oother cas, my leeve brother;
> But that thou sholdest trewely forthren me
> In every cas, and I shal forthren thee,—
> That was thyn ooth, and myn also, certeyn;
> I woot right wel, thou darst in nat withseyn.
> Thus astow of my conseil, out of doute.
> And now thou woldest falsly been aboute
> To love my lady, whom I love and serve,
> And evere shal til that myn herte sterve.
> Nay, certes, fals Arcite, thow shalt nat so.
> I loved hire first, and tolde thee my wo
> As to my counseil and my brither swoen
> To forthre me, as I have toold biform.
> For which thou art ybounden as a knight

---

116. *The Complete Works of Geoffrey Chaucer, ed. cit.*, pp. 50 f.
117. E. E. Slaughter, "Chaucer's Pandarus: Virtuous Uncle and Friend," *JEGPh*, XLVIII (April, 1949), pp. 186-95.
118. *Ibid.*, p. 195.

To helpen me if it lay in thy myght.
Or elles artwo fals, I dar well seyn." [119]

The language and suggestion of the oath put this relationship in the category of the sworn-brotherhood type of friendship rather than the Platonic. It would never do to present the Platonic form of friendship and then have one of the participants play false. For in the classical tradition friendship is higher than the love between man and woman, and Chaucer's recognition of this might have led him to avoid suggesting the Platonic form in those tales where he made love the principal motif.[120]

Lydgate's *Fabula duorum mercatorum* is the best example in Middle English literature of narrative action which has as its core the Platonic friendship motif. Based upon the *Gesta Romanorum* story of the Knights of Baldac and Lombardy, and on Petrus Alphonsus' *Disciplina clericalis,* the story emphasizes the perdurable qualities of friendship as opposed to love. According to the story, the merchant of Baldac has a strong desire for the merchant of Egypt. They exchange gifts, and eventually the Baldac merchant travels to Egypt and visits his friend. Here he falls in love with the girl whom the Egyptian merchant has reared to be his wife. But the bonds of friendship are so great that the Egyptian gives up his intended bride and has the wedding ceremony performed, with his friend as groom. Whereupon the newlyweds return to Baldac and live in happiness. Years later the merchant of Egypt, having fallen from fortune, is, while wandering through Baldac, falsely accused of a murder. He confesses to the crime, but the merchant of Baldac, recognizing his friend, likewise confesses, and the Egyptian is freed. Whereupon, the real murderer feels forced to confess, and the two friends are reconciled.

The love story is subordinate to the friendship plot, as is the case in any tale where Platonic friendship is represented. And there is ample evidence that this is Platonic friendship. There is, first, the idea that friendship is based on virtue. The merchant of Egypt was a good man:

---

119. *The Complete Works of Geoffrey Chaucer, ed. cit.,* p. 32, 11.1129-51.
120. The "Pardoner's Tale," and the "Shipman's Tale" both represent the characters as taking oaths of friendship, only the vows are broken by treachery. These are further examples of Chaucer's use of the sworn-brotherhood type of motif. Mills has suggested that the "Tale of Melibeus" is Platonic in its attitude toward treatment of one's enemies. The references Chaucer mentions, however, show non-Platonic sources. See Mills, *op. cit.,* p. 67.

> (For alle vertues in hym wern aggregat) ;
> Of vices voyd, pitous and merciable
> And of his woord, as any centre, stable.[121]

We learn that the merchant of Baldac

> was eek a worthy man,
> Ful weel belovid also in his contre:
> In trouthe he hadde al, that euyr he wan,
> And hym governyd evirmore in honeste.[122]

Likewise, there is a reference to the element of similarity:

> Kynde is in werkyng a ful myghty lorde:
> In love he lynketh hem, that be vertuous.[123]

And finally, there are references to unity in one soul:

> oon, as by affeccioun
> Ther may be maad no divisioun [124]
>
> So ful they were of oon accordement,
> As oon in too and too in oon for euere,
> That nought, but death, her love mau disseuere.[125]

The many indications of the existence of a classical friendship motif in the English literature of the Middle Ages suggests that Professor Mills's conclusions on the rarity of the motif may have been based on insufficient evidence. The friendship theme appears to be something of a commonplace in the Middle Ages, and, aside from the Christian attempts to adapt the motif to theology, exists in a state little different from its first appearance in Plato.

But even the Christian examples follow the familiar device of adapting to Christian ends an idea basically Neoplatonic. This is not to say that Christianity did not have as an inherent aspect of its belief a consciousness of the virtuous qualities of friendship; there are sufficient hints in Christ's ethical teachings to give evidence of the existence of Christian teaching on friendship entirely apart from Platonic influence. But in the corollary aspects of the theory—in finding the source of friendship in God, in seeing in the God-man relationship an equality based on friendship, and perhaps in the ideas on

---

121. Ed. Gustav Schleich, *Quellen und Forschungen,* LXXXIII (1897), p. 2, ll. 5-7.
122. *Ibid.,* ll. 43-46.
123. *Ibid.,* ll. 75-76.
124. *Ibid.,* ll. 88-89.
125. *Ibid.,* ll. 86-88.

communal ownership of property—the parallels to the Platonic tradition are so striking as to suggest a mixing of the two traditions.

In any case, the mediaeval literary exemplification of the concept in the Middle Ages seems to differ little, in frequency or degree, with the literary adaptations of the friendship motif in English literature of the Renaissance.

X

THE POETRY AND NOVELS OF
ROBERT PENN WARREN

By RICHMOND C. BEATTY

(Professor of English)

MR. WARREN is a poet, critic, novelist, short story writer, and dramatist. He was born in 1905. Prior to this fall he taught for a decade at the University of Minnesota, which is about as far north as a native Kentuckian can get, without crossing the border. Among the many men of letters identified with the Southern Literary Renaissance of the past quarter century—Faulkner, Tate, Wolfe, Ransom, and others—he is obviously the most versatile. It is also already evident that an excellence amounting to genius is present in almost everything he has published since his university days.

He is virtually all inclusive in that he refuses to limit his sensibility in any way; yet to compare him with Whitman on this score would be meaningless. For Warren has absorbed the formal disciplines of the schools—Vanderbilt, California, Yale, Oxford: no more learned writer is doing significant work in this generation. One should begin a discussion with some notice of his verse which is, intrinsically, as rewarding as his prose, although it has been overshadowed by a recent popular success in the latter form. And a mild quarrel seems necessary at the start.

In a generally penetrating review by Mr. John Crowe Ransom of Warren's *Selected Poems* (1944) we find this comment about "The Ballad of Billy Potts," the longest performance in the book. In brief the ballad tells about Young Billy's leaving his wretched home for the West to make his fortune, only to be killed by his parents, though in innocence, upon his return ten years later. "The Pottses, incidentally, are most unsympathetic characters; they are a nest of Kentucky rattlesnakes." This remark is certainly true. The basis of Ransom's complaint is that they are "mean and inarticulate." They do not know what tune they are playing, and the writer has to speak for them in parenthetical passages, passages which achieve, incidentally, the effect of a Greek chorus in the sense that they universalize the significance of the action of the ballad proper. "I wish

142

we had a way of holding this poet, whose verse is so beautiful when it is at his own height of expression," Ransom concludes, "to a level no lower than its height." But does not this wish amount to a plea that Warren abandon his fundamental conception of what poetry should be and do? The critic's objection would seem to imply that, by analogy, Shakespeare should not have drawn the characters of the Grave Diggers, or Bottom the Weaver, or even that of the lying, cowardly, and piggish if lovable Falstaff—since such creations are incapable of representing the "height" of Shakespeare's own "expression." Warren's concern is with the welter of modern man's experience, as comprehended by an artist to whom nothing human is alien.

Reiterated in his verses are the themes of Man's Personal History or Conscience, of Time's Violence, and of the Lost Innocence which the "frail reproachful *alter ego*" of childhood never permits the restless but tortured adult to forget. In a sense they are all subjective pieces, despite whatever brilliant objectification particular details may receive in separate poems.

What does it all mean, how can the protagonist define it—"the old houses and new-fangled violence" of "Ransom," for instance? The actors (his ancestors) are nameless and, with faces turned, "I cannot make them out." "At night, the old man [the parent] coughs"

> thus history
> Strikes sum, ere dawn in rosy buskins laced
> Delivers cool with dew the recent news-story.

At most he can with his love "endeavor definition," though he is aware that his success will be frail—"frail as the clasped dream beneath the blanket's wool." So it goes with the argument of an earlier poem, "The Return: An Elegy." The poet is coming back from a distant place to the home in which his mother lies dead, and the recalcitrant images which flood his mind insistently violate the sanctity of the occasion.

> Calcium phosphate lust speculation faith treachery
> it walked upright with habitation and a name
> *Tell me its name*

(What better summation of the complex nature of man excels in blunt honesty the above first line?)

> I have a name: I am not blind.
> Eyes, not blind, press to the Pullman pane

143

Survey the driving dark and silver taunt of rain
What will I find
What will I find beyond the snoring pine?
O eyes locked blind in death's immaculate design
Shall fix their last distrust in mine.

But the irony, the dogged unwillingness to avoid the full context of the experience—of this irony more presently—evokes the following brutal passage:

Give me the nickels off your eyes
from your hands the violets
let me bless your obsequies
if you possessed conveniently enough three eyes
then I could buy a pack of cigarettes.

Again,

the old bitch is dead
What have I said!

reinforces the complex tone of the situation the poet is trying faithfully to render, as on the train he pursues "past culvert cut fill embankment semaphore" the ghostly parallels. The Elegy concludes with one of Warren's finer passages:

If I could pluck
Out of the dark that whirled
Over the hoarse pine over the rock
Out of the mist that furled
Could I stretch forth like God the hand and gather
For you my mother
If I could pluck
Against the dry essential of tomorrow
To lay upon the breast that gave me suck
Out of the dark the dark and swollen orchid of this sorrow.

The total relationship between mother and son is rendered without any evidence of timidity about suggesting the selfish human concomitants of death. An awareness of this stubborn unwillingness on Warren's part to violate any subject is one of the keys to the basic intention of his poetry.

He has himself, in collaboration with Mr. Cleanth Brooks, termed this practice the method of irony. It is a deliberate attempt to include the discordant and contradictory without evasions, and the result is that such poetry may be said, when successful, to achieve an added dimension. To illustrate from the use of metaphor:

In the poetry of the Nineteenth Century (or for that matter of the Eighteenth) the relation between the emotional associations of the two terms of a comparison is one of similarity. Shelley is not much concerned with the physical likeness of his skylark to the glow-worm in a dell of dew, or for that matter to a high-born maiden in her bower. But he is careful to make the maiden "high-born" and in general to make all of the objects in his comparison "poetic." And in this he reflects the general Nineteenth Century view of poetry.

The protagonist in Warren's most mature poetry is a man accursed. And what is the nature of his curse? Mr. Ransom's analysis of perhaps the most successful of the *Selected Poems,* "Original Sin," seems to reach the heart of the question. The opening stanzas read as follows:

> Nodding, its great head rattling like a gourd,
> And locks like seaweed strung on the stinking stone,
> The nightmare stumbles past, and you have heard
> It fumble your door before it whimpers and is gone:
> It acts like the old hound that used to snuffle
> > your door and moan.
>
> You thought you had lost it when you left Omaha,
> For it seemed connected then with your grandpa, who
> Had a wen on his forehead and sat on the veranda
> To finger the precious protuberance, as was his
> > habit to do,
> Which glinted in sun like rough garnet or the rich
> > old brain bulging through.

"But this nightmare, the vague, inept and not very presentable ancestral ghost, is not to be exorcised. It appears even in Harvard Yard, for the victim's handsome secular progress had led him so far, where the ghost is ill at ease indeed. But you must not think the illusion of the ghost is the form of the speaker's simple nostalgia, for that is painful too, but goes away:

> You were almost kindly then in your first homesickness
> As it tortured its stiff face to speak, but scarcely mewed;
> Since then you have outlived all your homesickness,
> But have met it in many another distempered latitude:
> Oh, nothing is lost, ever lost! at last you understood.

"This ghost will not be laid. Yet it is an ineffectual ghost, unlike that portentous apparition of Hamlet the Elder, which knew so much about 'theatre,' including how to time and how to make an entrance: our ghost does not interfere with the actions of the living:

> But it never came in the quantum glare of sun

To shame you before your friends, and had nothing to do
With your public experience or private reformation:
But it thought no bed too narrow—it stood with lips askew
And shook its great head sadly like the abstract Jew.

We must return to the title, [Ransom adds] and take its consequences: Original Sin. And here it may be of some moment that we
ourselves have had dire personal inklings of Original Sin, hustled
and busybody creatures as we are yet perhaps painfully sensible of
our treachery to some earlier and more innocent plan of existence;
or, on the other hand, that we know it by theology and literature. . . .
Briefly, Original Sin is the betrayal of our original nature that we
commit in the interest of our rational evolution and progress. . . .
We should take into account the phenomenon of recapitulation; for
it is understood that individually we re-enact the evolution of species.
We do it physiologically, but there is a conscious side to it too. We
have a nature, and proceed to condition it; and more and more, from
age to age, are subjected to the rule of reason, first the public reason
which educates us, and then, when we have lost our native spirits,
our own reason which draws corollaries to the public reason.

The imagery of Warren's verse is one of its most arresting fea-
tures. There is the general in "Pursuit" who, after the battle, with-
draws from the dead and from his gorgeous subalterns:

Or stares from the thicket of his familiar pain, like a fawn
That meets you a moment, wheels, in imperious innocence is gone.
. . . .
. . . history held to your breath clouds like a mirror.

Or consider the similes in the first stanza of "Original Sin," together with its closing lines:

Later you may hear it wander the dark house
Like a mother who rises at night to seek a childhood picture;
Or it goes to the back yard and stands like an old horse cold in the
    pasture.

The cold heart heaves like a toad

But again, on a happier occasion:

And the faithful heart inside you purrs like a cat.

Yet Warren is perfectly capable of managing the Homeric simile,
as in the opening stanza of "Love's Parable":

As kingdoms after civil broil
Long faction-bit and sore unmanned,
Unlaced, unthewed by lawless toil,

146

Will welcome to the cheering strand
A prince whose tongue, not understood,
Yet frames a new felicity,
And alien, seals domestic good:
Once, each to each, such aliens, we.

The mother rising at night, the old horse cold in the pasture, the heart heaving like a toad or purring like a cat—they are all figures drawn from an awareness of the timeless cycle of nature. They succeed because of their conciseness and accuracy; they are never blurred.

Warren's liberties extend to metrics as well as to content. Even the early poems reflect a bold attitude toward formal convention: no stanzaic pattern, once established, is permitted to recur unmodified, if it gets in the way of a freer expression of a given mood. Oddly enough, he reminds one again of Whitman, though whatever freedom he may take with accent he invariably compensates for through rhyme. It is an oral poetry, with frequent cadenzas, so to speak: it reads well aloud and attests a uniformly sensitive ear, but it will not be bound. The first line of the "Last Metaphor," an early poem, is this:

The winds had blown the leaves away and left

But in stanza three, line one, of this series of quatrains he writes,

He passed by a water, profound and cold

Variations in the number of unaccented syllables are continuous.

The later poems are even more loose in their incidental structure. The following are concluding lines of the five stanzas of "Pursuit":

That meets you a moment, wheels, in imperious innocence is gone.
Till you feel like one who has come too late, or improperly clothed, to
a party.
What matter what crevice, cranny, chink, bright in dark, the pale
tentacle find.
Of spume-tooth and dawnless sea wave, salt rimes the lookout's devout
eye.
And rattles her crutch, which may put forth a small bloom, perhaps
white.

147

This is no place to quarrel about hovering accents; the lines are basically irregular. Yet a study of each of the stanzas will reveal that the elaborate rhyme scheme of number one (abba, cddc, ee) is scrupulously maintained to the end. This formal tension within each unit which finds its fluid release at its close is a unique attribute of Warren's verse.

Nor is wit absent, when Warren is disposed to use it. The section called "Mexico Is a Foreign Country: Five Studies in Naturalism" is playful enough on the surface. But it is not wholly playful by any means. Number II he entitles "Siesta Time in Village Plaza by Ruined Bandstand and Banana Tree." The poet is not sleeping on this occasion; he is meditating over his last beer:

> If only Ernest now were here
> To praise the bull, deride the steer.
> And anatomize for chillier chumps
> The local beauties' grinds and bumps;

This sound critical appraisal of one phase of Hemingway is likely to be overlooked because of the tone of the stanza; the author is obviously having a good time with his subject. Later he writes:

> Or if the Baptists would undertake
> To dip local sinners in the picturesque lake,
> And not too obsessed in spiritual pride
> Bring a nationally advertised insecticide;
> Or if Henry Wallace and cortege
> Could get this far with friendship's message,
> And smile his smile of the bashful Jesus
> On these poor Indians and their diseases;
> Or even if the Standard Oil
> Would come and puncture this parched soil,
> And corrupt the pomaded politicos
> And load the peons with fresh woes—

The stanzas are interesting because they reveal so plainly the range of effects inherent in the ironic method. No institution, person, or corporation is quite perfect: Standard Oil, the Baptists, Henry Wallace—they all have their limitations when conceived in terms of the total picture his method seeks to reveal.

Only one brief unit of Warren's *Selected Poems,* "Kentucky Mountain Farm," is Southern in any special sense. Here he is admittedly writing about the section in which he was born, but they are early poems, some going back to student days:

> The hound's black paw will print the grass in May,
> And sycamores rise down a dark ravine,
> Where a creek in flood, sucking the rock and clay,
> Will tumble the laurel, the sycamore away . . .
> Under the shadow of ripe wheat
> By flat limestone, will coil the copperhead
> Fanged as the sunlight, hearing the reaper's feet.

Here once, in the autumn orchards, young men lay dead—gray coats, blue coats. Yet,

> Their reason is hard to guess, remembering
> Blood on their black moustaches in moonlight.
> Their reason is hard to guess and a long time past.

There are other pieces about the cardinal, the jay, the watershed—objective, rather slight presentations of particularities. And in the last, "The Return," the protagonist comes in a final sense to know that nothing is there to call his image back, the familiar faithless things—the sycamore, the leaf falling, the stream—being voiceless. The unrelenting sweep of time and change has left him alone with his ghosts, which are his tradition, his past. It is out of this past, which seems always present to him, that the impressive achievement of Warren's poetry has found its definition.

In his first three novels Warren has dealt with subjects that may be called, in a rough sense, contemporary; that is to say, they do not take us behind our own century. The period of *Night Rider* is 1905, of *At Heaven's Gate* 1929, of *All the King's Men* 1935. An informal criticism I have heard from one of his older friends, who is also a novelist, runs to this effect: "He lifts his subjects from the newspapers." I should like to comment on this judgment immediately.

Warren is certainly and in the fullest sense a modern writer and a modern personality in that he knows, as we say, "what is going on" in political and literary affairs. He shares the technical advantages along with the major curse of our time—the curse of dissociation. It is a curse which he has gradually yet successfully surmounted as artist in the primary act of giving it convincing representation in fiction. Willie Proudfit's story in *Night Rider* is less integrated into the structure of the novel itself than is the "Statement of Ashby Windham" in *At Heaven's Gate*. Without the narrative of "Cass Mastern's Wedding Ring" *All the King's Men* would be, structurally, little more than another tale about a state dictator. Warren, in other words, seems to prefer to undertake a presentation of history in simultaneous terms. The past and the present adumbrate each other; contrasting characters accent similarities along with differences. But Fate, or "the awful responsibility of time," is the albatross which, in one way or another, we all wear about our necks. A man of genius can find dramatic conceptions of this truth wherever he turns.

When characters are dissociated, a primary quest becomes a search which, over and over, drives the lost people of Warren's narratives to their private catastrophes. For actually his moderns are all doomed and damned people: Percy Munn in *Night Rider,* Sweetwater and Sue Murdock in *At Heaven's Gate,* or Willie Stark, the Scholarly Attorney, and Dr. Adam Stanton in *All the King's Men.* Those who preserve a measure of integrity are characters whose mores are rooted in an earlier and alien tradition, a simpler tradition in the sense that its way of life possessed form and meaning— Proudfit, Windham, Mastern, along with Jeremiah Beaumont of *World Enough and Time.* To dismiss this juxtaposition of values as myth—as opposed to the factual realities of history—as has been done, represents, I think, a major failure on the part of the reader's imagination. All significant writers think in terms of myths. Milton had his Christian myth, Yeats his myth about the cycles of history, Eliot his about the inferiority of the present to the past. The important question is: What insights into human nature does any given author afford us, once we have suspended our disbelief and accepted his vision in its own terms?

Yet if damned, the moderns in Warren's fiction are never stereotyped villains, and it is his fundamental and instinctive awareness of the human frailties in all people that makes his characters rewarding subjects for contemplation at whatever level one elects to consider them. On the surface, in *At Heaven's Gate,* for example, the principal figures are as disgusting as the bloated monstrosities of Hogarth: Jerry Calhoun, weak, morally spineless ex-athlete; Bogan Murdock, a crooked financier; Sue, his bitch daughter; Sarrett, a fake artist, liar, homosexual son of a whore and eventual murderer; Sue's mother, a dipsomaniac; Duckfoot Blake, a cynical statistician (Ph.D., Chicago!).

"Put them all together," as the sad old song goes, and "they spell Mother!" In a sense the sentimental line is appropriate, for these people to Warren are typical of the many miserable wretches to whom our century has given birth. Yet Sue can exclaim, brushing her hair and watching her face in the mirror: "Oh I wasn't like this. I wasn't like this always!" These are words which imply a violation of that same innocence which preoccupies the narrator of "Original Sin." Similarly, Slim Sarrett can write as follows about Shakespeare:

> The tragic flaw in the Shakespearean hero is a defect in self-knowledge. Macbeth comes to ruin, not because he kills (Shakespeare could scarcely have been so naive as to believe that men have not killed and then ruled in prosperity and dreamless sleep—he had, we know, read Holinshed), but because he does not realize upon what grounds it is possible for him, Macbeth, to kill. Bacon wrote: Knowledge is power. Bacon was thinking of knowledge of the mechanisms of the external world. Shakespeare wrote: Self-knowledge is power. Shakespeare was thinking of the mechanisms of the spirit, to which the mechanisms of the external world, including other persons, are instruments. In other words, Shakespeare was interested in success. By success, he meant: Self-fulfillment. But his tragedy is concerned with failure. Naturally. The successful man—saint, murderer, politician, pick-pocket, scholar, sensualist, costermonger—offers only the smooth surface, like an egg. Insofar as he is truly successful, he has no story. He is pure. But poetry is concerned only with failure, distortion, imbalance—with impurity. And poetry itself is impurity. The pure cry of pain is not poetry. The pure gasp and sigh of love is not poetry. Poetry is the impurity which an active being secretes to become pure. It is the glitter of pus, richer than Ind, the monument in dung, the oyster's pearl.

And Jack Burden, of *All the King's Men,* thinking of the deaths of his Boss and the Doctor, recalls Willie's last words: "It might have been different, Jack. You got to believe that." The novelist goes on, though never quite in *propera personae:*

> He had seen his two friends, Willie Stark and Adam Stanton, live and die. Each had killed the other. Each had been the doom of the other. As a student of history, Jack Burden could see that Adam Stanton, whom he came to call the man of idea, and Willie Stark, whom he came to call the man of fact, were doomed to destroy each other, just as each was doomed to try to use the other and to yearn toward and try to become the other, because each was incomplete with the terrible division of their age. But at the same time Jack Burden came to see that his friends had been doomed, he saw that though doomed they had nothing to do with any doom under the godhead of the Great Twitch. They were doomed, but they lived in the agony of will. As Hugh Miller (once Attorney General under Willie Stark and much later Jack Burden's friend) said to him when they were discussing the theory of the moral neutrality of history: "History is blind, but man is not."

What is Warren saying in his fiction, or to phrase the matter differently, what is his vision of reality? Basically, as in his poetry, his theme is the Problem of Evil, something before which, in Schleiermacher's words, the understanding of man is dumb. The artist's advantage over the philosopher with respect to this question is that he is not obligated to attempt a solution; his responsibility is to present it in human and concrete terms. Warren's people are constantly violating the original innocence of their natures; their experiences are, in sum, the record of these violations, whether they are committed in the interest of outwardly plausible and even noble causes or through a blind lust for temporal power.

Night Rider is the story of a cooperative movement among tobacco growers in Kentucky, the growers agreeing to hold their product until it can bring a better price. At first public and conventional, their program soon moves into a second and secret stage: violence will be used upon those who refuse to join. Percy Munn, a somewhat ineffectual lawyer, becomes involved in the program, innocently and in a negative way. He simply drifts into it. Near the end of the story he kills a man, Bunk Trevelyan, whom he had formerly saved from death at the hands of the court. He is destroyed because he surrendered himself to the advocacy of a movement purely economic in character. The contrast between this type of loyalty and that which the old Confederate Captain Todd had once given to his Cause is implicit throughout the later stages of the book. The values which dignify group loyalty became perverted, cheapened, and therefore evil, as represented in the character of Munn.

The basic theme in *At Heaven's Gate* is similar. It contrasts the representation of a sophisticated and therefore corrupt society in the capital of a Southern state with that of the illiterate mountaineer preacher, Ashby Windham. The calamities that befall both groups, however, are more sharply presented and defined than in the earlier novel. How Evil overtakes Windham is told in his own words:

> We come to a big markit where folks brung vegitibles and chickins and such to sell and folks in the city comes and buys it. We stood where they come in and went out and I read to them out of the book.
> A police man come and said, for Christ sake you all git on somewheres else so I won't have to run you in.
> I said to him how we done come in Gods name.
> Well for Christ sake, he said, you go somewheres else in Gods name and quit worryin folks.
> I read to him what the book said.
> Save it for Sunday, he said, and git on.
> We went round to another door where folks was.

Old Man Lumpkin said how he was worrit how Mrs. Lumpkin was makin out. I said I would go down to the boat and see how she was makin out. He was a old man and it was hard for him to climb back up the hill. I said I would git a doctor if she was not makin out so good and come tell him. I told him and Jasper to wait and not do no readin or testifyin or nuthin. I did not want them to git in no trouble and me not there.

I come to the boat and Mrs. Lumpkin was still porely. I said I was aimin to git a doctor and she said naw, for the money. I said the money was not nuthin and her layin there and not makin out no better. She said naw, and I was argyin with her and of a sudden Pearl yelled somethin. Pearl was out front of the house part. She yelled agin, and I come out.

It is Murry, she yelled.

I seen Murry runnin down the hill. Then I seen a man behind him. It was a police man. The police man was yellin for him to stop but he never paid him no mind. They was another police man back up the hill was comin too. The first police man had a pistol in his hand I seen. I yelled for Murry to stop but he never.

The police man shot off his pistil but I seen he did not mean to shoot Murry.

Murry run up the board we had laid to the boat. He yelled they done taken Jasper and Old Man Lumpkin. He kicked that board in the water and he tried right quick to cut that rope as helt the boat. He taken out his knife to cut it. They says how Murry taken out his knife to cut the police man but he never. He is a good boy and has got true peace in his heart. He did not mean nuthin when he broke loose from the police man up to the markit and tripped him up and run. He was afeard lak a young un, and taken no thought.

The first police man got there and he grabbed that big board out of the water. He was tryin to lay it to the boat. Murry tried to kick it loose but he slipped and fell.

The other police man got there and he was yellin.

Then Pearl yelled right behind me. I looked round and seen her. She had that there old squirril rifle of Jasper in her hand.

It looked lak I could not say nuthin. It all come of a sudden.

Them police men throwed the board on and was yellin. One of them put his foot on the board.

Oh God, Pearl said out loud.

Pearl, I yelled, Pearl. And I aimed to grab holt of that rifle.

She shot off that old squirril rifle.

I seen that police man put his hands on his stummick afore he fell in the water. . . .

They taken us to the jail.

The conception of tragedy revealed here is basic in that it befalls a man who is innocent and yet who, even when in the light of his best or instinctive impulse, is overtaken by the Evil which is inherent and inescapable in the world. Wyndham represents simply a single facet of the universal human predicament. Wherever man goes and whatever his condition—be it exalted or humble—his doom follows him like his own sinister shadow in a westering sun.

Warren has made a statement about the motivation of *All the King's Men*. Taken at face value, it should obviate controversy or conjecture about the way a serious novelist works out creatively the raw material of experience. Mr. Robert Gorman Davis, in the New York *Times* (August 18, 1946), declares that Warren "is writing about the real Huey Long." He adds: "the novel must be judged, then, in political as well as literary terms, for its total effect is to justify Long and the intellectuals who played ball with him." Yet consider Warren's own words, as printed in the Chicago Sunday *Tribune* of May 11, 1947:

Anyone who lived in Louisiana under the consulship of Huey P. Long could not help speculating about the irony of means and end in politics, or, perhaps to state the question more accurately, about the irony of process, product, and byproduct. The assassination of Long in the fall of 1935 seemed to give that irony its proper dramatic summation. But after the assassination, other and more complicated ironies, and more deep seated issues, began to unfold themselves.

By the fall of 1937 I had begun to think of a play concerning a political boss in a southern state. So the career of Long and its sequel did suggest the material and some of the issues which were to appear in "All the King's Men." But in 1937 I was engaged in writing my first published novel, "Night Rider," and postponed any work on the political play. But the more I thought of a political play, the more I was convinced that the ironies and issues which presented themselves in the action of politics were manifestations of other ironies and issues more fundamental in our contemporary situation.

By the spring of 1938 I began to feel that I had some notion of how to relate the two levels of meaning, or some hope of how I might relate them. So I wrote a few exploratory fragments on a play then called "Proud Flesh." In the summer of 1938, in fascist Italy, other relations began to suggest themselves. In the winter of 1938-'39, back in Louisiana, the play began to assume its basic structure. In the summer of 1939 I returned to Italy on a Guggenheim fellowship to finish the play. Then in the winter of 1939-'40, between watching troops in the streets and listening to radio reports of the war, I finished the first draft of the play, but I felt too close to it to undertake revision. So I laid it aside to work on another novel, which was later published under the title of "At Heaven's Gate."

In the winter of 1942-'43 I dug out the draft of "Proud Flesh" and tried to revise it. But the revision went slowly, and I began to work on a novel involving the same material. Somewhat earlier I had thought of the possibility of doing a novel if the revision of the play did not recapture for me the original heat of the idea, but I felt handicapped by my ignorance of the practical stage. And so I undertook the novel

"All the King's Men." The last rewriting and revision of proofs were finished in the early spring of 1946. The novel was published in August, 1946. In the fall of the year I returned to the play and began revising it. Its title was changed from "Proud Flesh" to that of the novel.

As for the relation of the play and novel to the facts of recent Louisiana history, the facts of that history gave the original suggestion for the project. By the time actual composition began I felt that I had cut myself off from the facts of that history and could create a fable for my own ideas, using only such facts as could be detached for that purpose. But it is useless to belabor that point, for readers who do not realize this from the text of the novel or play cannot be expected to abandon their preconceptions, prejudices, or convenience because of any statement of mine.

The richly figurative context of Warren's prose is of a piece with his poetry. No modern writer with whose work I am acquainted can command with so little apparent effort the limitless possibilities of the English language. He has inherited, of course, the rewards of the revolution in diction (the repudiation of the "poetic" or otherwise special language) which T. S. Eliot and his contemporaries inaugurated some thirty years ago. But Warren has profited by their experiments in much the same way that Shakespeare learned from Kyd and Marlowe; he has taken from them what he could use within the framework of his own always questing imagination. Consider, for instance, the following figurative expressions:

> With her eyes closed, she felt the whisky flower inside her, and then its tentacles reached out delicately into her body. She thought: the light had never been like that before, green-gold light and bright after the storm and you thought it came from the underside of the leaves, too, and from the grass, for it was everywhere, and I held the kitten in my arms and I loved it and I knew it was going to die, but he came and looked down from his horse and said, Poor little thing. She thought: But that was then, not now, and I was that then and now I don't know what I am.

> He never drank—he didn't like the taste, he said—and rarely smoked. But he bought whisky for his parties, when he had the money—a vile pale-yellowish whisky, which purported to be distilled from corn mash, back in the hills, by the loving hands of simple independent folk of pure Anglo-Saxon stock who had passed the skill down from father to son, but which had actually been distilled, in tin, by Negroes in a slum shanty from a mess of potato parings, brown sugar, corn meal, and anything else which would ferment. He paid three dollars a gallon for it, and had sometimes stinted himself in order to buy it. Though he did not drink, and, in fact, needed no whisky to sit up and talk and argue until the sky began to thin and pale in the distance beyond the river, he got a peculiar and profound stimulation from its effect on other people, from

155

the mounting noise, the sudden, aimless laughter, the self-appreciated wit, the refractions and distortions of personality, the twisted glimpses and unveiling, the flashing eyes and moist lips.

. . . They all believed in a great number of things, and they spoke of those things in the same familiar tone they used to name the dead names of people whom he had never seen, whose faces were featureless to him, as they were now featureless under the sod, who had died, long back, of child-bed, minnie-ball, weak lungs, burst bowels, or the fall from the horse when the girth slipped.

. . . He would lie in the dark beside her, after she had gone to sleep, and be happy. He would be happy, at least when he did not think of anything in the world but just looked at her, as she lay there with her eyes gravely closed. . . . A chunk of Sweetie Sweetwater, L.L.D., Chaplain, C.S.A., and old men with congress gaiters and silver-headed sticks and bad breath and old ladies who peered at you and Vyvian Sweetwater who was buried in 1660 in a little brick church which still stood in the dead field beside the salt estuary in Virginia, and a chunk of Bogan Murdock and Mrs. Murdock, who they said, was a drunkard, and of that old half-wit bastard Murdock, who was a murderer, and of all the Murdocks before, whose names he had never heard of, and chunks of people who had been dead a thousand years. The little devil sure-God had an assortment of junk and plunder stored in there with him while he hunched up and didn't have to do any breathing and try to make sense of it yet. Maybe he would be able to make sense of it. He had him a time trying to make sense of the chunk which was just Sweetie Sweetwater.

The figure of speech is a way of tying together the disordered fragments of human experience, is a way of achieving one's identity. Practically every page of Warren's poetry or prose is a commentary upon this fundamental quest. James Joyce could manage this kind of effect, but his procedure was relatively clumsy in the sense that it demanded a great degree of violence upon the conventions of the language—running words together, inventing words, indulging in esoteric allusions, and the like. Warren could probably not write as he does had he not studied carefully the work of this distinguished predecessor. His mastery and refinement of modern technics are further apparent in passages like the following, from *All the King's Men:*

I walked across the hot pavement toward the green polka-dot figure which stood there behind the glass like something put in a show window for you to admire but not touch. So I walked past the eyes of which the whites were like peeled hard-boiled eggs and past the sad big mouth which didn't know what to say.

These are the lessons of Impressionism (compare E. E. Cumming's statement in *The Enormous Room:* "I followed the back and holster toward the door"); yet Warren can bring to fiction, time after time, the disciplined but intensely figurative language of poetry at its most rewarding level:

> After one of my exhibitions Lois would try to discipline me by withholding the sweets of her gender.

> He had been put in at the second quarter because the regular at left end had been performing like a constipated dowager.

> And with that I slammed his door and was running and stumbling down the dark stairs, for it was the kind of apartment house where the bulb burns out and nobody ever puts a new one in and there is always a kiddie car left on a landing and the carpet is worn to ribbons and the air smells dankly of dogs, diapers, cabbage, old women, burnt grease, and the eternal fate of man.

> Yes, Adam Stanton, Anne Stanton, and Jack Burden, back in Burden's Landing, had a good time when they were children by the sea. A squall might, and did, pile in off the Gulf, and the sky blacked out with the rain and the palm trees heaved in distraction and then leaned steady with the vanes gleaming like wet tin in the last turgid, bilious, tattered light, but it didn't chill us or kill us in the kingdom by the sea, for we were safe inside a white house, their house or my house, and stood by the window to watch the surf pile up beyond the sea wall like whipped cream.

It is all there: the echo from the past—Poe, in this case—the present focused against its vanished and now ridiculous meaning, along with the electric but apparently effortless language.

Wordsworth remarked in his famous Preface to the *Lyrical Ballads* that though poetry might be the spontaneous overflow of powerful feelings, first-rate poetry could be written only by a person who had thought long and deeply about his subject. The generalization applies to any kind of creative composition. *World Enough and Time* (1950), Warren's most recent novel, is subtitled "Romantic," by the author—Romantic, presumably, in the sense that two levels of early nineteenth century Kentucky society—its frontier and its more sophisticated elements—conflict in what becomes almost an orgy of violence. Yet if its action is extravagant, it is not unreal; it is set down with the convincing particularity one associates with his earlier prose.

Jeremiah Beaumont has murdered Colonel Fort because of an alleged violation of the honor of his wife, Rachel, and he is being pursued by four vigilantes:

> But the older man cut in. "Mr. Beaumont, we'll come straight to the point, and I hope you won't get offended. There is some suspicion of

you in Frankfort, you being a stranger there that night and all, and we . . ."

"One moment," Jeremiah said. "Do you wish to tell me that you have come for me?"

"Yes, sir-ree-bobbin," the familiar face said, and the fellow made himself big in the saddle, "and we're aiming . . ."

"Stop," Jeremiah commanded. "I do not know who you are, or on what authority you come, but . . ."

The man patted his pocket. "I got heaps of authority right here," he said, and leered.

"I don't care what you have in your pocket, unless it is a warrant for my arrest. Which I gravely doubt, if there is any decency and justice in Frankfort. But unless you have a warrant, I will not submit to you as a prisoner. I am unarmed, but you will have to shoot me down in cold blood in my own yard. Do you understand?"

The man took out his pistol.

"Put that thing up," Jeremiah said. "You might hurt yourself."

"By God, I'll show you, you can't git uppity with me, I'll show . . ."

Jeremiah turned his back square on the pistol, and addressed the older man. "I don't know who this fellow is," he said, "but if . . ."

"Aw, he's Mr. Bumps, Mr. Carlos Bumps," one of the other men volunteered, a young peeled-faced fellow, not more than boy, and his voice had a tinge of reverence, as he added, "why, Mr. Bumps is on the patrol, up in Frankfort."

Then Jeremiah remembered in a flash why that fleshy raw face was familiar. The man was the third member of the patrol on the street in Frankfort, the one who had stared at him passing while the others jollied the drunks about missing their dark meat. But Jeremiah continued to address the older man. "It does not matter that Mr. Bumps—if he rejoices in such a name—can bully niggers and drunkards in Frankfort. He should learn better manners when he comes to Saul County and enters a man's yard or . . ."

"Ain't no man gittin funny about my name, by God!" the man behind Jeremiah exclaimed.

"Put up your pistol, Bumps," the older man said quietly. Then to Jeremiah: "We have no thought of making you a prisoner, Mr. Beaumont. We come in friendship and to . . ."

"A prisoner?" And at that word, spoken in Rachel's voice, Jeremiah turned to see her standing at the head of the steps, looking very pale but quite calm. His heart went full of a great pride in her, she was so clear and possessed.

She gazed from surprised face to face of the men below, then asked Jeremiah: "Who are these men? If they come in friendship, why don't you ask them in to breakfast?"

"They come from Frankfort," Jeremiah explained. "You remember I told you last night that Colonel Fort had been killed. Well, they come to tell me I am suspected and . . ."

"Suspected?" she echoed incredulously. She came down the steps and stood by her husband's side, laying a hand on his arm. "Jerry," she said (And he thought, *how long has it been since she called me Jerry, and her voice like that?*). "Jerry," she said, "why don't you ride to Frankfort with these gentlemen and clear everything up?"

"Lady," the older man said, "that's all we . . ."

"Listen," Jeremiah interrupted. "I have never said that I would not go to Frankfort. I am happy to go, and be sure that my name is not bandied about by every loose tongue. But I will not go as a prisoner. Is that clear?"

"That's all we come for," the older man said.

"Good," Jeremiah agreed. "And now if you will kindly tell me your names, I shall present you to my wife."

The older man's name was Crawford, the boy's was Showforth, the other man's was Jarvis. Jeremiah presented the three quite formally, passing over Bumps, and Rachel acknowledged them. Then Jeremiah feigned to discover Bumps. "Oh," he said to her, nodding at Bumps, "this man calls himself Bumps."

The boy Showforth snickered at that, and Bumps sat sullen and unhappy under the eyes of the other men, and Jeremiah felt that he had scored a point, for, as he records, "You can always turn the members of a group, however solid, against one of their own if you discover his weakness or comicality to them, for such is vanity that they will repudiate him to join you." *Dividere et,* Jeremiah writes and takes pleasure in his victory at the first little skirmish.

"Won't you come in for some refreshment?" Rachel urged. "I'll call a boy to take care of your horses." Then she let her gaze fall on Bumps. "Or," she said, as at a sudden inspiration, "perhaps Mr. Bumps would be good enough to do that."

The boy snickered again, and the men, even the older man, suppressed grins, so that Jeremiah wasted an instant of pity on poor, hulking Bumps, whose fleshy face had gone crimson. "Lady," he blundered sullenly, "listen, lady, I ain't no nigger."

"Why, Mr. Bumps," she said, with a voice full of contrition and surprise, "whoever thought you were? I knew you were white immediately I laid eyes on you."

This somewhat extended passage reflects not merely Warren's realism; it echoes, as well, his central theme. "If you discover his weakness!" The point is that *everyone* has his weakness, his tragic flaw. It is the inevitable condition of man; it is embodied in the myth of original sin. As old as *Genesis,* it remains as everlastingly certain as death. Beaumont's flaw is that of idealism; he would live and act by a code of honor which is uncomprehensible to the world; and he dies because, becoming involved with the world, he finds himself powerless to withstand its inexorable laws. The "pure idea," he hoped, would comprise the sphere in which he moved. This failed him in fact; yet with death imminent he could still wonder: "Was all for nought?" Warren ends his book with the same question, a question the answer to which is afforded only in the implicit assumptions of the narrative itself.

The primary tension in Warren's prose arises from the fact that it will at any moment fly off into the inexhaustible extravagances, or texture, of poetry. Few more melancholy observations can be recorded than that most modern readers are too impatient to appreciate his almost page-by-page revelations. Perhaps original sin is with us here as elsewhere.

XI

THE HAPPY CAPTIVITY OF
FRANCISCO NÚÑEZ DE PINEDA Y BASCUÑÁN

By MAXWELL LANCASTER

(*Associate Professor of Romance Languages*)

IN 1550 while Dr. Juan Ginés Sepúlveda and Bartolomé de las Casas were bitterly debating in Valladolid the question of whether Indians should be included in Aristotle's category of men born to be slaves, the conquistador Pedro de Valdivia, on the far-off embattled frontier of Chile, dispatched the report to his sovereign Carlos Quinto that he had cut off the hands and noses of two hundred Indian prisoners "because of their rebellion, when I had many times sent them messengers and given them *Requirements,* as ordered by your Majesty." [1]

In an earlier letter to his king, Valdivia had praised the land of Chile, but had damned its recalcitrant inhabitants. "It is a beautiful land," he rhapsodized, "tal que para vivir en ella no la hay mejor en el mundo," [2] but "every prisoner I have taken has cost me and my men one hundred drops of blood and two hundred drops of sweat." When he himself was taken captive, Valdivia paid for his cruelty with his life, being either bludgeoned to death by a wasp-tempered old Araucanian warrior, or forced to drink molten gold by his former *yanacona* (domesticated Indian servant) Lautaro, if we are to believe the suspiciously colorful legend.

Not all Spanish prisoners of the Araucanians were entertained so roughly, especially if they held high military rank. They were in most cases held as hostages and liberated in exchange for *caciques* who had fallen into the power of the Spaniards. In a little known personal history, *El Cautiverio Feliz y Razón de las Guerras Dilatadas del Reino de Chile,* [3] Francisco Núñez de Pineda y Bascuñán, a century after the publication of Alonso de Ercilla's first

---

1. Lewis Hanke, *The Spanish Struggle for Justice in the Conquest of America,* (Philadelphia: University of Pennsylvania Press, 1949).
2. "so much so that in the world there is none better wherein to live."
3. *The Happy Captivity and an Account of the Long-extended Wars of the Kingdom of Chile.*

book of *La Araucana,* and more than a half century after the appearance of Pedro de Oña's *Arauco Domado,*[4] describes his unusual experiences as a captive among the Araucanians. He had studied for nine years in a Jesuit monastery where he had acquired considerable knowledge of Latin literature and Holy Scripture, but because of "juveniles desaciertos"[5] was ordered by his father to enter the Spanish infantry. Francisco wanted to be made a captain immediately, but his austere father don Álvaro, who had already lost one eye and had both his legs "imposibilitadas"[6] in military service, was so infuriated by his son's presumptuous ambition that he had to take to his bed. "He began to assail me," explains Francisco, with

> palabras desabridas y ásperas, (diciendo) que no sabía ni entendía lo que hablaba, que cómo pretendía entrar sirviendo al rey nuestro señor con oficio de capitán, si no sabía ser soldado, que cómo pretendía entrar a ordenar ni mandar a los experimentados y antiguos en la guerra sin saber lo que mandaba; que sólo serviría de darles que notar y que decir porque quien no había aprendido a obedecer era imposible que supiese bien mandar.[7]

It was probably at the beginning of 1625 that Francisco enlisted during the interim command of the *maestre de campo* don Francisco de Alba y Norueña. He quickly rose from the rank of standard-bearer to that of corporal, and finally to a captaincy. There were frequent incursions of the barbarians from the mountains on the other side of the Bio-Bío River. In 1629 these invasions became more formidable, and the legion of Francisco, called the legion of San Felipe, was stationed near Yumbel. This legion was engaged in the disastrous siege of las Cangrejeras on the 15th of May, 1629. Francisco was shocked by the death of a Spaniard occasioned by a trigger-happy compatriot. An harquebuse had gone off accidentally and the Spanish victim had been unable to speak a word. "Aquel desastre era de otros mayores prenuncio." "That disaster foreboded other greater ones." The rainy weather and strong north wind

---

4. Arauco Tamed.
5. "youthful blunders."
6. "incapacitated."
7. "sour and harsh words, (saying) that I didn't know or understand what I was talking about, [and] how did I presume to enter the service of the king our Lord with the rank of captain, if I didn't know how to be a soldier, [and] how did I think I could come in and order or command veterans seasoned in warfare without knowing what orders to give; that I would only serve to give them a spectacle to talk about because it was impossible for one who hadn't learned how to obey to know how to command well."

hampered the Spanish firearms and 80 Spanish infantrymen were surrounded when the cavalry fled, leaving them unprotected.

The following is don Francisco's account of his own capture.

> Estando yo haciendo frente a la vanguardia del pequeño escuadrón que gobernaba con algunos piqueros que se me agregaron, oficiales reformados y personas de obligaciones, considerándome en tan evidente peligro, peleando con todo valor y esfuerzo por defender la vida, que es amable, juzgando tener seguras las espaldas y que los demás soldados hacían lo mismo que nosotros, no habiendo podido resistir la enemiga furia, quedaron muertos y desbaratados mis compañeros; y los pocos que conmigo asistían iban cayendo a mi lado algunos de ellos, y después de haberme dado una lanzada en la muñeca de la mano derecha, quedando imposibilitado de manejar las armas, me descargaron un golpe de macana, que así llaman unas porras de madera pesada y fuerte de que usan estos enemigos, que tal vez ha acontecido derribar de un golpe un feroz caballo, y con otros que se me asegundaron, me derribaron en tierra, dejándome sin sentido, el espaldar de acero bien encajado en mis costillas y el peto atravesado de una lanzada; que a no estar bien armado y postrado por los suelos, desatentado, quedara en esta ocasión sin vida entre los demás capitanes, oficiales y soldados que murieron. Cuando volví en mí y cobré algunos alientos, me hallé cautivo y preso de mis enemigos.[8]

Luckily Bascuñán awoke as the prisoner of the kind and intelligent chief Maulicán, who considered himself honored to have the son of the respected Álvaro Maltincampo in his custody, and who was so grateful to Francisco for not having tried to escape after a most perilous crossing of the Bío-Bío that he swore to restore him to his countrymen at the very first opportunity. The good faith of Maulicán was put to the test when, in a council of war chiefs, Putapichún, Antegüeno, Lincopichún and Nailicán offered to buy

---

8. "While I was standing before the vanguard of the little squad I commanded with some pikemen who were added as reinforcements, reformed officers and persons of integrity, [and] while I considered myself to be in such evident peril, my companions fighting [alongside me] with all courage and energy to defend their lives, [a possession] that is precious [to all of us], judging that their rear was secure and that the other soldiers, unable to resist the enemy's fury, were doing the same as we, were left slain and routed; and some of the few who stayed with me to assist me kept falling at my side, and after I was given a lance-thrust in the wrist of my right hand so that I was left incapacitated to handle arms, [the foeman] discharged on me a blow with a bludgeon, for that's what they call the clubs of heavy, stout wood that these enemies use and that sometimes have felled a ferocious horse with a single blow; and with other repeated blows with which they smote me, they knocked me down to the ground, leaving me senseless, with my steel shoulder-piece jammed into my ribs and my breastplate pierced through with a lance-stab. If I hadn't been well armed and lying prostrate and dazed on the ground, on this occasion I should have remained lifeless amongst the other captains, officers and soldiers who died. When I regained my senses and recovered some breath, I found that I was a captive and prisoner of my enemies."

his distinguished captive and sacrifice him in the ceremony of *Pruloncon*. Despite their bids of necklaces, horses, diamonds, saddles, "ovejas de la tierra," [9] and Spanish prisoners, Maulicán remained adamant. Don Francisco was an eyewitness of the horrible torture to which these chieftains wished to subject him. The crafty Maulicán won Francisco's eternal gratitude by refusing to deliver him into the hands of these bloodthirsty extremists.

Here is a description of the ceremony from which Bascuñán escaped by the skin of his teeth.

Seguimos a los dos caciques mensajeros y llegamos al lugar donde nos aguardaban los demás ministros que se fueron poniendo en orden. En medio pusieron al soldado que trajeron liado para el sacrificio y uno de los capitanes cogió una lanza en la mano en cuyo extremo estaban tres cuchillos, a modo de tridente, bien liados, y otro tenía un toque, que es una insignia de piedra a modo de una hacha astillera. Cogió en la mano el toque o en su lugar una porra de madera que usaban entonces sembrada de muchos clavos, el valiente Putapichún como más estimado cacique y en el lenguaje, veloz y discreto. Y haciendo la salva a todos los compañeros, habiéndose puesto en pie en medio de la plazoleta, se acercó adonde a aquel pobrecito soldado le tenían asentado en el suelo, y desatándole las manos, le mandaron coger un palillo y que dél fuese quebrando tantos cuantos capitanes valientes y de nombre se hallaban en nuestro ejército, y como el desdichado mozo era novel en la guerra, no tenía noticia de los que en aquel tiempo tenían opinión entre los enemigos, y le mandaron los fuese nombrando. Dijo que no conocía a los valientes. A que replicó Putapichún:—¿Pues no conocéis a Álvaro Maltincampo (que así llamaba a mi padre)? —Sí, conozco y tengo muchas noticias de él, respondió el desdichado.—Pues cortad un palito y tenedlo en una mano. ¿Al Apó no conocéis?—Muy bien, dijo. —Cortad otro palito.

De esta suerte fué nombrando el sargento mayor y hasta diez o doce de los más renombrados, y le mandó cortar otros tantos palitos los cuales le hizo tener en una mano, y le dijo:—Tened en la memoria a todos los que hemos nombrado y haced un hoyo para enterrar esos valientes. Y lo puso luego en ejecución. Putapichún le entregó a mi amo una porra de madera pesada, sembrada toda de clavos de herrar, las cabezas para fuera y el cuchillo que había puesto en medio de los dos y los otros dos cuchillos mandó a los acólitos. Con ellos y sus lanzas arboladas se pusieron a los lados del sacrificante, el cual se fué acercando al lugar donde aquel pobre mancebo estaba y lo tenían asentado, despidiendo de sus ojos más lágrimas que las que en los míos sin poder detenerse se manifestaban.

Conque cada vez que volvía el rostro a mirarme me atravesaba el alma, y correspondiéndonos con unos suspiros y sollozos desmedidos, muchos de los ministros circunstantes daban muestras de hallarse

---

9. "Sheep of the land." Probably a reference to llamas, guanacos or alpacas, wool-bearing ruminants or camcloid beasts-of-burden of South America.

condolidos. Porque hay algunos entre ellos que se duelen y lastiman de los miserables. Allegóse Maulicán al desdichado y le dijo:—¿Cuántos palillos tienes? Contólos y respondió que doce. El miserable turbado dijo: —Este representa al primer valiente, y este otro al gobernador. Y los echó en el hoyo. Conque fué por sus turnos sacando desde el maestro de campo general y sargento mayor hasta el capitán de amigos llamado Diego Monje, que ellos tenían por valiente y gran corsario de sus tierras; y acabado de echar los doce palillos en el hoyo, le mandaron fuese echando la tierra sobre ellos y los fué cubriendo con la que había sacado del hoyo; y estando en esto ocupado, le dió en el celebro tan gran golpe que le echó los sesos fuera con la macana claveteada. Al instante los acólitos que estaban con los cuchillos en las manos, le abrieron el pecho y le sacaron el corazón palpitando y se lo entregaron a mi amo que después de haberle chupado la sangre, le trajeron una quita de tabaco, y cogiendo humo en la boca, lo fué echando a una y otras partes como incensando al demonio a quien habían ofrecido aquel sacrificio. Pasó el corazón de mano en mano y fueron haciendo con él la propia ceremonia que mi amo; y en el entretanto andaban cuatro o seis de ellos con sus lanzas corriendo a la redonda del pobre difunto, dando gritos y voces a su usanza y haciendo con los pies los demás temblar la tierra. Acabado este bárbaro y mal rio volvió el corazón a manos de mi amo y haciendo de él pequeños pedazos entre todos se lo fueron comiendo con gran presteza.[10]

---

10. "We followed the two messenger-chiefs and we came to the place where we were awaited by the other ministers who were arraying themselves in orderly formation. In the middle they put the soldier whom they brought, bound for the sacrifice, and one of the captains [leaders] seized in hand a lance at whose extremity were three knives, in the manner of a trident, well bound together, and another held a *toque*, which is an insignia of stone like a timber-ax. The valiant Putapichún, as the most esteemed chieftain and the most swift and adept in language grasped up in his hand the *toque* or in its stead a wooden club that they used then, sown with many nails. And making a salute to all his companions and having stood up in the midst of the small square, he approached the place where they were keeping that poor soldier seated on the ground, and untying his hands, they ordered him to pick up a little stick and break it into as many pieces as there were valiant and renowned captains in our army, and as the unfortunate youth was new and inexperienced in war, he had no knowledge of those who at that time held a high reputation among the enemy, and they commanded him to name them off. He said that he didn't know the brave ones. Whereupon Putapichún replied: 'Well, don't you know Álvaro Maltincampo (that was my father's name)?' 'Yes, I know him and I've heard a lot about him,' answered the unlucky fellow. 'Well then, cut off a little stick and hold it in one hand. Don't you know the Apó [commander-in-chief]?' 'Very well,' he said. 'Cut off another little stick.'

"In this fashion he repeated the names of the sergeant-major and even ten or twelve of the most renowned officers, and [the Indian] ordered him to cut off as many other splinters which he made him hold in one hand, and he said to him: 'Hold in your memory all those that we have named and dig a pit to bury those valiant ones.' And straightway he put it into execution. Putapichún handed my master a heavy wooden club entirely sown about with horse-shoe nails, with heads sticking outward, and the knife that he had put in the middle of the two, and the other two knives he offered to the acolytes. With these and their lances upheaved they placed themselves at the sides of the sacrificer who approached the place where that poor lad was and where they had him seated, shedding from his eyes more tears than the tears that manifested themselves in mine without being able to stop flowing.

Flutes were made from the victim's bones, drums from his flesh, and his head was stuck on a pike for exhibition to the yelling, frantic multitude.

Maulicán, after falsely promising the other chieftains to deliver Francisco into their hands, in a *cojau,* or powwow a fortnight from then, set out for his village, fording the Bío-Bío and stopping in the settlement of Colpoche, who, in the midst of a wild *borrachera*[11] and sumptuous feast of partridges, capons, lambs, chickens, sausages and potatoes, aired his grievances against the Spaniards. During the festivities another Spanish prisoner was forced to don his armor and dance with his musket on his back, firing it from time to time. Bascuñán was hailed as an honored guest and invited to join in swimming parties, wood-chopping expeditions and the ball games of *peuco* and *palican.* Continuing their journey, chief Maulicán and Francisco were overtaken by a storm, lost their horses in a swamp, and carrying their saddles over their heads, arrived in the village of the hater of Spaniards, Inalicán. This *cacique,* during the customary drunken brawl on that evening, quarreled with Maulicán, accusing him of being a Spaniard-lover and swearing to seize Francisco, his prisoner, or to kill him. Maulicán, who had no intention of giving up

---

"And so, every time he turned his face to look at me, he pierced my soul, and joining us with measureless sighs and sobs, many of the ministers standing by gave signs of being sympathetic. Because there are some among the Indians who grieve and feel pity for the wretched. Maulicán stepped up to the hapless boy and asked him: 'How many little sticks do you have?' He counted them and answered that he had twelve. The wretched boy, disturbed, said: 'This one represents the first courageous man, and this other, the governor.' And he threw them into the pit. And so, he went along drawing out, in turn, [all the symbolic splinters], from the general grand-master of the camp and the sergeant-major to the captain of friends called Diego Monje, whom they considered as valorous and a great corsair of their lands; and after he had finished flinging the twelve splinters into the pit, they ordered him to throw earth on them, and he proceeded to cover them with the dirt he had taken out of the pit, and while he was occupied with this, he was given such a great blow on the head that his brains were knocked out by the nail-studded bludgeon. Immediately the acolytes who were standing with the knives in their hands, opened his chest and drew out his heart still palpitating and handed it to my master, who after having sucked the blood of it, was brought a strip of tobacco, and collecting smoke in his mouth, he blew it out in every direction as if he were burning incense to the demon to whom they had offered that sacrifice. The heart passed from hand to hand and [the others] performed with it the same ceremony as my master had observed; and in the meantime four or six of them started running around the poor dead victim with their lances, giving yells and shrieks according to their usage and the rest of them making the earth tremble by stamping their feet. When this barbaric and evil ritual was concluded, the heart returned to the hands of my master, and after it was cut up into small pieces, they all started eating it with great speed."

11. drunken-spree.

his captive, rushed Bascuñán out of the chieftain's hut and put him
in a little shed of wild reeds that served as a chicken-roost. Don
Francisco spent a bedeviled night.

> Quise arrimarme a lo que me pareció más enjuto y abrigado y me
> encontré con algunas gallinas que empezaron a gritar y a hacer ruido
> que me obligaron a que me asentase en medio donde combatía el viento
> y el agua. Por una parte, el agua, el viento, y frío me molestaban y por
> otra, el estiércol de las gallinas que sobre mi cabeza muy de ordinario
> caía. Si intentaba mudarme, se alborotaban.[12]

A more cordial welcome awaited the Spaniard and his Indian master in the village of Antegüeno. In the company of the latter's sons
don Francisco discovered the *pengu* tree, whose bark and fruit have
medicinal value for abdominal disturbances. Antegüeno was loath
to see his visitors part from him. Despite the princely entertainment
he offered them, Maulicán, who was homesick, refused to tarry. On
his arrival in his poor frontier village he consulted his old father
Llangareu about the best means of safeguarding his prisoner from
the murderous tribesmen of the cordillera. When their ambassadors
arrived to demand the surrender of Bascuñán in return for payment, Maulicán insulted them and drove them away. In consequence,
it became necessary to hide don Francisco in a dense tree-lodge,
where food was brought him by the little daughter of his captor. In
the meanwhile, because of the treachery of Lemullanca, a chief of
Maulicán's *parcialidad*,[13] raids were made on Maulicán's domain.
Maulicán accepted the invitation of chief Ancanamón in Pellaguen,
who wished to give a seven-day feast and *borrachera* in honor of his
notable captive. Francisco's clothes had worn out and he was re-
luctantly compelled to don primitive Indian garb. At night, in order
to keep warm, he slept with Llancareu's grandsons, whom he instructed in the Christian religion by day. Bascuñán possessed a
signal advantage in his work of proselytizing because he was thoroughly familiar with the Araucanian language. He taught them to
make the sign of the cross, translated the Lord's Prayer into Araucanian for them to commit to memory, carved a makeshift cross

---

12. "I wished to huddle up near what appeared to me to be the driest and best
sheltered spot and I met up with some hens that began to cackle and make
noise and that obliged me to sit down in the middle where I had to fight the
wind and the rain. On one side, the water, the wind and the cold plagued me,
and on the other, the chicken-droppings that quite often fell on my head. If I
tried to move, the chickens went into an uproar."
13. territory.

with his knife and instructed them in Christian ethics. God is the great *Pilli,* he explained, who can be seen by the pure soul even as the human face is reflected in the quiet clearness of a crystal pool. The *Machis* or witch-doctors, he said, have a pact with the Devil and are like mud cast into limpid waters, contaminating and blurring man's pure vision of God.

The Christian Heaven should supplant the Araucanian concept of Gulchemán, where the *Pilli,* after leaving the body at death, "goes to eat black potatoes behind the snow-capped mountain ranges." The sun was explained as God's agent "that protects us from the rigors of weather, clothes the fields and fructifies plants."

Bascuñán's sincerity as a Christian was put to the test on his arrival in the village of Ancanamón. He was overwhelmed with gifts of meat and *chicha* wine and was invited to engage in the *Hueyelpurun,* "un baile deshonesto." [14] From the open platform on which he was stationed he heard *romances* sung in his honor and saw the

> danzantes ridículos que traían ceñidas a la cintura unas tripas de caballo bien llenas de lana, más de 304 varas a modo de cola colgando, tendidas por el suelo y dando coladas a las indias chinas y muchachos, que andaban tras ellos riéndose de su desnudez y desvergüenza.[15]

Ancanamón offered Francisco his granddaughter, who was half Spanish and unmarried, and the Spanish captive was forced to employ all his diplomatic tact and even to lie to the maiden in order to escape temptation. Ancanamón afterwards let him know that he, unlike most Spaniards, had proved himself worthy of respect by living up to the standards he professed. Bascuñán had already won the heart of chief Maulicán's daughter, who had brought him food in his refuge in the tree-loft. His battle with temptation is described thus: "Siempre que la veía venir sola, me temblaban las carnes. Si fuese vieja y no de tan buen parecer como lo era, sobre muchacha, no tuviera tantos recelos ni su vista me alborotara tanto." [16] His

---

14. "an indecent dance."
15. "ridiculous dancers who had some wool-stuffed horse-entrails wound about their waists, more than three hundred and four yards like a tail hanging down and stretched out over the ground, and giving tail-flicks and swishes to the Indian girls and boys who went behind them laughing at their nakedness and shamelessness."
16. "Every time I saw her coming alone, my very flesh trembled. If she had been old and not so good-looking as she was, in addition to being a girl, I shouldn't have had so many misgivings nor would the sight of her have stirred me up so much."

firm rejection of excess and his hard-won self-mastery, which at first was misunderstood as arrogance, opened the way to effective missionary work among the Indians. Maulicán's daughter was later captured by the Spaniards and bought out of slavery by Bascuñán, but she refused to return to her country and insisted on being baptized.

Ancanamón, with genuine admiration, took Francisco into his confidence and explained why he had murdered some Jesuits in reprisal for the theft of his wives. According to the aged Quillalebo's later statement, the first conquistadors were especially lustful, Valdivia's murder was fully justified in payment for his cruelty and even the treacherous slaughter of General Loyola by the Purenians, which was so gorily dramatized in Álvarez de Toledo's historical epic *Purén Indomito*,[17] was explainable, if not codonable, as a grim expression of the Araucans' hatred of their oppressors. Quillalebo also made sly hints about misbehavior in the Spanish convents, which Bascuñán reports with great diffidence.

Left for safekeeping with Maulicán's friend, chief Luancura, Bascuñán continued his work of christianizing young Indians. It was impossible, he claims, to touch the hearts of the mature Indians, who were unwilling to give up all wives but one. He taught the chief's son the Lord's Prayer in Araucanian: *Inchi in ta inchao huenuneuta mileimi,* baptized him by pouring water on his head from a pitcher, and used to advantage his knowledge of curative herbs by attempting to save the life of the chief's dying child. He was unsuccessful in staving off the child's death, but rejoiced for having converted the little Indian to Christianity and for having instilled in him a loathing for the *Machi* witch-doctors. In great detail Pineda y Bascuñán describes the *Machi's* ceremony of fumigation. "He resembled Lucifer," swears Bascuñán, "as he entered the sick boy's room. He wore no breeches, but a woman's girdle. He was very ugly, with long braided hair, a cloud or cataract in one eye; he was dwarfish and crippled in one foot. The mere sight of him caused horror and fear. I sat in a corner of the room and watched him hang cinnamon boughs about the room, slaughter a sacrificial sheep, accompanied by the weird wails of the women bystanders, and fill the room with tobacco smoke. He had the patient's chest and stomach uncovered and

---

17. *Indomitable Puren.*

began to touch his body with his filthy nails. Then, in the midst of a more doleful chant, he returned to the sheep, cut out its heart, sucking it and fumigating it. With the sacrificial knife he opened up the chest of the pain-racked boy so that the liver and entrails were manifestly exposed. Out of the boughs we saw a dark mist hovering that blurred our vision. The enchanter then fell like a dead man, his body jerking upward and jumping like a ball, and the tambourine in his hand twitched as much as its master. While the whites of his eyes were showing, they asked him whether the sick boy would be healed and on what occasion the boy's enemy had put poison in his veins. With a flutelike voice the *Machi* replied that the spell was wrought at a *borrachera,* but he refused to reveal the identity of the one who had caused the illness. Recovering from his trance, the *Machi* went back to the table where the tobacco was lighted, smoked it and fumigated the boughs anew. The stick where the sheep's heart had been nailed had mysteriously disappeared, either hidden by the quack-doctor or stolen away by the Devil, who, according to their superstition, eats the heart. Finally the *Machi* reclined among the cinnamon boughs to sleep and rest, his hideous ceremony being over."

Francisco in a conversation with the little sick boy condemned the *Machis* as perverted homosexualists and vampires who have a pact with the Devil, and proceeded to explain how Mary, though a virgin, gave birth to the child Jesus.

> El celestial rocío con un plácido elapso se deslizó al virgíneo ve-
> llocino y toda la onda de la Divinidad se encubrió en el pasoso vellico
> de nuestra carne. ¿No habéis reparado cuando alguna noche se
> queda fuera de casa un ovillo de lana o pedazo suelto, que sólo del
> rocío amanece empapado en agua y parece que está enjuto, y llegando
> a exprimirlo, sale el rocío que se embebió en él? Pues en el vellocino
> de María se embebió la divinidad de Cristo.[18]

That night the dying lad saw in a dream a huge black man trying to gag him and suddenly driven away by the appearance of a "pichigüinca muy blanco,"[19] a child more golden-blonde than the

---

18. "The celestial dew with a gentle falling slipped into the virginal fleece and all the wave of Divinity was hidden within the dry down of our flesh. Haven't you noticed when some night a skein of wool or a loose piece of it remains outside the house, that only from the dew it is soaked in water when the morning sun rises, and seems to be dry, and when one comes to squeeze it, the dew that was soaked into it runs out? Well then, the divinity of Christ was absorbed like that into the fleece of Mary."

19. "very white babe" corresponding to the North American Indian *papoose*. Sometimes, also called *guagua* in Chile.

sun, with dazzling hair and a face adorned with every grace, who climbed a tree near the fountain, and surrounded by flying children and a lovely lady seated amidst the green branches, poured water on his head from a pitcher. Bascuñán interpreted the dream as a sign of God's wish that the little Indian should be baptized. Happily the child was made a Christian before he died and was buried on a hill near a rough cross hewn from the *pengu* tree.

Moving from one Indian settlement to another, Bascuñán was hailed as a greater healer than the *Machis* and a sincere Christian. He won the affection of the old Hispanophobe Quillalebo, and cured a sick Indian woman by the skilled application of herbs, while he sojourned in the village of Chief Quillalebo. Maulicán, in the meantime, had sent ambassadors to the Spaniards and had arranged for the exchange of Bascuñán for three prisoner-chieftains. Francisco was accompanied to the Spanish fort of Nacimiento by his old friend Quillalebo, Mollbunante, a kinsman of Maulicán, and Millalipi, the son of his former host Tureupillán. On the 29th of November, 1629, "I kissed Spanish earth," says Francisco, "and I embraced the pillars of the Church." His Indian friends were kept waiting outside the garrison, but were afterwards treated to a succulent Spanish meal by Captain Marcos Chavari. The boat on which one of the captured *caciques* was to be brought was late in arriving and the Indians were regretfully preparing to take Bascuñán back into captivity on the second day. The boat came in the nick of time, however, and Bascuñán took leave of his friends and former captors, lavishing on them rich present of garments and adornments. On December 7th he reached Chillán, where his father resided. Overjoyed to see his son, the crippled don Álvaro arose from his sickbed and with the aid of crutches, accompanied him to confession and Holy Communion. Thus ends Bascuñán's chronicle.

In 1654 Francisco was made governor of the southern frontier, Boroa, Toltén, Villarica and their environs. He was with Juan de Salazar in 1655 when the latter attempted to avenge the rout that he and his forces had suffered earlier on the banks of the Bio-Bío. When Toltén was sacked by the Indians, Bascuñán was warned to escape by friendly chieftains who had been ordered to seize him. He and four other men were the only Spaniards uncaptured. More than 5000 Indians attacked Toltén where Bascuñán's estate was under

171

the management of his son. In the long defense of this fort he had to use 3000 pesos of silver to make bullets; his property was ruined and all the clothing that he possessed was distributed among the defenders of the fort. For his losses don Francisco was paid only half damages which he was forced to collect piecemeal from the soldiers. Small wonder then that Bascuñán should have so often and so virulently inveighed against the corruption of Spanish magistrates, who rewarded fawners, flatterers and rich favor-seekers, and left faithful soldiers of the king, who had grown old in harness, to starve and suffer the humiliation of begging their due. "Yo soy el menos digno entre todos," says Bascuñán,

> que a imitación de mis padres he continuado esta guerra más de cuarenta años, padecido en un cautiverio muchos trabajos, incomodidades y desdichas, que aunque fué feliz en el tratamiento y agasajo, no por eso me excusé de andar descalzo de pie y pierna, con una manta o camiseta a raíz de las carnes, lleno de pulgas y otros animalejos que me daban fastidio; que para quien estaba criado en buenos pañales y en regalo, el que tenía entre ellos no lo era: y con todo esto me tuviera por premiado si llegase a alcanzar un pan seguro con que poder sustentarme y remediar en algo la necesidad de mis hijos.[20]

Apparently Bascuñán was rewarded. While corsairs were prowling about Chile's southern coast in 1674, Francisco Núñez de Pineda y Bascuñán was appointed Governor of Valdivia by the *Real Audiencia de Lima*.[21] The *relación* certifying his appointment is the last notice we have of him.

Were it not for his tedious digressions, Latin quotations and sententious moralizing, Bascuñán might be favorably compared with Bernal Díaz del Castillo or Góngora Marmolejo. He spoiled half of his work with rhetorical tinsel. He appreciated the Araucanians, not for their warlike qualities as did Ercilla, but for their hospitality, their kindness and tolerance of Christianity. In his book the customs of the Araucanians, their festivities, their drinking sprees and dances,

---

20. "I am the least worthy amongst all, I, who in imitation of my parents have continued this war for more than forty years, suffered in captivity much hardship, inconvenience and misfortune, for although I was happy in the treatment and gracious regalement that I received, I was not on that account exempt from going about bare of foot and leg, with a blanket or under-shift next to my skin, full of fleas and other little animals that pestered me. For one who was reared in good swaddling clothes and in dainty comfort, the life I led amongst them was far from convenient; but despite all this, I should consider myself rewarded if I might have some security of getting my daily bread wherewith to sustain myself and, in some wise, remedy the need of my children."

21. Royal Court of Lima.

their games and domestic life, their military tactics, and social and political organization are etched with accuracy and fidelity. Even more important is Bascuñán's detailed revelation of their character, a certain hard-headed distrust of Spaniards, their craftiness in inventing temptations to prove or snare the moral fiber or weakness of their Spanish prisoners, and their absolute integrity in the fulfillment of promises to friends. Interesting and authentic sidelights are the descriptions of colonial government, the scoring of the abuses of the *encomienda* [22] system and the condemnation of the *encomenderos*,[23] of the rapacity of those who trafficked in Indian slaves, bought high offices and lived in luxury while deserving men were tossed into the corner of poverty, hunger and neglect.

---

22. The vicious practice of pressing a group of Indians into virtual slave-labor on farms by royal edict and "commission." Fray Bartolomé de las Casas gained the ear of Charles V and succeeded in having the "encomiendas" suppressed for a while. The *mita* provided for the forced labor of the Indians in mines.
23. The Spanish beneficiaries of the *encomienda* system in the New World.

XII

KEATS'S PHILOSOPHY OF NEGATIVE CAPABILITY IN ITS PHILOSOPHICAL BACKGROUNDS

CLAUDE LEE FINNEY

(Professor of English)

Men of Genius are great as certain ethereal Chemicals operating on the Mass of neutral intellect—by [*for* but] they have not any individuality, any determined Character—I would call the top and head of those who have a proper self Men of Power.
Keats to Benjamin Bailey, November 22, 1817.[1]

I had not a dispute but a disquisition, with Dilke upon various subjects; several things dovetailed in my mind and at once it struck me what quality went to form a man of achievement especially in literature, and which Shakespeare possessed so enormously—I mean *Negative Capability*, that is, when a man is capable of being in uncertainties, mysteries, doubts, without any irritable reaching after fact and reason, Coleridge, for instance, would let go by a fine isolated verisimilitude caught from the Penetralium of mystery, from being incapable of remaining content with half-knowledge. This pursued through volumes would perhaps take us no further than this, that with a great poet the sense of Beauty overcomes every other consideration, or rather obliterates all consideration.
Keats to George and Thomas Keats, December 28, 1817.[2]

KEATS'S philosophy of negative capability, which he first formulated in the autumn of 1817, developed through the remaining years of his life into his mature philosophy of life and art. Various critics of Keats's poetry, including myself,[3] have explained this philosophy from his letters and poems; but no one, so far as I know, has connected it with the philosophic currents of his age.

Keats's philosophy of negative capability is based on two of the primary philosophical problems of the eighteenth century—the problem of personal identity and the problem of disinterestedness versus selfishness of the human mind. The problem of personal identity, or unity of consciousness, arose when Descartes[4] founded modern

---

1. *The Letters of John Keats,* edited by Maurice Buxton Forman (New York: Oxford University Press, 1935), p. 67.
2. *Ibid.,* p. 72.
3. C. L. Finney, *The Evolution of Keats's Poetry* (Cambridge, Mass.: Harvard University Press, 1936), I, 324-26, II, 472-79, 579-83, 599-603, *passim.*
4. *The Method, Meditations, and Philosophy of Descartes,* translated by John Veitch (New York: Tudor Publishing Co., 1901), pp. 170-72.

philosophy upon consciousness. Establishing doubt as his organon, and clarity and distinctness as his criterion of truth, Descartes discovered that he could doubt everything except the consciousness of a definite moment, the particular sensation, image, desire, will, emotion, or concept of a definite moment of consciousness. To doubt whether there is a consciousness at a definite moment is to be conscious of the doubt at that moment. Descartes inferred self-existence *(sum)* from self-consciousness *(cogito)* not as a logical deduction but as a simple intuition of the mind. One's sensation or concept in a definite moment is the means of revealing his existence in that definite moment. One cannot think his being conscious without thinking his being. His being conscious in a single moment is his being in that moment. Thus the momentary existence of the ego was secured: *cogito, ergo sum.*

Personal identity, or the continued existence of the ego through successive states of consciousness, is not established, however, by the simple intuition *cogito, ergo sum.* It was inferred by Descartes from doubtful assumptions. Defining the ego or the mind as a thinking substance and matter as an extended substance, he said:

> I am—I exist: this is certain; but how often? As often as I think; for perhaps it would even happen, if I should wholly cease to think, that I should at the same time altogether cease to be.

The mind as a thinking substance, Descartes asserted, is always thinking, although, because of the weakness of cerebral impressions, it does not always remember the thoughts of which it was conscious. Therefore, he concluded, the mind always exists. Descartes' intuition of the momentary existence of the ego or mind was accepted as self-evident but his argument for personal identity, or the continuous existence of the ego, was soon questioned.

The *cogito, ergo sum,* the basic principle of Cartesian idealism, contained within itself the germs of both spiritualism (or spiritual monism) and scepticism. On the Continent it developed through Descartes, Malebranche, and Leibnitz into spiritualism but in England it developed through Locke, Berkeley, and Hume into scepticism. The course of our problem of personal identity leads through the English sceptics and their opponents.

Locke adopted principles and methods of Descartes' rational idealism, although he was essentially an empiricist of the tradition of

Bacon, Hobbes, Gassendi, Bernier, and Boyle. Like Descartes he based philosophical enquiry upon an analysis of consciousness. He accepted the *cogito, ergo sum,* the existence of the ego in a definite moment of consciousness:

> 'Tis past controversy [he said] that we have in us something that thinks; our very doubts about what it is confirm the certainty of its being, though we must content ourselves in the ignorance of what kind of being it is.[5]

Although Locke accepted the Cartesian intuition of the existence of the ego or mind, he was not so sure as Descartes was of the nature of its being. He pointed out that reflection does not give us a knowledge of the mind but only of its operation. He expressed doubt also of Descartes' assertion that the mind always thinks.

Locke perceived the chasm between ideas or presentments and objects or things in themselves. He divided the qualities of objects into primary (extension, solidity, figure, motion or rest, and number) and secondary (color, taste, smell, sound, temperature, etc.). The primary qualities are real qualities in objects, but the secondary qualities are ideas in the mind, produced by the action of primary qualities upon the organs of sense. Ideas of primary qualities resemble qualities in objects but ideas of secondary qualities do not resemble qualities in objects at all. Redness, for example, is an idea in the mind, not a quality in an object, although it is produced by the action of some quality in an object upon the organ of sight. The empirical epistemology which Locke supported by his theory of primary qualities was the basis of theories of poetry according to which the poet imitates the qualities, the ideas, the laws of being which he perceives objectively in nature.

Locke made a careful analysis of the problem of personal identity.[6] He attempted to solve the problem by distinguishing identity of person from identity of substance and identity of organization, two very different kinds of identity, with which it has been confused. A man does not possess identity of material substance, because the substance of his body is constantly changing from birth to death. He does possess, however, identity of living organism, an organization of parts in one coherent body, partaking of one common life. He pos-

---

5. *An Essay Concerning Human Understanding, The Philosophical Works of John Locke,* 2 Vols., edited by J. A. St. John (London: George Bell and Sons, 1898), II, 146.
6. *Ibid.,* I, 466-79.

sesses also identity of person, a thinking being who can consider himself the same thinking being in different times and places. He may possess, finally, identity of spiritual substance, an immortal soul.

On its metaphysical side, Locke's theory of personal identity is set over against the theological theory that identity of person or self consists in identity of spiritual substance. A man is a person, Locke said, by means of his consciousness of his present thoughts and actions, and he is the same identical person as far as his consciousness can extend into his past and future thoughts and actions. Personal identity consists in identity of consciousness, not in identity of spiritual substance. If the same immaterial soul which once animated Plato afterwards animated Plotinus but if Plotinus did not have the same consciousness as Plato—that is, if he did not remember the thoughts and actions of Plato—then he would be a different person from Plato. And, on the other side, if Plotinus should have the same consciousness as Plato, he would be the same person as Plato. To take another example, if two distinct incommunicable consciousnesses could act the same body, the one constantly by day, the other by night, the day and night man would be two persons as distinct as Socrates and Plato, or, as Stevenson afterwards feigned, as Dr. Jekyll and Mr. Hyde. And, on the other side, if the same consciousness acted by intervals two distinct bodies, then there would be one person in two distinct bodies. Locke did not free himself entirely, however, from theological bias. He conceded that "the more probable opinion is, that this consciousness is annexed to, and the affection of, one individual immaterial substance." "But," he added, "let men, according to their diverse hypotheses, resolve of that as they please."

Berkeley, although an idealist, represents the second stage in the development of English scepticism. He rejected Locke's division of qualities of objects into primary and secondary. He argued that all of our ideas of qualities of objects are mental, that there is no proof of identity between our impressions of objects and the inherent qualities of objects, and that therefore we can never know the object or thing in itself. Berkeley did not deny the existence of material objects. He only contended that matter had no existence independent of mental perception. He believed that existence and perceptibility are convertible terms (esse est percipi); that real existence belongs only to knowing and willing beings such as ourselves; and that we, together with God, constitute the real. He believed like Descartes not only in the existence of the mind in a moment of consciousness but also in its personal identity or continued existence through successive moments of consciousness. Berkeley's subjective idealism supported a subjective theory of poetry according to which the poet infuses the whole range of his ideas of beauty, truth, and goodness into nature. Coleridge learned this theory from Berkeley before he became acquainted with the systems of the German transcendentalists, Fichte and Schelling.

Hume represents the climax in the development of English scepticism. He constructed his system on the empirical principle of Hobbes and Locke that all of our ideas are derivatives or developments of our sensuous impressions and on Berkeley's principle of idealism that all of our impressions and ideas are purely mental, having no identity with the qualities of material objects.

"It is certain," Hume said, "there is no question in philosophy more abstruse than that concerning identity, and the nature of the uniting principle, which constitutes a person."[7] He argued that all of our sensuous impressions are distinct and separate existences which have no unity or connection and that therefore the identity which we ascribe to the mind is a fiction—a fiction of the imagination. "Some philosophers," he said, "imagine we are every moment intimately conscious of our self, our personal identity, its existence and its continuance in existence." [8] They say that our strongest sensation, our most violent passion, "instead of distracting us from this view, only fix it the more intensely and make us consider their influence on self either by their pain or pleasure."[8] But "for my part, when I enter most intimately into what I call *myself,* I always stumble on some particular perception or other, of heat or cold, light or shade, love or hatred, pain or pleasure. I never can catch *myself* at any time without a perception, and never can observe anything but the perception." [8] Hume therefore denied personal identity. "What we call a mind," he concluded, "is nothing but a heap or collection of different perceptions united together by certain relations, and supposed, though falsely, to be endowed with a perfect simplicity and identity."[9]

---

7. David Hume, *A Treatise of Human Nature,* Everyman Edition, 2 Vols. (New York: E. P. Dutton & Co., Reprinted 1920), I, 184.
8. *Ibid.,* I, 238-39.
9. *Ibid.,* I, 200.

Hume attributed to imagination instead of to reason our belief in personality. By casting doubt upon the validity of the faculty of reason which the scientific rationalism of the period had exalted into an infallible instrument of truth, especially by attacking the law of cause and effect, the chief law of reason, and by attributing to the imagination most of the mental activities which had been assigned to the reason, Hume prepared the way for the development of a constructive theory of the imagination by Coleridge, Wordsworth, and Hazlitt.

The problem of the selfishness versus the benevolence of the human mind, the second principle in the genesis of Keats's philosophy of negative capability, became a living issue in English philosophy in Thomas Hobbes's *Human Nature* in 1650 and *Leviathan* in 1651. Hobbes's philosophy may be defined as a form of scientific determinism. He maintained that all our conceptions or thoughts are derived from sensations which are the impressions of external objects upon our organs of sense; that, since nothing exists out of the mind except matter and motion, the mind with all its operations is nothing except matter and motion; that, besides sensations and thoughts and trains of thoughts, the mind has no other motion; that trains of thoughts are regulated either by association or by desire (or appetite) ; and that the mind, therefore, acts from necessity.

Hobbes maintained that pleasure and pain, or love and hatred, or desire and aversion, which are different names for different considerations of the same thing, are the principles of human action. He derived these passions as follows: Thought, which is motion in some internal substance in the head, proceeds to the heart and either helps or hinders the motion of the heart which is called vital. If it helps the vital motion, it is called pleasure but if it hinders, it is called pain. Pleasure and pain, with reference to the objects of thought, are called love and hatred, and, with reference to the solicitation to draw near to the objects which please or to retire from the objects which give pain, are called desire and aversion. The passions, therefore, are thoughts that arouse desire for apparent goods or aversion to apparent evils.

The theory of power, reflected in Keats's classification of men into men of power and men of genius, is derived ultimately from Hobbes's argument for the selfishness of the human mind. The power of a

179

man, Hobbes said, consists in his present means of obtaining some apparent good.

> . . . the Felicity of this life, consisteth not in the repose of a mind satisfied . . . Nor can a man any more live, whose Desires are at an end, than he, whose Senses and Imaginations are at a stand. Felicity is a continuall progresse of the desire, from one object to another; the attaining of the former, being still but the way to the latter. The cause whereof is, That the object of mans desire, is not to enjoy once onely, and for one instant of time; but to assure for ever, the way of his future desire . . . So that in the first place, I put for a generall inclination of all mankind, a perpetual and restless desire of Power after power, that ceaseth onely in Death.[10]

Hobbes reduced the various passions, therefore, to various manifestations of the desire of power.[11] "Glory," for example, " . . . is the passion which proceedeth from the imagination or conception of our *own power* above the power of him that contendeth with us." Humility is "the passion . . . proceeding from apprehension of our own infirmity." "Reverence is the conception we have concerning another, that he hath the *power* to do unto us both *good* and *hurt,* but not the *will* to do us *hurt.*" "The passion of laughter is nothing else but *sudden glory* arising from some *conception* of some *eminency* in ourselves, by *comparison* with the *infirmity* of others, or with our own formerly." "Weeping is the sudden *falling out* with ourselves, or sudden conception of defect." "Pity is imagination or fiction of *future* calamity to *ourselves,* proceeding from the sense of another man's calamity."

Hobbes resolved all benevolence, or disinterestedness, into self-love. He asserted that there is no such principle as benevolence in the mind of man but that every act of benevolence springs from self-interest.

> There is yet another passion sometimes called *love,* but more properly *good will* or *charity.* There can be no greater argument to a man, of his own power, than to find himself able not only to accomplish his own desires, but also to assist other men in their's: and this is that conception wherein consisteth *charity.* In which, first, is contained that *natural affection* of parents to their children, which the Greeks call ῎Ερως, as also, that affection wherewith men seek to *assist* those that adhere unto them. But the affection wherewith men many times bestow their benefits on *strangers,* is not to be called charity, but either *con-*

---

10. *The English Works of Thomas Hobbes,* edited by Sir William Molesworth, Bart. (London: John Bohn, 1839), III, 85-6.
11. *Ibid.,* IV, 40-6.

tract, whereby they seek to purchase friendship; or *fear,* which maketh them to purchase peace.[12]

Upon this principle of the selfishness of the human mind, Hobbes based his theory of the condition of man in a state of nature.[13] All men are so equal in the faculties of body and mind, he said, that any man may claim for himself any benefit to which another may pretend. From this equality of ability arises equality of hope in the attaining of ends. Therefore, if two men desire the same thing, they become enemies and, to attain their desire, endeavor to subdue or destroy each other. "Hereby it is manifest, that during the time men live without a common Power to keep them all in awe, they are in that condition which is called Warre; and such warre, as is of every man, against every man." A state of nature, therefore, is a state of war, and "the life of man" in such a state is "solitary, poore, nasty, brutish, and short."

Hobbes's philosophy of egotism was continued in England by Mandeville and in France and Switzerland by Condillac and Helvetius. "Against Hobbes, says Warburton, the whole Church militant took up arms. The answers to the Leviathan would form a library."[14] His chief opponents in England were the Cambridge Platonists, Cudworth and More; Dr. Samuel Clarke, who resembles the Cambridge Platonists; and Dr. Richard Cumberland who is a connecting link between the Cambridge Platonists and the sentimental optimists.

The course of our enquiry lies, however, in the philosophy of sensibility or sentimental optimism, which proposed a system of universal benevolence as an answer to Hobbes's system of universal egotism. This philosophy was developed by the Earl of Shaftesbury, Archbishop King, Dr. Hutcheson, and Bishop Butler. Reid, who substituted the term common sense for Shaftesbury's moral sense, and his followers, Gerard, Campbell, Beattie, and Dugald Stewart, extended this philosophy of benevolence down into the early years of the nineteenth century.

Sentimental optimism was a modified form of traditional English Neoplatonism. The rising tide of rationalism, nourished by the

---

12. *Ibid.,* IV, 48.
13. *Ibid.,* III, 110-13.
14. *The Miscellaneous Works of Sir James Mackintosh, Modern British Essayists* (Philadelphia: Carey and Hart, 1848), VIII, 116.

progress of natural science, impaired the faith of philosophers in the Platonic theory of the νοῦς or *mens* or intuitive reason which apprehends ultimate truth. The Cambridge Platonists were the last school of philosophers in this period to maintain Plato's intellectual mysticism. Thinkers were unable, however, to abandon belief in truths which could not be proved by scientific rationalism. Lord Herbert of Cherbury proposed natural instinct as the faculty which apprehends those common notions upon which all rational knowledge must be based. And Shaftesbury posited a moral sense which intuits the true, the good, and the beautiful. The transfer of this intuitive power from the intellect *(mens)* to a sense, a feeling, prepared the way for a flood of sensibility and feeling in religion, philosophy, and literature.

The sentimental optimists like the Neoplatonists posited a beneficent God who created the best possible world, consisting in a chain of being from God through angels, men, animals, and plants to inorganic matter. Men occupy a middle position in the chain of being, a position which some order of beings must occupy. In comparison with angels they are miserable but in comparison with animals they are fortunate. The good of the whole is paramount to the good of the individual. So whatever is, is right.

Men are originally and innately good and benevolent creatures. They have inherent social or benevolent passions which tend to preserve their species, all nature, and the universe, and inherent private or self-regarding passions which tend to preserve the individual, both of which are natural and good when the latter are subordinate to the former. For the sentimental optimists, the whole system of morals is reduced to a principle of universal benevolence, a love for mankind as a whole.

William Hazlitt, whom Keats knew personally and whose philosophical and literary essays he admired very much, was the chief and immediate source of Keats's philosophy of negative capability. Hazlitt wrote *An Essay on the Principles of Human Action*[15] to prove that man is a benevolent as well as a selfish being. He anticipated Keats in combining the two philosophical problems which we have been surveying. The doctrine of selfishness, he said, is founded on the metaphysical notion of self or of personal identity. A man, it is as-

---

15. *The Complete Works of William Hazlitt,* edited by P. F. Howe, 21 Vols. (London and Toronto: J. M. Dent and Sons, Ltd., 1930), I, 1-49.

sumed, being always the same has necessarily the same interest in whatever happened to him yesterday, happens to him today, or will happen to him tomorrow. Because a man is not and cannot be another, he has no possible interest in what happens to another except as it is in some indirect way connected with him.

Hazlitt attacked the philosophy of selfishness by dividing personal identity, the principle upon which it is founded, into three parts— past, present, and future. A man, he said, has an interest in his present self by means of consciousness which he cannot have in the feelings of any other individual, because his consciousness does not extend beyond his personal identity to that of any other being. A man has an interest in his past self and a continued identity with it by means of memory which he cannot have in or with that of any other being, because his memory is strictly confined to his own past consciousness. So, in regard to his past and his present self, a man is a purely selfish being. In regard to his future self, however, a man has no faculty which gives him a knowledge of his future sensations and ideas and consequently a selfish and exclusive sympathy with them. In regard to his future self, therefore, a man is not necessarily a purely selfish being. The past and the present, in which a man is a selfish being, are not subjects of voluntary action, whether selfish or benevolent, because nothing in the past or present can be altered. The good which a man pursues is always in the future and therefore the future alone is the subject of voluntary action. Any interest which a man may have in any good, whether relating to himself or to others, whether selfish or benevolent, belongs to the future. And the only way in which a man can project himself into the future is by means of the imagination, the same faculty by means of which he projects himself into the minds of other men. And so, Hazlitt concludes, a man is as capable of benevolence as of selfishness, for both belong to the future and both are built up by imagination and reflection. Men may become predominantly selfish by habitually narrowing their minds to their own feelings and interests or they may become benevolent by accustoming their minds to sympathize with the feelings of others.

Hazlitt's analysis of personal identity reflected Hume's scepticism. In the first place, he pointed out, every individual is an aggregate of dissimilar things. The greatest difficulty is not to distinguish one individual from all other individuals but to explain how many dissimilar things can form one individual. There is no connection in sense experience between the different sensations, images, and thoughts of an individual. To insist on an absolute simplicity of nature as essential to individuality would be to destroy all individuality, for it would lead to the conception of as many individuals as there are feelings, thoughts, actions, and properties in the same being. In the second place, each individual, acted upon by external objects and modified by inner thoughts and feelings, is perpetually changing. The individual is never the same for two moments together. To get rid of this difficulty, the imagination creates a double individual part real and part imaginary, by transferring the identity which is based on the continuity of past and present consciousness into the future and by stamping the image of self on an imaginary future state of being which does not as yet exist.

Hazlitt like Hume attributed great powers to the imagination but unlike Hume he maintained that it is an instrument of truth as well as of fiction. And unlike Wordsworth he saw nothing mystical in the activity of the imagination. He believed that the imagination functions on the basis of observation and experience. The child who has been burnt by fire can transfer the idea of pain to his future self. "The child seeing himself in danger of fire," he said, "does not think of his present and future self as two distinct beings but as one and the same being: he as it were *projects* himself forward into the future, and identifies himself with his future being." This identification of himself with his future self, "as if it were incorporated with his actual substance, and weighed upon the pulses of his blood, is itself the strongest instance that can be given of the force of the imagination . . . " And as a man may project himself forward into his future self and feel imaginatively the sensations of his future self, so he may project himself into another person and feel the sensations of that person. In both cases, his imagination projects his feelings beyond the bounds of his own senses. The mind, Hazlitt remarked, can so identify itself with something "as to be no longer master of itself."[16]

Hazlitt anticipated Keats also in the distinction between men of genius and men of power. Being a pluralist, he disapproved of any

16. *Ibid.*, VII, 328.

system of philosophy which is founded upon a single principle whether egotism, benevolence, sympathy, or utility.

> Truth is not one, but many, and an observation may be true in itself that contradicts another equally true according to the point of view from which we contemplate the subject.[17]

He said that the complex frame of the mind is composed of distinct and dissimilar principles, that the elementary feelings of pleasure and pain, regarded as the primary motives of thought and action, should be separated into distinct feelings in respect to the objects which stimulate them, and that, besides the sensibility to pleasure and pain, there are other independent principles, the two most significant of which are the love of truth and the love of power. Employing this distinction, he divided men into those who seek truth and those who seek power, into men of genius and men of power. He followed Hobbes in defining men of power as men who are dominated by strong selfish or egotistic impulses. And he based his concept of men of genius upon the theory of imagination which we have outlined above. In some men, he believed, the imagination is strong enough to enable them to escape from the fetters of egotistic impulses and to project themselves into external reality, into natural objects and into the minds of other men.

Hazlitt was the first critic, so far as I can discover, to fuse together the epistemological problem of personal identity and the ethical problem of egotism versus benevolence, to transfer these principles to literary criticism and to transform them into principles of literary composition and standards of aesthetic judgment. He distinguished the Romantic poets of his own day from the humanistic poets of the Renaissance by these principles.

Certainly one of the chief characteristics of romantic poetry of the eighteenth and nineteenth centuries is what Hazlitt called egotism or what later critics, borrowing a term from German transcendentalism, call subjectivity, in which the poet infuses the feelings and thoughts of his own personality into natural objects and persons. The prevalent subjectivity of eighteenth century literature was inspired by the intensive study of psychology by every philosophic school of the period and by the emphasis which the sentimental optimists placed on feeling or passion. Every philosophical and critical treatise of the

17. *Ibid.*, IX, 228.

period contains an extensive and minute analysis of the passions. Kames and Alison, representative critics in the late decades of the eighteenth century, explain the principles of this aesthetic subjectivity. Kames's [18] theory of personification approaches Ruskin's theory of the pathetic fallacy and a subjective form of the very modern theory of empathy. And Alison made subjectivity the basic principle in his theory of the beautiful and the sublime. "Matter," he said, "is not beautiful in itself, but derives its beauty from the expression of mind." This principle which he called Platonic he attributed to "Lord Shaftesbury, Dr. Hutcheson, Dr. Akenside, and Dr. Spence." It "has been maintained," he added, "nowhere so firmly and so philosophically as by Dr. Reid in his invaluable work *On the Intellectual Powers of Man.*"[19] When a "man of sensibility" gazes at a natural scene or reads a passage of descriptive poetry, Alison explained, he "will be conscious of a variety of great or pleasing images passing with rapidity in his imagination, beyond what the scene or description before him can, of itself, excite." He explained the chain of images passing through the mind by David Hartley's psychology of association. "It is then, indeed, in this powerless state of revery, when we are carried on by our conceptions, not guiding them," he said, "that the deepest emotions of beauty or sublimity are felt . . ." [20] Coleridge, in the Prefaces to his *Poems* of 1796 and 1797, and Wordsworth, in the Preface to *Lyrical Ballads* of 1798, defended egotism or subjectivity by the same arguments. Hazlitt answered Alison and the associationists with an argument drawn from their own psychology. "It has been the fashion of late," he said, "to pretend to refer everything to association of ideas (and it is difficult to answer this appeal, since association, by its nature, mixes up with everything), but as Hartley has himself observed, who carried this principle to the utmost extent, and might be supposed to understand its limits, association implies something to be associated, and if there is a pleasing association, there must be first something naturally pleasing from which the secondary satisfaction is reflected, or to which it is conjoined." [21]

18. Henry Home of Kames, *Elements of Criticism,* 2 Vols. (Edinburgh: Bell & Bradfute, etc., 1807), II, 228-54.
19. Archibald Alison, *Essays on the Nature and Principles of Taste* (New York: Harper & Brothers, 1870), p. 444.
20. *Ibid.,* p. 51.
21. *The Complete Works of William Hazlitt,* XX, 390.

For Hazlitt all poetry is essentially imaginative projection (or empathy). Poetry "signifies the excess of the imagination beyond the actual or ordinary impression of any object or feeling. The poetical impression of any object is that uneasy, exquisite sense of beauty or power that cannot be contained within itself . . . "[22] The poet, feeling this beauty or power in an object or person, enters imaginatively into it. At this point Hazlitt made an essential distinction between an egotistic (or subjective) and a disinterested (or objective) projection of the poet into the object or person. In egotistic projection, the poet, feeling his own identity intensely and exclusively, absorbs the object or person into himself and expresses himself through it. In disinterested projection, the poet is absorbed, loses his own identity, and becomes the object or person, and expresses its sensations, feelings, and thoughts. Hazlitt regarded the romantic poets of his day, especially Wordsworth, Coleridge, Southey, and Byron, as egotistic poets:

> The great fault of a modern school of poetry is, that it is an experiment to reduce poetry to a mere effusion of natural sensibility; or what is worse, to divest it both of imaginary splendour and human passion, to surround the meanest objects with the morbid feelings and devouring egotism of the writers' own minds.[23]

Wordsworth "sympathizes," Hazlitt said, "only with what can enter into no competition with him, with 'the bare trees and mountains bare, and grass in the green field.' " In his review of Wordsworth's *Excursion,* he said:

> An intellectual egotism swallows up every thing. Even the dialogues introduced in the present volume are soliloquies of the same character, taking different views of the subject. The recluse, the pastor, and the pedlar are three persons in one poet . . . The power of his mind preys upon itself. It is as if there were nothing but himself and the universe. He lives in the busy solitude of his own heart; in the deep silence of thought.[24]

Hazlitt said that Byron's characters are all himself.

> There is nothing more repulsive than this sort of ideal absorption of all the interests of others, of the good and ills of life, in the ruling passion and moody abstraction of a single mind, as if it would make itself the centre of the universe, and there was nothing worth cherishing but its intellectual diseases. It is like a cancer, eating into the heart of

22. *Ibid.,* V, 3.
23. *Ibid.,* 53.
24. *Ibid.,* IV, 113.

poetry. But still there is power; and power rivets attention and forces admiration.[25]

In contrast to the romantic poets who are egotists or men of power, Hazlitt regarded Elizabethan poets as men of genius who can escape from the impulses of their own egos and view the world in a disinterested manner. Shakespeare's indifference to fame, Hazlitt said,

> may be accounted for from the very circumstance, that he was almost entirely a man of genius, or that in him this faculty bore sway over every other . . . He seemed scarcely to have an individual existence of his own, but to borrow that of others at will, and to pass successively through "every variety of untried being,"—to be now *Hamlet,* now *Othello,* now *Lear,* now *Falstaff,* now *Ariel.*[26]

In Shakespeare's plays, especially in his characters, Hazlitt found the perfect examples of disinterested or objective imaginative projection:

> The striking peculiarity of Shakespeare's mind was its generic quality, its power of communication with all other minds . . . He was the least of an egotist that it was possible to be. He was nothing in himself; but he was all that others were, or that they could become . . . There was no respect of persons with him. His genius shone equally on the evil and on the good, on the wise and the foolish, the monarch and the beggar . . . He was like the genius of humanity, changing places with all of us at pleasure, and playing with our purposes as with his own . . . He had only to think of any thing in order to become that thing, with all the circumstances belonging to it. When he conceived of a character, whether real or imaginary, he not only entered into all its thoughts and feelings, but seemed instantly, and as if by touching a secret spring, to be surrounded with all the same objects, "subject to the same skyey influences," the same local, outward, and unforeseen accidents which would occur in reality . . .[27]

> That which distinguishes the dramatic productions of Shakespear from all others, is the wonderful variety and perfect individuality of his characters. Each of these is as much itself, and as absolutely independent of the rest, as if they were living persons, not fictions of the mind. The poet appears for the time being, to be identified with the character he wishes to represent, and to pass from one to the other, like the same soul, successively animating different bodies. By an art like that of the ventriloquist, he throws his imagination out of himself, and makes every word appear to proceed from the very mouth of

---

25. *Ibid.,* V, 153.
26. *Ibid.,* IV, 23.
27. *Ibid.,* V, 47-8.

the person whose name it bears . . . One might suppose that he had stood by at the time, and had overheard what had passed.[28]

The character of Shylock is another instance of Shakespear's powers of identifying himself with the thoughts of men, their prejudices, and almost [their] instincts.[29]

Keats's distinction between men of power and men of genius which was quoted at the beginning of this essay may now be expanded as follows: Men of power, in whom egotistic impulses control the intellect, have strong, dominant personalities. Their minds, being egotistic, shape and color their intuitions of the world in accordance with their practical desires. Men of genius, in whom the intellect is free from the fetters of egotistic impulses, have no individuality, no identity. Their minds, being disinterested, interpret the world impartially.

Keats, finding no appropriate name for this philosophy which he was adapting from Hazlitt, invented the striking term Negative capability. A negatively capable man of genius, such as Shakespeare, is "capable of being in uncertainties, mysteries, doubts, without any irritable reaching after fact and reason," but a man of power, an egotist such as Coleridge, "would let go by a fine isolated verisimilitude caught from the Penetralium of mystery, from being incapable of remaining content with half-knowledge." This concept of negative capability came into Keats's mind in the midst of a conversation with Charles Dilke about various subjects. It was inspired, it is probable, by his perception of the egotistic, rationalizing character of Dilke's mind. Two years later he wrote his brother George:

That Dilke was a Man who cannot feel he has a personal identity unless he has made up his Mind about every thing. The only means of strengthening one's intellect is to make up one's mind about nothing —to let the mind be a thoroughfare for all thoughts . . . Dilke will never come at a truth as long as he lives; because he is always trying at it. He is a Godwin-methodist.

Keats's theory of the imagination is the key to his philosophy of negative capability. He drew an explicit distinction between the imagination, the faculty by means of which a negatively capable genius intuits truth, and the reason, the faculty by means of which the egotist deduces truth. The reason, by nature, seeks to construct an absolute and comprehensive system of philosophy into which it

28. *Ibid.*, V, 185.
29. *Ibid.*, V, 296.

can fit all the facts of human experience. The imagination, on the contrary, apprehends truth in individual, isolated intuitions. In a letter to his friend Benjamin Bailey, November 22, 1817, Keats explained his belief in the "authenticity of the imagination." In this letter his philosophy of negative capability is interwoven with the Neoplatonism of *Endymion* which he later outgrew and which we may disregard in this connection. "I am certain of nothing," he said, "but of the holiness of the Heart's affections and the truth of imagination . . . " He defined his own mind as "simple imaginative" and said that "What the imagination seizes as Beauty must be truth—whether it existed before or not . . . " He defined a second type of mind as rational and said that he was unable to believe that even the greatest philosophers could discover truth by "consequitive reasoning" and arrive at their goal "without putting aside numerous objections." He defined a third type of mind as complex—"one that is imaginative and at the same time careful of its fruits—who would exist partly on Sensation partly on thought—to whom it is necessary that years should bring the philosophic Mind." "Such a one," he told Bailey, "I consider yours and therefore it is necessary to your eternal Happiness that you not only drink this old Wine of Heaven [imaginative apprehensions of beauty and truth] . . . but also increase in knowledge and know all things." Keats formed his concept of the complex mind from his study of Wordsworth with Bailey at Oxford.

Keats's philosophy of negative capability made him an agnostic in the sphere of religion. In the religious controversy which Shelley provoked among Keats's friends, Keats took a position of suspended judgment, considering impartially arguments for and against the validity of Christian dogma. On March 13, 1818, he wrote his friend Bailey, who had been ordained recently and who had published his first sermon:

> I have never had your Sermon from Wordsworth, but Mrs. Dilke lent it to me. You know my ideas about Religion. I do not think myself more in the right than other people, and that nothing in this world is proveable. I wish I could enter into all your feelings on the subject merely for one short 10 Minutes and give you a Page or two to your liking . . .

After quoting a sceptical sonnet on the four seasons of man's life, he concluded:

Now my dear fellow I must once for all tell you I have not one Idea of the truth of any of my speculations—I shall never be a Reasoner because I care not to be in the right, when retired from bickering and in a proper philosophical temper.

In the sonnet which he composed on the top of Ben Nevis on August 2, 1818, during his walking tour in Scotland, Keats expressed the vanity of man's endeavor to know himself, his source, and his destiny:

> Read me a lesson, Muse, and speak it loud
>   Upon the top of Nevis, blind in mist!
> I look into the chasms, and a shroud
>   Vaprous doth hide them,—just so much I wist
> Mankind do know of hell; I look o'erhead,
>   And there is sullen mist,—even so much
> Mankind can tell of heaven; mist is spread
>   Before the earth, beneath me,—even such,
> Even so vague is man's sight of himself!
>   Here are the craggy stones beneath my feet,—
> Thus much I know that, a poor witless elf,
>   I tread on them,—that all my eye doth meet
> Is mist and crag, not only on this height,
> But in the world of thought and mental might!

The principle of Keats's ethics was the negatively capable imagination. His ethical ideal was the imaginative identification of himself with other men, by means of which he could understand and sympathize with their feelings and thoughts, their impulses and motives. Referring to a recent quarrel between his friends Benjamin Robert Haydon and John Hamilton Reynolds, he wrote Benjamin Bailey on January 23, 1818:

It is unfortunate—Men should bear with each other—there lives not the Man who may not be cut up, aye hashed to pieces on his weakest side. The best of Men have but a portion of good in them—a kind of spiritual yeast in their frames which creates the ferment of existence —by which a Man is propell'd to act and strive and buffet with Circumstance. The sure way Bailey, is first to know a Man's faults, and then be passive—if after that he insensibly draws you towards him then you have no Power to break the link. Before I felt interested in either Reynolds or Haydon—I was well read in their faults yet knowing them I have been cementing gradually with both. I have an affection for them both for reasons almost opposite—and to both must I of necessity cling—supported always by the hope that when a little time—a few years shall have tried me more fully in their esteem I may be able to bring them together—the time must come because they have both hearts—and they will recollect the best parts of each other when this gust is overblown.

Keats considered the ethical problem of evil from the two opposing principles of the human mind—the principle of egotism and the principle of disinterestedness. "It is an old maxim of mine," he said, " . . . that every point of thought is the centre of an intellectual world—the two uppermost thoughts in a Man's mind are the two poles of his World; he revolves on them and every thing is southward or northward to him through their means." In March 1819, he wrote his brother George:

> Very few men have ever arrived at a complete disinterestedness of Mind: very few have been influenced by a pure desire of the benefit of others—in the greater part of the Benefactors to Humanity some meretricious motive has sullied their greatness . . . From the manner in which I feel Haslam's misfortune I perceive how far I am from any humble standard of disinterestedness. Yet this feeling ought to be carried to its highest pitch, as there is no fear of its ever injuring Society—which it would do I fear pushed to an extremity. For in wild nature the Hawk would lose his Breakfast of Robins and the Robin his of worms—the Lion must starve as well as the swallow.

This principle of egotism, Keats perceived, is as inherent in men as in animals.

> The greater part of Men make their way with the same instinctiveness, the same unwandering eye from their purposes, the same animal eagerness as the Hawk.

In men, however, there is a principle of disinterestedness as well as a principle of egotism.

> But then, as Wordsworth says, "we have all one human heart"—there is an electric fire in human nature tending to purify—so that among these human creature[s] there is continually some birth of new heroism. The pity is that we must wonder at it: as we should at finding a pearl in rubbish. I have no doubt that thousands of people never heard of have had hearts completely disinterested: I can remember but two—Socrates and Jesus—their Histories evince it.

Keats perceived therefore that the evil which natural creatures, including human beings, inflict upon one another is inspired by their instinctive and egotistic impulses. He perceived also that this evil is not only present in nature but that, nature being what it is, evil is also necessary in nature. These speculations reveal the negative capability of Keats's mind. He believed, we remember, that a negatively capable genius such as Shakespeare had a double mind, one part of which served the instinctive impulses of his ego, while the other part intuited and speculated about the world in perfect freedom. While Keats was speculating about the principle of egotism, the principle of evil, in nature, he was, he knew, outside and above nature. At the same time, he was, he knew equally well, a part of the egotistic order of nature.

> Even here though I myself am pursuing the same instinctive course as the veriest animal you can think of—I am, however, young—writing at random—straining at particles of light in the midst of a great darkness—without knowing the bearing of any one assertion[,] of any one opinion. Yet may I not in this be free from sin? May there not be superior beings amused with any graceful, though instinctive attitude my mind may fall into, as I am entertained with the alertness of a Stoat or the anxiety of a Deer? Though a quarrel in the Streets is a thing to be hated, the energies displayed in it are fine; the commonest Man shows a grace in his quarrel. By a superior being our reasoning[s] may take the same tone—though erroneous they may be fine. This is the very thing in which consists poetry, and if so it is not so fine a thing as philosophy—For the same reason that an eagle is not so fine a thing as a truth.

In this striking speculation, Keats transferred his argument from the realm of ethics to that of poetics. By a bold imaginative intuition of truth, he perceived that the natural and the egotistic animal, which manifests power in its unswerving pursuit of its instinctive impulse, is beautiful and poetic. In another speculation, which we shall quote presently, he perceived that inanimate natural objects, such as the sun and moon, which have an "unchangeable attribute," are also beautiful and poetic. In both cases, this always being themselves, this unchangeable quality of their being, gives them identity.

By a strange and confusing shift of thought, Keats made a distinction not only between a speculative man and an instinctive animal but also between a superior being and a man. As a man, such as Keats, may receive aesthetic pleasure from the instinctive actions of an animal, so a superior being may receive aesthetic pleasure from any instinctive attitude the mind of man may fall into. Keats, the negatively capable thinker, made this distinction to indicate the absence of dogmatism in his speculations. "I am," he said, ". . . young —writing at random—straining at particles of light in the midst of a great darkness—without knowing the bearing of any one assertion[,] of any one opinion."

The conclusion that "This is the very thing in which consists poetry, and if so it is not so fine a thing as philosophy—For the same reason that an eagle is not so fine a thing as a truth" is ambiguous in statement although its meaning is clear in the context. Poetry consists in the natural, the instinctive, and therefore the beautiful, such as the eagle, and philosophy consists in the truth which the mind discovers in free speculation. The basic distinction which Keats made in this period, however, is the distinction between negative capability and egotism. As there is a negatively capable philosopher and an egotistic philosopher, so there is a negatively capable poet and an egotistic poet.

Keats like Hazlitt made a sharp distinction between the egotism of contemporary romantic poets and the negative capability of Elizabethan poets. On February 3, 1818, he wrote John Hamilton Reynolds:

> It may be said that we ought to read our contemporaries, that Wordsworth etc. should have their due from us. But, for the sake of a few fine imaginative or domestic passages, are we to be bullied into a certain Philosophy engendered in the whims of an Egotist[?] Every man has his speculations, but every man does not brood and peacock over them till he makes a false coinage and deceives himself. Many a man can travel to the very bourne of Heaven, and yet want confidence to put down his half-seeing. Sancho will invent a Journey heavenward as well as any body. We hate poetry that has a palpable design upon us, and if we do not agree, seems to put its hand in its breeches pocket. Poetry should be great and unobtrusive, a thing which enters into one's soul, and does not startle it or amaze it with itself, but with its subject.—How beautiful are the retired flowers! how would they lose their beauty were they to throng into the highway crying out, "Admire me I am a violet!—dote upon me I am a primrose!" . . . I don't mean to deny Wordsworth's grandeur and Hunt's merit, but I mean to say we need not be teazed with grandeur and merit when we can have them uncontaminated and unobtrusive. Let us have the old Poets, and Robin Hood.

Keats made his most striking distinction between the negatively capable poet and the egotistic poet in the letter which he wrote Richard Woodhouse on October 27, 1818:

> 1st. As to the poetical Character itself (I mean that sort of which, if I am anything, I am a member; that sort distinguished from the wordsworthian or egotistical sublime; which is a thing per se and stands alone) it is not itself—it has no self—it is every thing and nothing—It has no character—it enjoys light and shade; it lives in gusto, be it foul or fair, high or low, rich or poor, mean or elevated—It has as

much delight in conceiving an Iago as an Imogen. What shocks the virtuous philosopher, delights the camelion Poet. It does no harm from its relish of the dark side of things any more than from its taste for the bright one; because they both end in speculation. A Poet is the most unpoetical of any thing in existence; because he has no Identity— he is continually in for and filling some other Body—The Sun, the Moon, the Sea and Men and Women who are creatures of impulse are poetical and have about them an unchangeable attribute—the poet has none; no identity—he is certainly the most unpoetical of all God's Creatures. If then he has no self, and if I am a Poet, where is the Wonder that I should say I would write no more? Might I not at that very instant been cogitating on the Characters of Saturn and Ops? It is a wretched thing to confess; but is a very fact that not one word I ever utter can be taken for granted as an opinion growing out of my identical nature—how can it, when I have no nature? When I am in a room with People if I ever am free from speculating on creations of my own brain, then not myself goes home to myself: but the identity of every one in the room begins to [so?] press upon me that I am in a very little time an [ni] hilated—not only among Men; it would be the same in a Nursery of Children ...

The negatively capable poet, Keats believed, projects himself by means of his imagination into the minds of other men and so completely identifies himself with them as to lose his own identity. Such a poet may enter imaginatively into the instincts of birds and beasts and even into the mysterious energy of inorganic matter. "If a Sparrow come before my Window," Keats wrote Bailey, "I take part in its existence and pick about the Gravel." And Richard Woodhouse reported that Keats "has affirmed that he can conceive of a billiard Ball that it may have a sense of delight from its own roundness, smoothness & volubility & the rapidity of its motion."

Keats possessed this objective empathy, this power of imaginative identification with external nature, in a very high degree. And he strove consciously to make his imagery and the characters in his poems emphathic. An analysis of empathy in his poetry, however, is beyond the scope of this essay. I shall bring this study of Keats's philosophy of negative capability to an end with two examples of Keats's emphatic response to the imagery of Spenser and Milton. When Keats read Spenser's *Faerie Queene* with Charles Cowden Clarke in 1813, Clarke said that

he especially singled out epithets, for that felicity and power in which Spenser is so eminent. He *hoisted himself up, and looked burly and dominant,* as he said, "What an Image that is—'*sea-shouldering whales!*'"

Perhaps the following annotation on Milton's *Paradise Lost,* Book IX, 179-191 is more intense in its imaginative identification:

Satan having entered the Serpent, and inform'd his brutal sense—might seem sufficient—but Milton goes on "but his sleep disturb'd not." *Whose spirit does not ache at the smothering and confinement—the unwilling stillness—the "waiting close"? Whose head is not dizzy at the possible speculations of Satan in the serpent prison?* No passage of poetry ever can give a greater pain of suffocation.

XIII

THE NATURE OF THE CONFLICT IN
JONSON'S *SEJANUS*

JOSEPH ALLEN BRYANT, JR.

(Assistant Professor of English)

BEN JONSON'S first Roman tragedy, *Sejanus His Fall,*[1] has never been in any sense a popular play, either in the theater or out of it.[2] In the pages that follow I propose to examine the work from a new point of view and show why it merits serious consideration as something more artistically respectable than a reconstruction of Roman history [3] or a rhetorical curiosity in the Jonsonian canon.[4]

Most of the specific objections to *Sejanus* as drama may be found in an introductory essay which Professor W. D. Briggs wrote some years ago for his edition of the play.[5] Two of these objections, that the play is wordy and that too much attention is given to preparation for scenes that are never presented to the eye, are at least partially valid and help to explain why *Sejanus* was a failure at the Globe in

---

1. Jonson's *Sejanus* was first performed, unsuccessfully, at the Globe in 1603; it was published in quarto two years later. His second Roman tragedy, *Catiline His Conspiracy,* was performed in 1611 and published in quarto in the same year. These were the only tragedies to appear in the 1616 and 1640 folio texts. In this study all references to the works of Ben Jonson are to the edition by C. H. Herford and Percy Simpson, 8 vols. (Oxford, 1925-47), hereafter referred to as *Works.* References to the text of *Sejanus,* which appears in *Works,* IV, are to act and line.
2. For typical favorable comment see Felix E. Schelling, *Elizabethan Drama 1558-1642,* 2 vols. (Boston, 1908), II, 26 ff., and F. S. Boas, *An Introduction to Stuart Drama* (Oxford, 1946), pp. 75 ff. The most favorable comment of all, however, is that by William Hazlitt, who is sometimes oddly misquoted to make him seem a contemner of the play; see his *Lectures on the Dramatic Literature of the Age of Elizabeth,* in *The Complete Works of William Hazlitt,* ed. P. P. Howe, 6 vols. (London, 1930-34), VI, 262-263.
3. For an example of this point of view see S. T. Coleridge, "Notes on Ben Jonson," *The Complete Works of Samuel Taylor Coleridge,* ed. Shedd, in 7 vols. (New York: 1858), IV, 193.
4. See Swinburne's estimate of both tragedies, which concludes: "There is fine occasional writing in each, but it is not dramatic: and there is good dramatic work in each but it is not tragic."—*A Study of Ben Jonson,* in *The Complete Works of Algernon Charles Swinburne,* ed. Sir Edmund Gosse and T. J. Wise, in 20 vols. (London, 1925-27), XII, 42; see also pp. 19-23, 40-42.
5. W. D. Briggs, ed., *Sejanus* (Boston, 1911), pp. xliii-xlvi.

1603.[6] The remaining objections, however, derive from a basic assumption that the play has a simple, two-threaded story, consisting mainly of the plot of Sejanus and Tiberius against the family of Agrippina and the plot of Sejanus against Tiberius.[7] Briggs insisted, first, that about one fifth of the dialogue is spoken by a group of characters whose only function is to serve as chorus, "mingling in the plot and commenting on it for the spectator's benefit." [8] Second, he saw in the construction of the play "a real failure in proportion, with the result of a shift of emphasis in the middle of the play." [9] Third, he could find no explanation for the attention given to the trials of Silius and Cordus, business which comes in the first 487 lines of Act III and "as far as the dramatic impression goes . . . is treated as though it were the climax of the play." [10] And finally, he agreed with Gifford that Jonson should have ended his play at line 749 of Act V, thus omitting 154 lines of comment by Arruntius, Terentius, Lepidus, and the nuntius.[11] In short, Briggs regarded the struggle between Tiberius and Sejanus as the only real conflict in the play, and he had necessarily to consider as either nonessential or irrelevant anything not directly related to that conflict.

This same point of view dominates several of the more recent criticisms of *Sejanus*. Professor Moody E. Prior charges that "the whole action can be stated in its essence without reference to the characters who uphold the traditional virtues of political freedom and personal decency, even though their speeches constitute a very large part of the play." [12] And Professor L. C. Knights, who feels that the

---

6. It should be noted, however, that, to support the second of these objections, Briggs cites examples which hardly prove his point (pp. xlv-xlvi). The execution of the plot against Drusus was not suited to dramatic representation, for it involved the use of a subtle poison which would produce the effect of a natural death. Moreover, the destruction of Agrippina's family does not properly come within the limits of the play.

7. *Ibid.*, pp. xliv-xlv.

8. *Ibid.*, pp. xliv, liv-lv.

9. *Ibid.*, p. xlv. Briggs feels that from the middle of the play to the end, our attention is diverted from Sejanus' plot against Tiberius to the more striking counter-intrigue of Tiberius and Macro, while Sejanus becomes in the main a purely passive figure.

10. *Ibid.*, p. xlvi.

11. *Idem.* See also W. Gifford, *The Works of Ben Jonson*, 9 vols. (London, 1875), III, 146 n. To end the play thus would be to omit the prophecy of Arruntius, Terentius' account of Sejanus' death, the nuntius' account of what happened to Sejanus' wife and children, and the concluding comments by Lepidus, Arruntius, and Terentius.

12. Moody E. Prior, *The Language of Tragedy* (New York, 1947), p. 117; see also pp. 112-119.

"good" characters in the play are "choric and denunciatory merely [and represent] no positive values," writes: "The stuff of the play is the lust of political power and the pettiness that so often accompanies political greatness. The world with which we are presented is completely evil." [13] The fallacy in all these judgments, it seems to me, lies in the assumption on which they are based—an assumption which precludes consideration of all but one of the conflicts in the play, relegates everything else to the rank of nonessentials, and reduces to the class of melodrama a play which, even if it is not great tragedy, at least has many of the characteristics of great tragedy. In this study, therefore, I shall begin with an assumption which takes into account all the elements in *Sejanus* and postulates none as merely "choric and denunciatory." I shall assume that the basic conflict is between good and evil, rather than between two evils, and that the "good" characters in the play have a valid function as protagonists. In any case, this assumption would seem to be justified by the structure of the play itself; but further justification comes to light when we bring to bear on the text some of that knowledge of Roman history which Jonson sanguinely expected the nut-cracking audience at the Globe to have with them, together with a few ideas about kingship and tyranny which were familiar enough to most Elizabethans. This really amounts to nothing more than reading *Sejanus* with the aid of the notes that Jonson himself provided for the readers of the quarto of 1605 [14] and the additional help of a few extinct commonplaces which clarify greatly the issues involved but which to Jonson's readers would have seemed much too obvious for footnotes. We can best begin by identifying the various representatives of the two forces that oppose each other throughout the play.

I

The characters representative of good in Jonson's play are all related in some way, either by blood or by sympathy, to the popular hero Germanicus, a grandson of Augustus' second wife, Livia, and

13. L. C. Knights, *Drama and Society in the Age of Jonson* (London, 1937), pp. 180-81.
14. Herford and Simpson print Jonson's notes from the quarto in *Works,* IV, 472 ff. Briggs (*op. cit.,* pp. 195 ff.) also prints the notes and helpfully adds the chapter references, omitted by Jonson. In preparing this study I have used as texts of Jonson's principal sources Tacitus' *Annals,* ed. trans. John Jackson for Loeb (London, 1931-37), and Dio's *Roman History,* ed. trans. Earnest Cary for Loeb, in 9 vols. (London, 1904-27).

at one time commonly regarded as Augustus' successor. Now, Germanicus has been dead four years when the action of the play begins; but Jonson gives us a glowing description of his qualities and sends us repeatedly to Dio and Tacitus for facts about him. From the sources which he cites we learn that Germanicus, while alive, was the only man whom Tiberius feared, and that it was not until after Germanicus' mysterious death in Antioch in A.D. 19 that Tiberius revealed himself openly as a tyrant.[15] Nevertheless, even though he is only a memory as far as the play is concerned, Germanicus can and does stand as a symbol of those ancient Roman virtues exemplified in the lives of such men as Cato, Brutus, and Cassius. His full significance becomes apparent early in Act I, when Arruntius remarks:

> His name was, while he liu'd, aboue all enuie;
> And being dead, without it. O, that man!
> If there were seedes of the old vertue left,
> They liu'd in him.
>
> (I. 117-120.)

And Sabinus, observing that "he had the fruits . . ./More than the seedes," thereupon initiates a long discussion of this man, in whom was all the best of Rome's best men:

> POMPEI's dignitie,
> The innocence of CATO, CAESAR's spirit,
> Wise BRVTVS temperance, and euery vertue,
> Which, parted vnto others, gaue them name,
> Flow'd mixt in him. He was the soule of goodnesse:
> And all our praises of him are like streames
> Drawn from a spring, that still rise full, and leaue
> The part remayning greatest.
>
> (I. 150-157.)

Arruntius' final comment at this point emphasizes still another important fact: Rome in her present state is unworthy to receive the blessing of such an unparalleled gift from heaven. "I am sure/He was too great for vs," he says, "and that they knew/Who did remoue him hence." [16] Thus at the outset, Germanicus is established as the symbol

---

15. See Dio, *Roman History*, LVII. xix.
16. According to the references cited in Jonson's marginal notes, the second half of Arruntius' comment refers to Tiberius' envy of Germanicus, his recall of Germanicus to Rome, and his part in the death of Germanicus after Germanicus had been sent to the east. See Tacitus, *Annals*, II. v, xxvi; and Dio, *Roman History*, LVII. xviii.

of all that was good in Rome; and by the same token he is the symbol of all that Rome now lacks.

Of those representatives of good who actually appear in the play, we have, first, Germanicus' cousin, Drusus Senior, who, though he is also Tiberius's own son, has never shared his father's fear and envy of the popular young favorite. The old admirers of Germanicus see in him "a riotous youth" but an "excellent brave prince," one who has shown his essential goodness by serving as protector to Germanicus' three sons and by opposing openly his father's minion, the ambitious Sejanus.[17] Next come Germanicus' widow, Agrippina, and her three sons, Nero, Drusus Junior, and Caligula, on whom Tiberius's fear has now fastened itself.[18] Sejanus fears them too; for he rightly sees in all four, and particularly in the sons, a potential threat to his own aspirations. Thus he counsels Tiberius:

> . . . in them apace
> The fathers spirit shoots vp. GERMANICUS
> Liues in their lookes, their gate, their forme,
> t'vpbraide vs
> With his close death, if not reuenge the same.
> (II. 191-194.)

Finally, we have a group of Germanicus' old admirers, composed of Lucius Arruntius, Caius Silius and his wife Sosia, Titius Sabinus, Marcus Lepidus, Cremutius Cordus, and Asinius Gallus. So many Roman names might seem a bit confusing at first glance, but one can readily see that Jonson has not confused them; nor has he lumped them all together in the category of a chorus. As will appear presently, each is distinct from the others, and each has his specific function to perform.[19]

In discussing the representatives of evil in *Sejanus,* the usual plan is to center remarks on only two characters, Sejanus and Tiberius, and to make the central conflict of the play a struggle for supremacy

---

17, See *Sejanus,* I. 106-115, 560-575.

18. The last of these, Caligula, of course turns traitor to his breed and becomes ultimately the worst tyrant of all; and it is he, ironically enough, who replaces Tiberius.

19. Since Asinius Gallus does not appear in the discussion that follows, a word should be said about him here. Gallus is married to Vipsania, once the wife of Tiberius, and on numerous occasions he has inadvertently aroused Tiberius's anger. Hence, we see him in the play, as in Tacitus, as one eager to give lip-service to the Emperor but privately loyal to the Germanicans. See *Sejanus,* III. 294, 356, 469, 493-4, and IV. 1-42. See also the passages cited by Jonson in *Annals,* I, viii, xii; II. xxxv-xxxvi.

between these two. It is no wonder, therefore, that Jonson's full-blown presentation of Marco, if it gets the attention it deserves, seems to be explicable only as the result of an inartistic shift of emphasis. Yet there is more to this play than a struggle between Sejanus and Tiberius, and there are more villains in it than two, or even three. Tiberius, of course, is the principal tyrant in the play, in spite of the fact that he is not the central figure; and Sejanus, whose rise and fall provide the focus for our view of a much wider sequence of events, is never more than Tiberius's minion and agent. As Jonson tells the story, Sejanus's actions, with one notable exception, are always those that Tiberius has wished to be successful.[20] Tiberius knows very well that Sejanus has ambition, and he makes use of it to carry out his own attack on Agrippina and her supporters. He quickly learns, too, that Sejanus's ambition extends to absolute rule; and it is for this reason that he engages a second minion, Macro, to direct the practical business of Sejanus's destruction, unaware of course that toying with such murderous agents has been the cause of the death of his only son. The result is that Sejanus, although he frequently thinks he is acting independently, acts for the most part with his master's knowledge and permission. Consequently, we cannot justly regard the central conflict as a valid struggle between these two. To do so is to see the situation only through Sejanus's eyes—in short, to share his fatal illusion.

With Macro, the third tyrannous figure in the play, the case is somewhat different. Like Sejanus, Macro is Tiberius's agent and does his bidding; and, like Sejanus, he plots against his master. Yet, unlike Sejanus, the "wittily and strangely cruel Macro" is a thoroughgoing Machiavellian and does not foolishly let his own ambition blind him to realities, at least not to the point that he underestimates Tiberius; consequently, he achieves an increasing measure of genuine independence.[21] In fact, Tacitus tells us that it was Macro who finally brought about Tiberius' death;[22] and Johnson has Arruntius comment (in the part of Act V which Gifford and Briggs would omit):

20. The exception, of course, is the plot against Drusus, Tiberius' son; see *Sejanus*, II. 1-162. Tiberius does not learn that his son has been murdered until after Sejanus' death, when Sejanus' wife, desperate at the sight of her own dead children, reveals the fact that Drusus has been poisoned and by whom.

21. Macro is Jonson's portrait of the Machiavellian villain. For an analysis of his character see Macro's first soliloquy, *Sejanus*, III. 714-749.

22. According to Tacitus, Macro, seeing Tiberius recover after he had been expected to die, ordered that the old man be suffocated in his bedclothes. Thus

I prophesie, out of this *Senates* flatterie,
That this new fellow, MACRO, will become
A greater prodigie in *Rome,* then he
That now is falne.

(V. 750-753.) [23]

Macro, however, fails to recognize the danger to himself in the fourth
and last tyrant, Germanicus's youngest son, whom Jonson calls by
his notorious nickname, "Caligula," rather than by the name "Gaius,"
which Tacitus and Dio properly use in referring to him.[24] Of Caligula
we see only enough in this play to know what he will ultimately become. We see his indifference to the fate of his mother and brothers,[25]
and we see his willingness to succumb to Macro's offer of protection
and pleasure.[26] But while appearances tell us that Caligula is Macro's
minion, foreknowledge tells us that Macro, believing these same
appearances, is in this one respect as blind as his ambitious predecessor; for Caligula too has in him the seeds of tyranny and is destined
to better the instruction of all his predecessors, including that of his
present tutor and protector.[27] Thus, if we look back at the succession of tyrants presented in *Sejanus His Fall,* we find, not one
struggle, but a series of struggles; and we can see emerging from
it all a rather definite pattern, one which was aptly and succinctly
described by the editor of Jonson's copy of Tacitus when he wrote,
"That vngodly men are forborne awhiles, but neuer forgiuen: And
that no man hath a sinne in his hart, but the same man carieth
Nemesis on his backe." [28] Judging from *Sejanus,* we might easily
conclude that tyrants invariably pave the way for their own downfall
and that the nemesis on their backs is almost always another tyrant.

We are not to find the central issue of Jonson's play in any conventional "warning to tyrants," however; for, interested as Jonson
is in tyrants and what happens to them, he does not make tyranny or
the lust for political power the primary stuff of his play. In *Sejanus*

he cleared the way for the emperor he himself had tutored, Caligula; see
Annals, VI. 1. Dio has a slightly different version of the incident; he reports
that Macro and Caligula committed the murder together, *Roman History,*
LVIII. xxviii.

23. It was Tacitus who first ascribed to Arruntius this ability to speak "vatis in
modum." The occasion, however, was not the death of Sejanus but the imminent
death of Tiberius six years later. At that time Arruntius, having endured
Tiberius, Sejanus, and Macro, announced that he had no desire to live through
another tyranny under Gaius and committed suicide. See *Annals,* VI. 48; and
also Dio, *Roman History,* LVIII. xxvii.

we see various aspects of tyranny, but the tyrants themselves are not dissected for us. We do not, as in *Macbeth* or in Fulke Greville's *Alaham,* peer into the tyrant's mind and soul and learn the main-springs of his action.[29] Jonson's portrayal of Tiberius's peculiar combination of wickedness and craftiness is simply that which he found in the histories of Tacitus, Dio, and Suetonius; and Sejanus, who in Tacitus's account has a slight motive for some of his evil-doing,[30] appears in Jonson's play simply as a man evil by nature, one who boasts like Seneca's Atreus or Herod in the miracle plays of the wickedness he will do.[31] Similarly, the Machiavellian Macro is inexplicably evil; it is by definition his nature to be willing and apt for any mischief that will advance him.[32] There is no hope for any of these men and nothing in them to arouse our pity; for, as Jonson put it elsewhere, *"Natures that are hardned to evill, you shall sooner breake, then make straight; they are like poles that are crooked, and dry: there is no attempting them."* [33] Now, one can readily grant that it

---

24. The nickname, of course, was given to him because of his footwear. Having been reared largely in the camp, he preferred to wear military boots rather than the sandals of the city-dweller.

25. *Sejanus,* IV. 233-258.

26. *Ibid.,* IV. 514-522.

27. For Caligula's disposition of Macro, after the unhappy minion had ceased to be useful to him, see Dio, *Roman History,* LIX. x.

28. *Two Bookes of Constancie,* trans. Sir John Stradling, ed. Rudolf Kirk with notes by Clayton Morris Hall (New Brunswick, New Jersey, 1939), p. 164. The passage continues: "For that Furie followeth them alwaies, and as I may say with Euripides, *Going silently and with a soft foot, she will in due time violently pluck the wicked from off the earth."*

29. A full treatment of tyranny might be expected to take into account both the external and the internal punishment that a tyrant receives. For a good typical discussion of the second kind, as well as of punishment in general, see Chapters XIV and XV of Lipsius' *Two Bookes of Constancie,* ed. Kirk, pp. 164-69. For a discussion of the various theories of punishment that were current during the period, see Roy W. Battenhouse, *Marlowe's* Tamburlaine: *A Study in Renaissance Moral Philosophy* (Nashville, 1941), pp. 99-113.

30. Tacitus (*Annals,* IV. iii) makes the striking episode serve as a motive for Sejanus' intrigue. As Herford and Simpson point out (*Works,* II. 12), Jonson departs from Tacitus's account to make Sejanus begin plotting against Drusus somewhat before Drusus strikes him. Jonson has Sejanus take advantage of the incident thus: "What was my practice late, I'le now pursue/ As my fell iustice." —I. 580-81. Jonson has some historical warrant for Sejanus' early plotting, however; for Dio's account of the incident (*Roman History,* LVII. 22) has it that Sejanus, and not Drusus, struck the blow.

31. See *Sejanus,* II. 150 ff.

32. *Ibid.,* III. 714 ff.

33. *Discoveries,* in *Works,* VII. 564. An expanded statement of the same idea may be found, *ibid.,* p. 581. Jonson seems here to be following Seneca; see "On Reforming Hardened Sinners," *Moral Epistles,* CXII, ed. trans. Richard Gummere for Loeb (London, 1918-25), III, 281-83.

is more entertaining to watch a Shakespearean analysis of growing evil in a tyrant than it is to contemplate these relatively static Jonsonian portraits of unmotivated, unrelieved, and incorrigible villainy. Even so, it is hardly fair to charge Jonson with lack of insight merely because he has not chosen to show us what happens to a soul that suddenly finds itself unhappily in league with the devil. For the problem in *Sejanus* is not why the tyrant becomes what he is, but why the tyrant should exist at all. In other words, the primary subject is not Sejanus, but Rome itself; and in Rome, remember, we have not only Tiberius, Sejanus, Macro, and Caligula, but Drusus, Agrippina, and all those noble Romans who admire the ancient virtues. To put it even more briefly, *Sejanus His Fall* shows us the body politic in the grip of a disease that threatens to become mortal. It answers two questions: First, how was the disease contracted? And, second, how should it be combatted?

II

In answering the first of these questions, it is not at all farfetched, I think, to say that Jonson presents his succession of tyrants as the "Scourge of God upon a sinful race." [34] To be sure, the phrase "Scourge of God" would be out of place in *Sejanus,* and Jonson does not use it there; but he does manage to suggest to us, through his parade of tyrants and potential tyrants, the full duration of a scourging that tore Rome and her people for twenty-two years, from the death of Germanicus in A.D. 19 to the death of Caligula in A.D. 41—in all, over two decades of terror and bloodshed. Now, the idea of a tyrant's being a judgment or scourge upon a sinful people is by no means the exclusive property of the Christian writers. Tacitus explains at the beginning of Book IV that Heaven's wrath against Rome was the ultimate cause for Sejanus's whole career:

Before long, by his multifarious arts, he bound Tiberius fast: so much so that a man inscrutable to others became to Sejanus alone unguarded and unreserved; and this less by subtlety (in fact, he was beaten in the end by the selfsame arts) than by the anger of Heaven against that Roman realm for whose equal damnation he flourished and fell. [35]

34. Early Christian writers took this concept from Isaiah 10:5 ff. For discussions of it see John Dickinson, ed., *The Stateman's Book of John of Salisbury* [*Policraticus*] (New York, 1927), pp. lxix-lxxiv; and Battenhouse, *op. cit.,* pp. 108-113. For an interpretation of Shakespeare's Richard III as the Scourge of God, see Lily B. Campbell, *Shakespeare's "Histories": Mirrors of Elizabethan Policy* (San Marino, California, 1947), pp. 313-317.
35. *Annals,* IV. 1.

This point Jonson elaborates at great length in the first part of Act I, using as his spokesmen those gentlemen of Rome who appreciated the worth of Germanicus. Sabinus explains that even Tiberius recognizes the unworthiness of his subjects to be free:

> . . . oft TIBERIVS hath beene herd,
> Leauing the court, to crie, ô race of men,
> Prepar'd for seruitude'. which shew'd, that, he
> Who least the publique liberty could like,
> As loathly brook'd their flat seruilitie.
> (I. 51-55.)

And Silius replies:

> Well, all is worthy of vs, were it more,
> Who with our ryots, pride, and ciuill hate,
> Haue so prouok'd the iustice of the gods.
> We, that (within these fourescore yeeres) were borne
> Free, equall lords of the triumphed world,
> And knew no masters, but affections,
> To which betraying first our liberties,
> We since became the slaues to one mans lusts;
> And now to many. . . .
> (I. 56-64.)

A bit later, when Sabinus remarks to Arruntius that the times have changed, he receives the following answer:

> Times? the men,
> The men are not the same: 'tis we are base,
> Poore, and degenerate from th' exalted streine
> Of our great fathers. . . .
> Those mightie spirits
> Lye rak'd vp, with their ashes, in their vrnes,
> And not a sparke of their eternall fire
> Glowes in a present bosome. All's but blaze,
> Flashes, and smoke, wherewith we labour so,
> There's nothing *Romane* in vs; nothing good,
> Gallant, or great: 'Tis true, that CORDVS say's
> *Braue* CASSIVS *was the last of all that race.*
> (I. 86-104.)

Even Terentius, a onetime follower of Sejanus, comes at last to realize the grave sickness that his state is in and turns to Lepidus and Arruntius, crying:

> O you, whose minds are good,
> And haue not forc'd all mankind, from your brests;
> That yet haue so much stock of vertue left,
> To pitty guiltie states, when they are wretched:

Lend your soft eares to hears, and eyes to weepe
Deeds done by men, beyond the acts of *furies*.
(V. 750-758.)

The disease of tyranny, then, is but the symptom of a greater disease
that comes whenever the people in a state so completely cease to love
virtue that they forget even what it is.[36]

The question of what to do under tyranny is also an old one and
easily answered, at least in principle. Traditionally, Stoic, Christian,
and neo-Stoic philosophers all agree that tyranny is in the nature of
things and must be endured. So Seneca writes:

> Whatever happens, assume that it was bound to happen, and do not be
> willing to rail at Nature. That which you cannot reform, it is best to
> endure, and to attend uncomplainingly upon the God under whose
> guidance everything progresses; for it is a bad soldier who grumbles
> when following his commander.[37]

And John of Salisbury, stating the traditional Christian position on
this matter, quotes Romans 13:2:

> "Who, therefore, resists the ruling power, resists the ordinance of
> God," in whose hand is the authority of conferring that power, and
> when He so desires, of withdrawing it again, or diminishing it. For
> it is not the ruler's own act when his will is turned to cruelty against
> his subjects, but it is rather the dispensation of God for His good
> pleasure to punish or chasten them.[38]

Similarly, Justus Lipius describes tyrants as "the Beadles & Ser-
geants of Gods seuere punishments vpon that vngodlie nation," [39] and
urges subjects to withhold their hands from even the most tyrannous
of rulers:

---

36. It is interesting to compare Milton's statement of this idea in *Paradise Lost*,
XII, 95-101:
> Tyrannie must be,
> Though to the Tyrant thereby no excuse.
> Yet sometimes Nations will decline so low
> From vertue, which is reason, that no wrong,
> But Justice, and some fatal curse annext
> Deprives them of thir outward libertie,
> Thir inward lost. . . .

37. Seneca, "On Obedience to the Universal Will," *Moral Epistles,* CVII. 9, trans.
Gummere, III, 227-229.

38. *Policraticus,* IV. i, trans. Dickinson, p. 4. This statement is not necessarily
inconsistent with John of Salisbury's famous doctrine of tyrannicide, according
to which a people might turn against the tyrant whenever they should have
fulfilled the time of punishment for which God had sent the tyrant to them;
see *Policraticus,* VIII. xx ff. As I shall show presently, there was always
some difficulty involved in knowing just which tyrant had been sent as a
scourge.

39. *Op. cit.,* p. 147.

... if the odious and infamous name of tiranny offend thee, change thy habitation so shalt thou free thy selfe. Fortune (if thou marke it) hath holpen thee, and prouided thee a place of more security. ...

But thou wilt say, death is dayly imminent to me by meanes of a tyrant. As though it were not so euery daye by nature. Yea but it is a shameful matter to die by execution or strangling. O foole, neither that nor any other kinde of death is infamous, except thy life bee such.[40]

Thus Jonson, without manifesting any love for tyrants, could set down as the practical lesson of his play, this stern general warning to rebels:

This do we aduance as a marke of Terror of all *Traytors, & Treasons;* to shewe how iust the *Heauens* are in powring and thundring downe a weighty vengeance on their vnnatural intents, euen to the worst *Princes:* Much more to those, for guard of whose Piety and Vertue, the *Angels* are in continuall watch, and *God* himself miraculously working.[41]

The tyrant must be tolerated, therefore, no matter how wicked. For there is always the hope that God will reform his wickedness into virtue, and there is always the certainty that God has a good purpose in permitting such wickedness to exist.

Almost immediately, however, the question arises: Are all oppressive sovereigns to be endured as ministers of God or Fate? Is there none evil without divine authority? As regards the lawfully established sovereign, of course, there is but one possible answer, and this answer all the virtuous pagans in Jonson's play know very well. Even the hot-headed Arruntius hesitates to lay a hand on Tiberius; and when he hears it rumored that Sejanus has ambitions to be emperor, he observes, "The name TIBERIVS/ I hope will keepe; how ere he hath fore-gone/ The dignitie, and power." [42] Another of the Germanicans, Sabinus, in spite of an ill-concealed contempt for his depraved sovereign, declares:

No ill should force the subiect vndertake
Against the soueraigne, more then hell should make
The gods doe wrong. A good man should, and must
Sit rather downe with losse, then rise vniust.

---

40. *Ibid.,* p. 179.
41. This passage Jonson appended to "The Argument," in larger type, in the Quarto of 1605. Peter Whalley suggested in his edition of Jonson's works (1811) that Jonson here had reference to the Gunpowder Plot. Briggs (*op. cit.,* p. 203) suggests that it may have had reference rather to the Essex affair. It is probably true, as Briggs further suggests, that Jonson added this paragraph for the purpose of forestalling unfavorable criticism on the choice of subject, but there is still no reason to suppose that Jonson would have disclaimed the sentiment expressed in it.
42. *Sejanus,* I. 244-246.

Though, when the *Romanes* first did yeeld themselues
To one mans power, they did not meane their liues,
Their fortunes, and their liberties, should be
His absolute spoile, as purchas'd by the sword.
(IV. 163-170.)

The best statement of this point of view, however, is given in Act IV by Germanicus's wife, Agrippina (ironically, the only virtuous character in the play who even so much as contemplates revenge on the tyrant Tiberius) when she urges her sons to meet violence, not with violence, but with fortitude:

Thinke on your birth, and bloud,
Awake your spirits, meete their violence,
'Tis princely, when a tyran doth oppose;
And is a fortune sent to exercise
Your vertue, as the wind doth trie strong trees:
Who by vexation grow more sound, and firme.
After your fathers fall, and vncles fate,
What can you hope, but all the change of stroke
That force, or slight can giue? then stand vpright;
And though you doe not act, yet suffer nobly:
Be worthy of my wombe, and take strong cheare;
What we doe know will come, we should not feare.
(IV. 65-76.)

Agrippina's doctrine is good enough to save her, if she could only practice as well as she preaches. It does not differ materially from that of Lepidus, the constant symbol of Stoic fortitude in the play, whose appearance a bit later in Act IV causes Arruntius to exclaim, "I see (what's equall with a prodigie) / A great, a noble *Romane,* and an honest,/ Liue an old man!" [43] To Arruntius's desperate query, "What are thy arts?" Lepidus replies:

Arts, ARRUNTIVS?
None, but the plaine, and passiue fortitude,
To suffer, and be silent; neuer stretch
These armes, against the torrent; liue at home,
With my owne thoughts, and innocence about me,
Not tempting the wolues iawes: these are my arts.
(IV. 293-298.)

What Lepidus gives us here is nothing more than the traditional Stoic-Christian attitude toward all forms of oppression, legal or otherwise; and he would have it taken by his friends as the proper attitude toward Sejanus as well as Tiberius.[44] Fortunately for the

43. *Ibid.,* IV. 274-276.
44. Sejanus himself plays lip-service to this principle; see I. 576 ff.

play, however, Lepidus's friends are not all so admirably equipped with fortitude as he.

III

Throughout the whole course of the play the problem confronting the Germanicans is whether to consider Sejanus as an evil to be eradicated (that is, as a would-be usurper) or as a legitimate extension of Tiberius's own wickedness, and much of our suspense comes from their various indecisive attempts to find a satisfactory solution to this problem. Early in Act I Arruntius makes it plain that, although he will dutifully tolerate Tiberius, he will on no account stay his hand if Sejanus gives signs of aiming at complete rule:

> By the gods,
> If I could gesse he had but such a thought,
> My sword should cleaue him downe from head to heart,
> But I would finde it out: and with my hand
> I'ld hurle his panting braine about the ayre,
> In mites, as small as *atomi*. . . .
>
> (I. 252-257.)

In fact, it is Arruntius who serves as a point of reference for the tension that exists among the protagonists. Thus, at the end of Act I, when Drusus, Tiberius's legitimate heir, strikes Sejanus and delivers him a humiliating verbal rebuke, Arruntius leads the rest in applauding what appears to be an authoritative check to a mere ambitious upstart.[45] Act II, however, brings renewed evidence of Sejanus's power in the form of a torrent of spies sent to watch Agrippina and her friends. Most of the protagonists grow "exceeding circumspect, and wary" again; but Arruntius, not realizing that his hope in Drusus is vain, rails openly at "these qualified hang-men," as he calls them, and will not be restrained.[46] In Act III, after Drusus' sudden death has proved all such bravado a bit premature, we find even Arruntius somewhat calm. He now describes himself and the others as the "good-dull-noble lookers on"[47] and during Tiberius' hypocritical address to the Senate contents himself with making caustic asides to Gallus and Sabinus. Yet when Caius Silius and Cremutius Cordus, two of his own number, are brought unjustly to trial at the same assembly, Arruntius breaks out again;[48] and throughout the rest of the

---

45. *Ibid.*, I. 560-575.
46. *Ibid.*, II. 405-427.
47. *Ibid.*, III. 16.
48. *Ibid.*, III. 191 ff.

scene, one of the most important in the whole play, he expresses openly such profound approval for the defendants as to arouse the anger of Tiberius himself. Arruntius escapes immediate destruction only because Sejanus, in a subsequent conference with Tiberius, urges that his noisy frankness will be useful in stalking the others.[49] And it is in this same conference, we recall, that Sejanus confirms the growing suspicions of Tiberius by asking for the hand of Livia, Drusus' widow, in marriage, and thereby precipitates action destined to bring about his own death at the end of the play.

Thus at the beginning of Act IV we find the protagonists in a position similar to that in which we found them at the beginning of Act II. Rumors are now circulating that Sejanus has lost favor with Tiberius, and once again the would-be usurper seems to be nothing more than an upstart. This time, however, he has on his hands not only the suspicion of Drusus's blood but also the blood of Silius and Cordus; and Agrippina, grieving that these admirers of Germanicus should have died because of loyalty to her, vows vengeance on the tyrants and pleads with those friends who yet remain alive to stand clear.[50] Even before she can decide what that vengeance will be, however, word comes that Sejanus has saved Tiberius' life and is returning to Rome more powerful than ever. Disillusioned, she turns to her sons and counsels them merely to stand firm and endure like princes the blow that is sure to fall.[51] Meanwhile Sabinus, whose cardinal principle we have seen is to respect duly constituted authority, relaxes his guard sufficiently to allow himself to be goaded into making a treasonous remark about Tiberius.[52] He is arrested immediately and put to death. Thus with these events, the return of Sejanus and the death of Sabinus, the picture blackens almost as quickly as it has brightened; and Arruntius, whom we last saw confident and aggressive enough to have joined Agrippina in seeking vengeance, now confusedly calls into question the justice of the gods and cries aloud to Lepidus for the secret of his equanimity.[53] We have already seen how Lepidus at this point tries to put Arruntius back on the only course on which he and the other protagonists can hope to triumph,

49. *Ibid.*, III. 488-501.
50. *Ibid.*, IV. 1-24. Concerning Asinius Gallus, who tries to dissuade Agrippina at this point, see note 19 above.
51. *Ibid.*, IV. 61-76.
52. *Ibid.*, IV. 115-232.
53. *Ibid.*, IV. 259-279.

the course of virtue, fortitude, and forbearance; but his words are not immediately effective. Arruntius takes refuge in a daydream and conjectures savagely that if Sejanus is strong, Tiberius may also be stupid; perhaps the mongrel will shortly be leaping at his master's throat. To this Lepidus replies that "Zeale,/ And dutie; with the thought, he is our Prince," forbid such impious hopes; and he further points out that Sejanus's seeming rehabilitation is really just the prelude to total collapse.[54] Lepidus himself does not convince his pupil, but he does restrain him long enough to permit subsequent events to send home the instruction. Act V shows us those events and (if we allow the play to stand as Jonson wrote it) the whole significance of Sejanus' fall.

IV

Before going on to Act V, however, we need to consider carefully one scene which could be given only passing mention in the foregoing summary. This is that scene of some 487 lines which since Gifford's edition in 1875 has customarily been referred to as Scene I of Act III. Actually, it takes up roughly two thirds of Act III and, as Briggs complained, is treated as though it were the climax of the play.[55] To make matters even more complicated, it gives us one of those rare examples of Jonson's deliberate manipulation of events. The scene is composed of three episodes which, according to Tacitus, were separate incidents, having no direct connection with each other; Jonson ignores the gaps in time and brings all three together.[56] In addition, he constructs an elaborate defense for Silius, including an impressive death-speech composed of passages from Seneca, Cicero, and Lucan. Tacitus, on the other hand, had merely reported that the indictment of Silius was presented, "with the defendant either holding his peace, or, if he essayed a defence, making no secret of the person under whose resentment he was sinking."[57] Obviously, therefore, it would be foolish to assume that Jonson stumbled on this scene by the simple accident of following his sources; for where there is so

---

54. *Ibid.,* IV. 446-472. Note also Arruntius's reply immediately following.
55. See note 10 above.
56. Tiberius' address to the Senate took place in A.D. 23, the trial of Silius A.D. 24, and the trial of Cordus in A.D. 25; see Tacitus, *Annals,* IV. viii-ix, xvii-xx, xxxiv-xxxv. See also Herford and Simpson, *Works,* II. 12-15.
57. *Annals,* IV. xix. For the sources which Jonson used in constructing his versions of Silius's speech, see Briggs's notes, *op. cit.,* p. 245, and also his "Source-Material for Jonson's Plays," *MLN,* XXXI (1916), 330.

much evidence of painstaking, we must assume that Jonson had a reason for what he did. Moreover, since it is clear, even to those who disapprove, that this carefully integrated scene occupies the climactic position in the play, it is perhaps not rash to assume that Jonson intended it to serve as the climax. As a matter of fact, the only obstacle to our so regarding it is that conventional interpretation of *Sejanus* which reduces the protagonists to the rank of a chorus and makes the basic conflict of the play a struggle between Sejanus and Tiberius, that is, a struggle between two evils.

The basic conflict here, as elsewhere throughout the play, is that perennial one between evil, in this case unadulterated evil, and that imperfect good which is all most mortals can hope to attain to. The evil is determined; for Tiberius and Sejanus, as we have seen, are merely the instruments of Heaven's just wrath. They have no choice, therefore, but to act and thereby accomplish the punishment for which they have been sent. The good characters, though far from perfect, are still free to elect their course. They cannot escape the divine punishment; but they may elect either to resist and thus be destroyed, spiritually as well as physically, or to submit to correction and either die as virtuous men or rise purged of human weaknesses. In the second of these choices lies their only sound plan for survival. It is the plan that Agrippina learns too late, that Sabinus knows already but forgets momentarily and fatally, and that Arruntius comes to understand only with the patient guidance of the wise Lepidus. This, too, is the plan that is set before us dramatically as well as rhetorically in that memorable scene in Act III, where for the first and only time in the play good and evil confront each other squarely, openly, and knowingly.[58] From it we learn three things: first, we see the enemy revealed beyond doubt; second, we see the enemy attack and learn the only way in which he can be successfully opposed; and, third, we see the justification for that kind of opposition which on the surface might easily appear to be no opposition at all.

The situation at the beginning of that scene may be stated briefly. Drusus, the white hope of all good men, has recently died, presumably the victim of Sejanus's plot; and it has since become apparent that Sejanus has plots on many others as well. Consequently, when a special meeting of the Senate is called, everyone wonders what new

---

58. We may except that brief encounter between Sejanus and Drusus in Act I, which is a purely accidental clash, not sought by either side.

mischief is brewing; for no one can believe that Tiberius will appear publicly so soon after his son's death. Tiberius with characteristic inscrutability surprises them all. He not only appears but even rebukes the assembled senators mildly for having the appearance of mourning; and he intrusts to them the three sons of Germanicus, whom until now Drusus Senior has had in his charge. Up to this point Tiberius's words have the ring of sincerity; the senators are moved, and Arruntius can hardly believe his ears. Immediately thereafter, however, he begins to mouth platitudes about wishing to see the republic restored and preferring to have some other Roman, more worthy, take over the reins of government. It is precisely at this point that Sejanus, as by a prearranged signal, steps in with a vigorous objection. "Ah! are you there, to bring him of?" whispers Arruntius as Sejanus continues his entreaties. Tiberius, of course, with pretended reluctance, indicates his willingness to accede to the "general demand," whereupon the Senate obediently offers a prayer for him, which Arruntius punctuates with sarcastic asides. By this time, however, there is no doubt in anyone's mind that whatever may have seemed sincere in Tiberius's earlier remarks must now be open to suspicion. It is clear, too, that no one stands higher in Tiberius's eye than the notorious Sejanus, the suspected murderer of the Emperor's own son. Shocking as all this is, what follows is even more so.

No sooner has Tiberius ordered the Senate, "Proceed to your affaires," than Domitius Afer, the orator, advances to cite Caius Silius on charges of treason brought by the Consul Varro. Varro is of course acting under the joint direction of Sejanus and Tiberius, and the charges that he brings are patently false. Moreover, as Silius himself points out, it is hardly legal for Varro to bring charges against a man whom he as consul must also judge. Tiberius, however, denies all appeal; and Silius, knowing that he is doomed, proceeds to defend himself, as we might say, "for the record." He denies the charges of treason and makes it clear that it is Sejanus's hatred which has been the immediate cause of this mockery of a trial. Then with the boldness of a man who has nothing left to lose, he turns to Tiberius and lays upon him an equal share of the blame. There is no air of desperation about Silius's remarks, though what he has to say so shocks the Tiberian faction that they take it for madness. Throughout the whole episode he clearly has the upper hand; and the reason for his su-

periority becomes evident in the last speech that he delivers, a speech
which is without question the high point of the play:

> Stay, most officious *Senate,* I shall straight
> Delude thy furie. SILIVS hath not plac'd
> His guards within him, against fortunes spight,
> So weakely, but he can escape your gripe
> That are but hands of fortune: Shee her selfe
> When vertue doth oppose, must lose her threats.
> All that can happen in humanitie,
> The frowne of CAESAR, proud SEIANVS hatred,
> Base VARRO's spleene, and AFERS *bloudying* tongue,
> The *Senates* seruile flatterie, and these
> Mustred to kill, I'm fortified against;
> And can looke downe vpon: they are beneath me.
> It is not life whereof I stand enamour'd:
> Nor shall my ende make me accuse my fate.
> The coward, and the valiant man must fall,
> Only the cause, and manner how, discernes them:
> Which then are gladdest, when they cost vs dearest.
> *Romanes,* if any here be in this *Senate,*
> Would know to mock TIBERIVS tyrannie,
> Looke vpon SILIVS, and so learne to die.
>   (III. 320-339.)

So saying, Silius stabs himself and dies. To Varro it is a "desperate
act," and to Tiberius "a sad accident." Arruntius's first comment,
however, is "An honorable hand!" And one must admit that here in
Silius's death-speech and suicide is the perfect summary of Stoic
virtue: self-sufficiency, the inner guard, knowledge of fortune and
contempt for her ways, a realization that life is to be endured rather
than loved, fortitude to endure that life and courage to end it when
Fate so wills. There is a touch of grim humor in Arruntius's eagerness to share in Silius's virtue. "My thought did prompt him to it,"
he says; but he adds more soberly, "Farewell, SILIVS./ Be famous
euer for thy great example."

The next item of business to be transacted is, of course, the trial
of the historian Cremutius Cordus, who has been accused of "biting
the present age" in his account of the Roman republic. It is not difficult to see why Jonson felt it expedient to bring in the trial of Cordus
at this point, even at the cost of violating chronology; for no other
incident in Tacitus demonstrates quite so dramatically and concretely
that virtue, aside from being its own reward, commands the admiration of posterity and that vice, however prosperous in its own day,
can purchase nothing but eternal ignominy. It takes a historian to say

this sort of thing authoritatively; and Tacitus not only lets Cordus say it in a long speech refuting the charges made against him, but also adds some general observations of his own.[59] Jonson reproduces Cordus' speech with complete fidelity and gives Tacitus's comments to Arruntius and Sabinus, who therefore represent the voice of History here no less than Cordus. "Oh, how ridiculous/ Appeares the *Senate's* brainlesse diligence," cries Arruntius, "Who think they can, with present power, extinguish/ The memorie of all succeeding times!"[60] And Sabinus adds:

> 'Tis true, when (contrarie) the punishment
> Of wit, doth make th'authoritie increase.
> Nor doe they ought, that vse this crueltie
> Of interdiction, and this rage of burning;
> But purchase to themselues rebuke, and shame,
> And to the writers an eternall name.
> (III. 475-480.)

Then with a comment by Lepidus that the times are indeed sore and an observation by Arruntius that Augustus "well foresaw, what we should suffer," the scene ends, and the stage is given back to the villains of the piece, Tiberius and Sejanus.

V

Jonson's climactic scene, therefore, has given us a clear picture of the conflict, it has indicated the only terms on which a desirable solution may be effected, and it has foreshadowed the ultimate justification of goodness and right. For most of us, however, it is not enough merely to know that goodness will be applauded hereafter. We prefer to see some indication that goodness will ultimately prevail over evil—if possible, in our own time. Jonson's play does not quite give us that, but it does show us good's potentiality for survival and offer a hope that it will ultimately survive. Shortly, after Silius' suicide we hear, for the first time in the play, the voice of Lepidus, urging that three fourths of the dead man's property rather than the suggested one half be given to his surviving children.[61] Arruntius comments here on Lepidus's general worthiness and moderation; and at the end of that scene we find Lepidus standing on the side of Ar-

---

59. See *Annals,* IV. xxxiv-xxxv.
60. Arruntius's first comment on Lepidus (III. 366-368) is also taken from Tacitus; see *Annals,* IV. xx.
61. *Sejanus,* III. 359-365.

runtius and Sabinus. Thus in Act IV, after Sabinus too has been taken away, Lepidus remains to provide a moral point of reference for the now morally confused Arruntius. Without Lepidus, we may believe, the survival of goodness, as far as this play is concerned, would be a dubious matter indeed; for it is due solely to his goodness and persuasive power that Arruntius is able to resist the temptations of his own fickle nature and endure patiently when things seem to be going counter to all honest hopes. It must also be credited to Lepidus, therefore, that at Sejanus' fall the misguided Terentius has men "whose minds are good" to turn to for strength and correction. As long as men like these stand together, there can be hope that good will prevail.

Act V shows us a part of the solution of our problem, but it is a part that illuminates the whole. Here we see Sejanus reach that species of total blindness that only ambition can lead to. So confident is he by now, that he can ignore the rumors that are circulating about his imminent fall; much to the dismay of his friend Terentius, he can even laugh aside the unmistakable omens that Fate has given to him [62] and challenge all the gods to mortal combat.[63] Thus with a calm born of rashness he sits quietly in the Senate while the letter from Tiberius, which he presumes will elevate him to the dignity of a tribune, veers from praise to criticism and from criticism to condemnation. The subsequent arrest of Sejanus leaves Macro in complete command of the situation, and we last see the Senate shouting, "Praise to MACRO, that hath saued Rome./ Liberty, liberty, liberty." [64]

The remaining portion of the act consists of those 154 lines which Gifford and Briggs would cut. These lines, to be sure, give us only talk; but the talk is perhaps more significant than some critics have allowed. In the first place, it gives us an account of the physical punishment that comes to Sejanus, and indicates clearly that Tiberius

---

62. Sejanus' statue in Pompey's theater first spouts fire and smoke and then is found to have a serpent inside (V. 25-30); later, a new head placed on that same statue is found to have a rope wreathed about it (V. 215-217). A bed falls, and a cat runs between the legs of Sejanus' followers (V. 51-57). A meteor appears above the city (V. 218-221). See also the famous scene in which the statue of Fortuna averts its face when Sejanus goes to make his observance (V. 171-210).

63. See the speech in which he declares "IOVE, but my equall: CAESAR, but my second" (V. 234-266), and also the one that begins, "O!/ How vaine, and vile a passion is this feare?" (V. 382-399).

64. *Sejanus*, V. 747-748.

is shortly to be punished with accurate knowledge of the manner of his son's death.[65] More important than this, which might be guessed from what has gone before, we have the prophecy of Arruntius,[66] later reinforced by the report of Macro's abominable behavior toward Sejanus' children, that Macro will prove a worse tyrant than Sejanus.[67] We have further reinforcement of that prophecy in the detailed description of the multitude, given by Terentius, Lepidus, Arruntius, and the messenger; and these four all agree that the people "neuer yet/ Knew why to loue, or hate, but onely pleas'd/ T'expresse their rage of power," [68] that they follow Fortune and their own affections, knowing nothing of reason,[69] and that they are stupid and flexible, even willing to have the tyrant back again.[70] All this is enough to let us know that no immediate happy ending is in sight, but there is still hope. Arruntius and Lepidus, who shortly before Sejanus' fall were marked for slaughter, are still standing to evaluate the situation for us, point by point. Without these last lines we should not be reminded of that important fact. Nor should we know of Terentius's escape from a mistaken attachment to evil and his genuine adherence to the cause of justice. In fine, Jonson's ending shows us that there is still more evil than good in the world, but it does show us clearly that good is there and that it is growing. Thus with the assurance that there are such men as Arruntius, Lepidus, and Terentius, who understand the evil and know the remedy, we can look beyond the days of Macro and Caligula to the hope of happier times.

To summarize, Jonson's play shows us a trial of the small remnant of virtue in a Roman commonwealth that is degenerate and, in fact,

---

65. See the messenger's account of how Sejanus' wife, Apicata, took the news of the loss of her family and subsequently revealed her husband's plot with Livia and Eudemus against Drusus, *ibid.*, V. 856-877.

66. *Ibid.*, V. 750-753. See also note 23 above.

67. *Ibid.*, V. 833-854.

68. *Ibid.*, V. 759-761.

69. Lepidus remarks, "They follow fortune, and hate men condemn'd,/ Guiltie, or not."—V. 799-800. Compare also Arruntius's remark that the multitude act "as both/ Their bulkes and soules were bound on fortunes wheele,/ And must act onely with her motion!" There is irony in this statement, coming from Arruntius; for he himself has only barely escaped that fate, and he has escaped it only with the aid of Lepidus.

70. The nuntius exclaims:
    Part are so stupide, or so flexible,
    As they beleeue him innocent; all grieue:
    And some, whose hands yet reeke with his warme bloud,
    And gripe the part which they did teare of him,
    Wish him collected, and created new.
                                                    (V. 883-887.)

all but doomed to destruction. The issue for that remnant, and for the commonwealth, is death or survival, and the only favorable solution is set forth in terms of the Stoic concept of virtue—a concept that unfortunately is foreign to most of us and, in any case, is perhaps incapable of being made consistently appealing dramatically. In a play in which fortitude and patience mark the only desirable course, those who follow that course must necessarily substitute rhetoric for action if they are to appear on the stage at all. Nevertheless, there is nothing wrong with the structure of Jonson's play. When read properly, as the story of how the virtuous Germanican faction in Rome learns the meaning of the evil that has beset it and comes to understand the only way consistent with virtue of dealing with that evil, the play has no loose ends, no cumbersome "chorus," and no awkward shift of emphasis in the third act. Nor is the ending, however rhetorical, merely a tag to the proceedings of the fifth act. Admittedly, as a play to be performed in the theater, Jonson's *Sejanus* was probably doomed to failure from the beginning. But it succeeds admirably in the study if, and in direct proportion as, the reader is prepared to accept it in terms of the ethical and metaphysical framework in which the author placed it. One should add also that the reader must be prepared literally to accept the framework too, at least for the duration of the play. Where Jonson erred, therefore, was not in constructing his play but in overestimating the general equipment for interpretation that most of his audience and perhaps most of his readers would have. It would be a pity indeed if a work so praiseworthy in total conception and execution as *Sejanus His Fall* should continue to be admired mainly for an occasional scene or two and be required to suffer with fortitude a perpetual neglect.

XIV
JUDAISM, JESUS, AND PAUL: SOME PROBLEMS OF METHOD IN SCHOLARLY RESEARCH

SAMUEL SANDMEL

(*Associate Professor, Hillel Professorship of Jewish Literature and Thought*)

I

WHEN one writes a paper on methodology, it is usually to express reservations about previous procedures, and to recommend new, and supposedly better, techniques. But this is only part of the present purpose.

Rather, it is proposed here to set forth an array of concerns, each of which impinges on studies in either Judaism or in Christianity of the first Christian century. Much of the inherited scholarship has dealt with less than the full array, and the difference in measure between parts and the whole is by and large the index to faulty method. I propose to discuss the relationships of Apocrypha, New Testament, rabbinics, Graeco-Jewish writings, and hellenistic literature.

Of all fields of study, none is so difficult of objectivity as the period of the birth of Christianity. Different from the scholar, the pietist is less interested in precision and accuracy than in expressing his religious devotion. In recent times novels, such as *The Robe* by Lloyd Douglas, or *The Nazarene* by Sholem Asch, have utilized materials of first-century Christianity for fictional purposes; this fiction is of course not to be regarded as interchangeable with scholarship. Again, other writers have looked to the New Testament (and to the Old) for the answer to specific modern problems. The procedure, invariably, is for such writers to ascribe a given solution to Scripture, and having put it there, exultantly proclaim that they found it there. Such studies, many of which are motivated by lofty purposes and characterized by noble content, are not in reality studies in first-century Christianity, but rather the search for an ancient authority for a modern program. Within this group can be listed efforts as diverse as the demonstration that liquor ought not be drunk (or might be drunk); that socialism is good (or bad); that pacifism is commendable (or reprehensible); or that the Renaissance view of the dignity of man rests on a fallacy. Such studies really use the Christian Scriptures only to begin with. A not unusual procedure is to lift some statement out of context: Jesus taught turn the other cheek; hence pacifism—overlooking the driving of money-changers out of the temple area. Or, to generalize about the New Testament view of something such as sin, righteousness, body or the like—generalizations which overlook both a variety of New Testament views and the presence of conflicting views. Or, to search for (and even find!) a single predominating view or motif which, it is averred, is not alone primary to but exclusive in the New Testament, for example, "love." [1]

Such procedures have been followed with great frequency to the annoyance of specialists in New Testament, and even to the point that a rift seems to have arisen in Protestant circles between the specialists in Bible and the specialists in modern theology; for New Testament scholars have often failed to find in the New Testament what such theologians have asserted was there.

For our purposes, however, neither the fiction nor the overtly tendentious essay is relevant for any more than a quick buttressing of the contention that objectivity is hard to obtain. It is not proposed to deal with either of these groups of modern writings, but rather only with the work of specialists, with the scholarship which aims at accuracy and precision, and whose purpose is not aborted in advance by a conscious or demonstrable special pleading. It is rather with the genuine scholarly studies, designed not to solve modern problems, but to elucidate the ancient that we are here concerned. It is not, indeed, the problem of the objectivity of the scholar (though I shall say some things about that) but rather with his horizons.

II

The fact that any literature arises at a given time and place presupposes that some understanding of background is significant. When literature, or segments of literature, are related to each other, it is all the more important for their relationships to be understood. The historical setting needs constantly to be borne in mind. Historically, Christianity arose as a quasi-sect within Judaism, conceived some sense of its individual identity, proceeded to assert its difference and independence of Judaism, and then created the beginnings of a sacred literature of its own. Within Palestine revolt against Roman sover-

---

1. See Cadbury, *The Peril of Modernizing Jesus,* New York, 1937.

eignty led to reprisals, the chief of which was the destruction of the Temple at Jerusalem in A.D. 70, and as a result the character of Judaism shifted from a religion presided over by priests to a lay type of religion. Outside Palestine, Jews lived in such abundance as to be self-sustaining. The larger context against which these developments occurred was the Hellenistic-Roman world, with its abundance of philosophical schools, religious sects, and literary figures.

III

Obviously, to understand either Christianity or lay Judaism in its own terms requires a knowledge of both the specific and the general literatures, and an embarrassment of riches rises to plague the scholar. Prior to the New Testament there appeared in Jewish circles a class of writings called Apocrypha, the term meaning "stored away," that is, books not admitted into the collections deemed sacred.[2] In addition to the Apocrypha there is a group of quite similar writings from roughly the same period of time whose superscriptions make the claim that they are the composition of very ancient worthies; to these scholars have given the name Pseudepigrapha.

Apparently the initial stages of the assembly by Jews of books deemed sacred were the canonization of Five Books of Moses and of the Prophets; this was accomplished by about 150 B.C. It was not until towards the end of the first Christian century that the Jewish canon was fixed for the Hagiographa.

That is to say, down into the first century there was an abundance of literature, the ultimate subordinate status of which was as yet not fully decided; and whether this literature is in truth subordinate, or perhaps equal in religious content to what was canonized, it is at all events a repository of doctrines, attitudes, sentiments, and narratives illustrative of times and movements and personalities.

When one recalls that there is an interval of at least two hundred years between the youngest book of the Old Testament and the oldest writing of the New, one can quickly discern that a knowledge of the intervening literature can help to trace the process of the extension of Old Testament ideas into the New, or elucidate doctrines which arose

---

2. An initial difficulty ensues from the circumstances that books deemed "apocryphal" in certain religious traditions are accepted as canonical in others; Catholics accept as canonical books such as First and Second Maccabees. Protestants in general regard as apocryphal those books which have not survived in Hebrew; the Catholic "canon" includes books which were preserved only in Greek.

between the latest Old Testament writings and the earliest Christian. For an example of the latter the word Messiah does appear, a single time, in the Old Testament, but never in the sense in which it is used in the later writings; but Apocrypha and Pseudepigrapha present frequent appearances of the term.

As scholarship essayed to put the study of the New Testament on the high plane of the study of other ancient literatures it was natural that this extra-canonical literature was studied in some minuteness. Essays on the religious ideas contained in them are often labeled "intertestamental studies." Their significance for understanding the New Testament cannot be overestimated. But the manner of using them can be the source of different scholarly opinions, and on fundamental issues. We shall see more of this in just a moment.

The western world, with Christianity as the dominating religion, so focusses on the time of Jesus as crucial in the history of mankind that it is startling to some people to know that within Judaism the Christian movement made very little impression until well into the second or third century, and that neither Jesus nor Paul figure in their own lifetime in the abundant literature which Jews preserved subsequent to the "intertestamental literature." A convenient term for this Jewish literature is "Rabbinics."

Rabbinic literature is a group of compilations of material originally transmitted orally, comprising the legal and ethical opinions of rabbis from a period beginning about 250 B.C. until about 500 A.D. It is in Aramaic and Neo-Hebrew. As indicated, where the rabbinic literature deals with Christianity, it deals with that which has already become a rival and antagonistic church, not just a sectarian movement within Judaism. Though rabbis contemporary with Jesus and Paul are quoted, and abundantly, neither Jesus nor Paul is ever cited. Jesus is mentioned, tendentiously, but these mentions are from periods long after the first century.[3]

And here an important observation is to be made. The rabbinic compilations are the results of assembly and redaction. The redaction of the most famous collection, the Talmud, was in two stages. First, a collection was made about the year A.D. 200 of terse, laconic legal statements; this is called the Mishnah, a kind of commentary on, and

---

3. Cf. J. Guttmann on Klausner's *Jesus of Nazareth,* in *MGWJ* (1931), 250 ff., and Solomon Zeitlin, "Studies in the Beginnings of Christianity," *JQR, 14* (1923-24), 111-139.

expansion of, the laws in the Bible. Next, the Mishnah itself was commented on, not laconically, but extensively; this commentary is known as the Gemara.[4] Two recensions of the Gemara exist, one made in Palestine about A.D. 450, and the other in Babylon about A.D. 500. Mishnah and Gemara comprise the Talmud. Thereafter the Babylonian recension became authoritative for Jews, who, when they speak of the Talmud, mean the collection with the Babylonian Gemara, and they specify *Palestinian* when they mean the less authoritative Talmud.

The Mishnah is a redaction of A.D. 200, and the Talmud of A.D. 450 or A.D. 500. The rabbis quoted, however, lived as early as 250 B.C. The oldest strata of Rabbinics are contemporaneous with the intertestamental literature. The question can be asked legitimately, how accurately can the Judaism of a given, early century, such as the first Christian century, be reconstructed from redactions which might possibly be selective, or incomplete, or tendentious? We know, from a variety of sources, that before the destruction of the Temple there were a number of sects, Pharisees, Sadducees, Essenes, and the like, vying with each other for supremacy. Rabbinic literature is the creation of the Pharisees; in view of the sharp rivalries between the Sadducees and the Pharisees, can we expect an impartial and even full picture of Sadduceeism from the later, selective literature of their opponents?

Obviously, some caution must be employed in using rabbinic literature for the reconstruction of the earliest periods. The need for such caution is the more understandable when one notices that the rabbinic literature reveals very little knowledge of the Apocrypha and Pseudepigrapha, ignores much of their contents, and was created by people who did not themselves preserve this extra-canonical literature. From the rabbinic literature alone we should know nothing substantial about Apocrypha, Pseudepigrapha, New Testament, and the writings of a good many Jews who wrote in Greek, including Philo and Josephus.

There are points at which modern scholarship discerns the meeting of the "intertestamental" literature and the rabbinic. But the biggest single impression is that of diversity rather than congruency. As this appertains to New Testament study, is one to interpret Jesus

---

4. These are the best-known rabbinic works. Equally important are the Midrash and the Tosifta.

and his teachings on the basis of the "intertestamental" literature or on the basis of the rabbinic literature?

Scholars have differed about the nature of Judaism at the time of Jesus. One elaborate construction, by Wilhelm Bousset,[5] was made almost exclusively on the basis of the intertestamental literature; and while the work was ostensibly scholarly, it was not without some condescending and superior attitudes towards Judaism which Jews with propriety resented. Perles,[6] a Jewish scholar, demonstrated that Bousset had not only set a convenient pattern for indicating the superiority of Christianity over Judaism, but had abused the small measure of rabbinic passages which he had cited. As the issue sharpened between Bousset and Perles, the scholarly world was to learn of an effort to distinguish in the Judaism of that time between the "folk," and their intertestamental literature, and the erudite and their rabbinic literature.[7]

Going a step further, a Christian scholar, George Foot Moore,[8] coined a new term which he used in great abundance in a book which was designed partly in reply to Bousset. Moore spoke of "normative" Judaism, implying, of course, that there was a type, or were types, which were not normative. Moore's book reconstructs Judaism primarily from the rabbinic literature.

When one begins with the assumption that there was a normative Judaism and that there was a non-normative, then such an assumption is fatal to the notion that a large collection, whether it is "intertestamental" or whether it is "rabbinic," will yield uniform points of view. The most significant fact about the Apocrypha and the Pseudepigrapha is their heterogeneous nature. Within the convenient laconic label there lies the greatest possible diversity of literary type, religious assumption, language of original composition, place and time of origin, and general purpose. It should therefore be obvious that a study of a doctrine in Apocryphal literature which assumes that one and the same view will abide in each book in that literature starts with a faulty premise. It is a commonplace that First Maccabees

---

5. W. Bousset, *Die religion des judentums in neutestamentlichen zeitalter*. Berlin, 1903; a second edition, edited by Gressman, is called: *Die religion des judentums im späthellenistischen zeitalter*. Tübingen, 1926.
6. Felix Perles, *Bousset's Religion des judentums in neutestamentlichen zeitalter kritisch untersucht*. Berlin, 1903.
7. W. Bousset, *Volksfrömmigkeit und Schriftgelehrsamkeit*. Berlin, 1903.
8. George F. Moore, *Judaism in the First Centuries of the Christian Era*. 3 Vols. Cambridge, 1927-30.

comes from the hands of a writer sympathetic to the viewpoint of the Sadduccees, but Second Maccabees is a version of the same historic incident from the hands of a pro-Pharisee. Ecclesiasticus was composed originally in Hebrew, probably in the second Christian century; Fourth Maccabees was written in Greek in the first pre-Christian or the first Christian century. Fourth Maccabees represents a quasi-philosophical approach strongly influenced by Greek attitudes; Jubilees, composed probably in Palestine, is a proto-rabbinic expansion of material found primarily in Genesis.

In the light of such diversity it is only with great reservation that one can accept a frequently encountered type of exposition which speaks of a particular doctrine as it is found in the Apocrypha and the Pseudepigrapha, especially when some generalization about this doctrine is to be made. The infinite variety of possible variations, which on scrutiny actually emerge, are obstacles too great for the glib generalizer. It is not sound to speak of a particular view in a particular book as the total view; it is always necessary to concede the presence of divergent and even antagonistic views.

Against such a background, it is quite obviously improper to assume that there were only two modes of Jewish interpretation in the period under consideration, the normative and the marginal. The marginal, if that term is to mean anything, must include a plurality of views, and it should not be assumed that each type of marginal Judaism was interchangeable with each other type of marginal Judaism. Moreover, it is to be recognized that normative Judaism itself presents a diversity of viewpoints; and, indeed, rabbinic literature offers the student many differences of opinion, ofttimes sharp, within normative Judaism itself. Within normative Judaism one must, at a minimum, distinguish between what might be said to be the prevailing view and what can be spoken of as a minority view, or views. In a welter of types of Judaism, it is most infelicitous to speak of first century Judaism without some specification or some qualification. To omit the qualifying adjective, such as normative, apocalyptic, or hellenistic is in effect to fashion a meaningless sentence.[9a]

9a. It is thus meaningless when W. F. Howard, *Christianity According to St. John*, Philadelphia, 1946, tells us again and again that the background is Jewish, not Greek. Conceding for a moment that the statement is correct, the insistent question is, what specific type of Jewish background? But, confer below the discussion of the motive in labelling a doctrine Jewish or Greek.

The sense in which one may properly speak of the intertestamental doctrines or rabbinic doctrines in terms which have meaning is in terms of relative, prevailing trends, which are always accompanied by a receptivity to reservation. To give a dangerous example, one might say that Apocryphal literature represents a Judaism in which legalistic conformity is as yet not dominant while rabbinic literature represents attitudes in which legalism is dominant. In Apocryphal literature we can expect to read quasi-prophetic works, such as apocalypses, to make another dangerous simplification. Within the diversity of normative Judaism there is a relatively greater measure of uniformity and inner consistency; in Apocryphal literature there is no such inner consistency and uniformity. One might go even further and say that the Apocryphal literature comes from a period before the Jewish synagogue was consolidated into a rather stable and crystallized form, and therefore the Apocryphal literature represents a "freer" type of speculation than would the opinions emerging from a settled and relatively serene type of objective religious experience.

Now having made these contrasts, I should be the first to proclaim that these are glib generalizations. That is to say, they are mostly true and are mostly applicable. But also, they are in part very much untrue, and in specific matters of research where specific ideas and terms are crucial, the generalizations which I have given would be inimical to the attainment of any well-rounded and sound scholarly understanding of a given doctrine.

This is relevant to the study of Christianity and Judaism in the first century, in that Apocrypha and rabbinic literature present too many variables for it to be possible for one to make nimble summaries of Judaism. The rabbinic literature, as indicated, comprises collections made centuries after the first century; there was no quasi-Christian interest specifically in the first century and hence no tacit or avowed purpose of demonstrating just what first century Judaism was; the literature was created by the descendants of Pharisees, only one of the various groups that flourished in Palestine in the first century, and it tends to overlook, or even to disparage, the groups in rivalry of the direct ancestors in the first century.

Moreover, the most pronounced shift within Judaism occurred in the first century; the destruction of the Temple, and the triumph of the synagogue. There are innumerable questions, the answers to which are elusive; had the synagogue already tended to supplant the Temple before the year 70? Had the Pharisees already emerged as the dominant party in Judaism before the year 70? Was apocalypticism as unknown in Palestine before 70 as the rabbinic literature would lead us to conclude? Do these relatively late collections read back into the past the conditions of their own time, or are the historical data which they occasionally include partly if not completely reliable? [9b]

With rabbinic literature representing the opinion of individuals separated in time as far as the second pre-Christian century is from the fifth Christian century and separated in place as far as Palestine is from Babylon, can we expect an unbroken uniformity throughout such long periods? Were there no significant differences evoked by the reason of the ingress of or exposure to hellenism, Parthian religion, gnosticism, and trinitarian Christianity? Was legalistic, objective Judaism the sole type of religious expression or do the laconic allusions in rabbinic literature to types of mysticism,[10] both theoretical and practical, represent movements wider in extent than the mere allusions in opposition indicate?

All these rhetorical questions point unmistakably to the conclusion: the precise status of Judaism in the first Christian century before the year 70 is well nigh not to be recovered. It is definitely not to be recovered in terms of convenient pigeon holes, simple categories, and unqualified assertions.

In the Synoptic Gospels there is considerable material which fits with much congruency into the milieu of the rabbinic literature. This material has to do with the life and teaching of Jesus. Can we elucidate obscure passages or amplify laconic ones in the Synoptic Gospels by a knowledge of rabbinic literature?

It is well to remind ourselves of some questions of chronology. Jesus belonged to first century Judaism. It is the Judaism of Palestine, if we include Galilee in Palestine. We shall have to assume, accordingly, that Galilee was in no way distinct from other parts of Palestine. Within such a framework it is to be conceded that much light can be thrown on matters discussed in the Gospels by a knowledge of rabbinic literature.

9b. See Mann, "Rabbinic Studies in the Synoptic Gospels," *HUCA*, I, 324-325; and Blau, "Early Christian Archeology from the Jewish Point of View," *HUCA*, III, 169-70.

10. Cf. on Maaseh Bereshith and Masseh Merkabah the section in G. Scholem, *Major Trends in Jewish Mysticism*. New York, 1946, pp. 39-78, 140.

But a number of scholars have tended to follow methods about which searching questions need to be asked. For well over a century rabbinic parallels to materials in the Synoptic Gospels have been gathered and published. In the last thirty years there has been made available a German work of staggering immensity in scholarship, Strack-Billerbeck, *Commentary on the New Testament*. This work is a verse by verse, indeed a word by word commentary, illustrating from rabbinic literature the text of the Christian Bible.

Strack-Billerbeck can hardly be overpraised. But unhappily it lends itself to frequent misuse by scholars. In the first place, some scholars who have themselves never read connected passages in the rabbinic literature, either in the original or in translation, utilize the excerpts in Strack-Billerbeck as the basis for judgments that are not always sound. The excerpts cited may have only a tangential connection with the New Testament, contained in the accident of a similar word or phrase, but its major tenor may be quite at variance. Nevertheless, the coincidence in part between a rabbinic and New Testament passage is taken to be total coincidence and congruency. Strack-Billerbeck tried in several places to define the use to which their *Commentary* can be put, but the method of piling up excerpts of doubtful relevance becomes a dangerous invitation to the imprudent. Frequently these focus their attention only on phases which coincide with rabbinic literature and fail to notice more abundant phases where coincidence gives way to incongruency. The convenient arrangement in Strack-Billerbeck has spurred many scholars, not to compare and contrast rabbinic literature and New Testament material, but to try to blend them together without thought or care as to meaning, context, date and place of provenance, and the like. It is assumed, not that Strack-Billerbeck provide interesting parallels or quasi-parallels to New Testament, but that Strack-Billerbeck provide the full means of explaining the New Testament.

Here a caution of a chronological nature has to be stressed. The earliest rabbinic activity precedes the composition of the Synoptic Gospels by a considerable length of time. This is attested to us by the presence in Jubilees and in the first century writer Josephus of proto-rabbinic expositions which reappear, either modified or unchanged in the later rabbinic collections. But that some rabbinic material is earlier is not to say that all rabbinic material is earlier. Even the later rabbinic material in addressing itself to a problem touched on in the New Testament may be an interesting parallel. In this sense, it may be described as background material. But background material of such time is illustrative material and without any necessary chronological precedent. That is to say, Jesus did not in the first century speak against a chronological background of opinions of rabbis of the fourth century in Babylon. A good many scholars, using Strack-Billerbeck, proceed from literary background to an assumption of chronological background, and thereafter assume that this or that attitude of Jesus is shaped by the supposedly antecedent rabbinic discussion.

When questions are raised about the legitimacy of such dubious procedure, a common retort is to say that the rabbinic material is after all relatively homogeneous. The retort would be interesting if it were universal and applicable in every situation, but for each scholar who asserts this kind of homogeneity in rabbinic literature, there is another who in a different context will prove his point by demonstrating the relative heterogeneity of the literature. To cite names, and to introduce still another facet, the writings of Philo, it is asserted by Bamberger [11] that rabbinic literature is all of a piece, and that Philo is dependent as it were even on the later rabbinic writings; while Marmorstein, [12] addressing himself to a striking difference between Philo and the rabbis explains the difference on the basis that in the second Christian century the rabbis underwent a change of heart and change of attitude. In the first case, dependency is proved by an assertion of homogeneity; in the second case differences are explained on the basis of heterogeneity.

Reverting to Strack-Billerbeck, the obvious difficulty in a set of excerpts is the likelihood of the rupture of context. It is not going too far to assert that a good many scholars who utilize Strack-Billerbeck do so even against the context of the rabbinic literature out of which the excerpts are made. [13]

But still another difficulty has to be encountered. If it has suc-

---

11. B. J. Bamberger, "The Dating of Aggadic Materials," *JBL*, LXVIII (1949), 115-123.

12. A. Marmorstein, *The Old Rabbinic Doctrine of God*. I, London, 1927, pp. 45 ff; and "Philo and the Names of God," *JQR(NS)*, XXII (1932), 295 ff. There intervened a protest against Marmorstein's first statement by Finkelstein in *JQR(NS)*, XX (1930), 363; Marmorstein's second is a rejoinder to Finkelstein.

13. A striking example of such procedure is W. D. Davies' greatly erudite *Paul and Rabbinic Judaism*. London, 1948.

cessfully been contended that the rabbinic literature, with its heterogeneity, provides us with one or more variables, then we must add that from the other side the New Testament provides a good many variables.

For well over a hundred years the chief impetus in the study of the Synoptic Gospels was the so-called recovery of the historical Jesus. This search rested on the quasi-theological notion, that the New Testament had undergone an incrustation of mythology and legend which hid fine ethical insights and guides for present-day conduct. All that was necessary was to remove the overgrowth and to find the historical Jesus, and thereby modern man would have a sufficient guide for himself.

In line with this assertion the Gospels were studied minutely. The results of the study have indicated the impossibility of recovering the historical Jesus. The reason for this is that in the Gospels legend and church interest of later times are so thoroughly interwoven with narratives about and words supposedly uttered by Jesus that it is quite impossible to disentangle the authentic from the inauthentic. While many conservative or fundamentalist Christians object to this scholarly conclusion, it is nevertheless a rather standard conclusion of the Protestant study of the New Testament.

Modern scholarship would assess the Gospels as throwing light not on the life and teachings of Jesus, but on the views of Jesus as they had crystallized at different stages throughout the developing church. More concretely, the Gospels reflect the time and place of their composition, rather than the events which they describe. While some oral tradition goes back to Jesus, this oral tradition has been so worked over by the church, that its pristine form is quite beyond isolation.

When one wishes to explain a New Testament passage by the rabbinic literature, he must remember from the New Testament side that the Gospels are products of the Christian community, coming after its self-conscious distinction from Judaism, and that they were written in Greek and in the Dispersion. Within any single Gospel there are heterogeneous views; the three Synoptic Gospels (Mark, Matthew, and Luke) provide an even greater measure of heterogeneity.

The Gospels, then, are themselves in the nature of a variable. For example, did Jesus teach that divorce under any conditions was

231

inadmissible, as Mark and Luke state, or did he permit it in the case of adultery, as Matthew states? Shall we look in Strack-Billerbeck for examples of both the total prohibition of divorce and for permission of divorce in the given type or situation?

The recognition that Luke and Matthew utilize Mark, expand him, alter him, and rewrite him should lead to the recognition that the changes and expansions in Luke and Matthew stem not from Palestinian Jewish soil, but from Diaspora soil. They are Diaspora reformulations of what is itself a Diaspora product. Accordingly, there is often little point to looking in rabbinic literature for the exposition of matters coming from a background and a set of interests completely alien to the rabbis.

The measure in which Strack-Billerbeck can be helpful in understanding the New Testament would seem by and large to be restricted to those passages in the New Testament where there is really a meeting of Judaism and early Christianity within a Palestinian Jewish setting. For such passages a considerably smaller number of total pages is needed than the five large volumes of Strack-Billerbeck.

IV

The mention that the Gospels are products of the Greek world can be a good point of departure for asking the question: how Greek was the Jewish world of Palestine? Most scholarship is in some way or other influenced by Matthew Arnold's famous distinction between the Hebrew spirit and the Greek spirit, and usually the question of Greek influence is approached with either one or more sets of mind. The standard assumption is that the rabbinic world and the Greek world were diverse in content as they were in form, and that at each point they represent divergency rather than congruency. The Hebrew world is intuitive, the Greek world philosophic; the Hebrew world is poetic, the Greek world speculative.

For our purposes it has to be borne in mind that the Greeks conquered Palestine at the end of the fourth pre-Christian century. Greek institutions were established in Palestine. The Greek language is represented in considerable abundance in the rabbinic literature. But essentially, how Greek did Jewish Palestine become? Was Dispersion Judaism, in the Greek regions, more intensively and extensively Greek than Palestinian Judaism?

It is known that about 175 B.C. the issue of Greek influence in

Palestine became a crucial one. Difficulties arising from political events, coupled with heavy-handedness on the part of the over-lord, the Syrian Greeks, led Jewish Palestine to a revolt, successfully accomplished under Maccabean leadership. Within the Jewish population there were anti-hellenizers as well as hellenizers. After the Maccabean Revolt, by and large any previous hospitality to Greek notions diminished, possibly nearly to the point of total exclusion.

Scholars differ as to the measure of Greek influence in Jewish Palestine, but the usual assumption is that the influence was surface or formal, but never penetrating or substantial. Accordingly, an intertestamental literary work is allocated for its place of origin largely by this assumption. For example, a work in Aramaic or Hebrew would come exclusively from Palestine and a Jewish work in Greek would come exclusively from outside Palestine.

In this light, one can allude to passages in the rabbinic literature (from the period considerably after Jesus) which speak with hostility towards the Greek language and Greek works such as Homer. Most scholars are inclined to agree that the rabbis forebade the reading of Homer. More recently a study has tried to show that it was the study of Homer as distinct from the cursory reading of him which the rabbis prohibited.[14] This latter study, an excellent one, represents a protest against the usual reconstruction of events, for it contends that hellenism was far less than unknown in Jewish Palestine.

The single and most dramatic distinction between Palestinian Judaism and Greek Judaism focusses on the translation of the Bible into Greek. The place of translation was probably Egypt, and more specifically Alexandria; traditions of some credibility allocate the translation there. Certainly by the time of Philo (20 B.C. – A.D. 40) the Greek Bible, called the Septuagint, was so pervasively the Scripture of Greek-speaking Jews in Egypt that the anniversary of its translation was celebrated as a holiday. Greek Jews (and Christians) considered it to have the fullest measure of inspiration. Considerably later in Palestine a rabbi was to declare that no misfortune was as great for Jews as the translation of the Bible into Greek. This attitude stemmed undoubtedly from difficulty with Christians who were utilizing the proof-texts based on divergences of the Greek from the

---

14. Saul Lieberman, *Hellenism in Jewish Palestine*. New York, 1950,

Hebrew for the substantiation of Christian contentions. But forgetting the fact that the festive observance and deep deploring are not attitudes of the same period, we still see a wide variance in the attitude of Jews, Palestinian or Diaspora, towards the Greek translation.

We know from passages in rabbinic literature that the rabbis were aware of certain places where the Greek diverges from the Hebrew. These divergences, the rabbis explained, were the results of efforts of the translators to avoid incurring the wrath or suspicion of Gentiles. For example the passage in Leviticus 11:6, which lists the rabbit as prohibited food was altered to avoid the "rabbit," since the Greek word for rabbit was the same as the surname of the reigning Ptolemy.[15]

The issue of how much hellenization was implicit in the translation of the Bible has been fought out in the scholarly circles. From time to time it has been alleged that Greek philosophical conceptions are woven into the translation. By and large such efforts have been shown to be ill-founded, and most of the hellenizations in the Greek Bible can properly be called surface. These include the Grecianizing of names and the equipping of these names with Greek case endings, and also the occasional use of Greek metrical forms where the original Hebrew metrical form was inappropriate.[16]

Yet even with the concession that the hellenizations are surface, it is obvious that there cannot be what Marcus has described as a word-to-word correspondence between the original and the translation, since the idiom of two different languages is not going to be identical. Accordingly, the Greek Bible is full of paraphrases and circumlocutions and the turning of a Hebrew phrase into an idiosyncratic Greek phrase. When the Greek Bible came to be studied by Greek Jews they searched Scripture as diligently as any other generation at any other time, and operating on the assumption that the Greek Bible was itself endowed with all the necessary qualifications of inspiration, they were ready to infer whatever they wished from the accidental wording of the Greek. In the same way that the study of Homer was accompanied by deducing elaborate lessons from the accident of the wording of a verse of the Iliad, so elaborate lessons

15. Max L. Margolis, *The Story of Bible Translations.* Philadelphia, 1917, pp. 35-36.
16. See Ralph Marcus, "Jewish and Greek Elements in the Septuagint," in *Louis Ginzberg Jubilee Volume.* New York, 1945, pp. 227-245.

were deduced from the Bible. And as rationalists among the Gentiles interpreted Homer allegorically so as to find in Homer the precursor and indeed the origin of their own philosophical systems, so Greek Jews began to interpret the Scriptures allegorically.

However little hellenization there might have been in the Bible itself in its Greek version, certainly the growth of allegorical interpretation increased rather than decreased the amount. Furthermore, as the allegorical interpretation took the form of deducing from the accidental readings of Scripture philosophical and religious notions from the Greek world, the hellenization had grown apace.

But it is quite a difficult question to decide in some cases where the Jewish aspect leaves off and the Greek aspect begins. For example, the Jewish notion that God is invisible to the eye and the Greek view that To On was discernible only to the intellect but not to the senses, are not dissimilar to each other. When one finds in the allegorical explanation of the Greek Bible the statement that God is not to be discerned by the senses, that view can stem either from the Jewish background or from the Greek background.

There are some areas that are congruous; there are some areas that are incongruous. For example, every harmonization which has been made of Greek philosophy and Jewish revelation has had to assert the primacy of certain Biblical notions. Accordingly, medieval philosophers who were Aristotelian in outlook could not square Aristotelianism with the creation story in Genesis; creation *ex nihilo* and the eternity of matter do not coincide.

Between the extremes of matters which are completely incongruent and matters which are congruent, there is quite a range where the issues are not as sharply drawn. By and large it can be said that the Jewish anthropology distinguished between man's body and man's soul, but not to the point of finding them antitheses to each other. By and large the Greek view was the view known as pessimism which ascribed positive virtues to the soul and negative qualities to the body. Yet there is implicit in the Palestinian Jewish distinction between body and soul, some of the contrast in a restrained form which becomes extreme in the Greek world and the Graeco-Jewish world. Accordingly, in passages in which Philo contrasts body and soul, we can sometimes find ourselves within the framework of the Jewish view of the congruency of body and soul but elsewhere we move into the Greek notion of the incongruency. The line of demarcation between the congruent and incongruent is not always easily discernible. This is particularly true where the Jewish and Greek notions are in their original form so parallel to each other that they can become merged in the same way that parallel lines seem to meet, as astronomers put it, in infinity.

To resume, it is not always possible to say of a given doctrine or view that it is either Jewish or Greek. Sometimes it is one or the other, but sometimes it is a mixture of both. Indeed space must be allowed in modern scholarly divisions for a broad area of a Graeco-Jewish world, of several centuries duration, sufficiently remote from Palestinian Judaism, but loyally Jewish in its own terms, so that its own peculiar character can be rather well defined.

Contrasts, indeed, can be noted between Graeco-Jewish thinking and rabbinic thinking, both in form and in substance. This is not to rule out the bare possibility that in Palestinian Judaism there was judaization of hellenism so advanced that the hellenistic background tends to be lost to view; and, conversely, that outside Palestine a hellenization of Judaism was so complete that the Palestinian origins in the Old Testament or of the early post-Old Testament period are well concealed. Hellenization, in the far-flung Jewish settlements, took place in varying measures and in varying degrees of penetration. Rabbinic Judaism, in its native Palestinian form, was not unmindful of hellenism. It did not embrace superficial forms or welcome philosophically involved aspects of hellenism. Its essential hebraic quality was never overshadowed. But as an organism living in the hellenistic world it could not help but be affected if only in minor aspects by the prevailing world intellectual and cultural streams.

It is possible to speak roughly of three degrees of hellenization. The rabbinic literature gives us only overtones of hellenistic influence. In the second degree, the writings of Josephus show us the hellenization of a Palestinian Jew who knows the Greek world rather well, but from the outside. He is hellenized, but only in limited measures, and he falls short of profundity in hellenization. Not only did he require Greek secretaries to assist him in writing his book, but also his efforts at reflecting Greek philosophy show that he had heard about it but not studied it. A third degree of hellenization is that of Philo who wrote theosophical works. Here hellenization is at its maximum. But let one not forget, it is a hellenization of Judaism.

That is to say, Philo is not a witness simply to hellenism, but to a specific kind of hellenism.

It may be well to pause and consider some concerns focussing on Philo. His writings, which are in the process of incorporation in the Loeb classics, have already reached nine volumes, of a planned eleven. Philo wrote in Greek; he wrote both sermonic tracts, based on a sequence of verses in the Bible (known as the Allegory of the Law) and a freer type of composition (known as the Exposition). Philo quotes extensively from Greek writers, whom he mentions by name—philosophers, poets, and playwrights. It is uniformly agreed that he is trying to demonstrate the congruency of Greek philosophy with Judaism, on the contention that Scripture, properly assessed by the allegorical method, yields an anticipation in time to the Greeks, and a profundity and truth beyond what the Greeks achieved. Later generations of the church said about him, either Plato Philonizes, or Philo Platonizes.

Despite a long history of Philonic research, an outstanding scholar declared only twenty-five years ago that the fundamental problem about Philo was still unsolved: was he a Greek philosopher with a Jewish background and loyalties, or was he a Jewish thinker who merely couched his Judaism in philosophic terms? [17] In our day, two extremes of interpretation exist, the one asserting that complete hellenization is to be discerned in Philo, and the other asserting that there is hellenization only in language and other external matters.[18]

Prepossession can control or even determine the judgment in such a matter. Some scholars, principally Jewish scholars, have started with the premise that loyalty to Judaism demanded a total rejection of hellenism, and hence it is to be assumed that Philo rejected all hellenism, utilizing only a philosophical shell. The prepossession consists of an unwillingness to admit of alien influences on a Jew so loyally Jewish.

A similar prepossession is to be found among Christian writers concerning Paul. Like Philo, Paul also wrote in Greek, and also utilizes Greek philosophical trappings and even terms from the Greek mystery religions. It is asserted by some scholars that Paul

17. Louis Ginzberg, *The Legends of the Jews*. Philadelphia, 1925, V, viii.
18. Harry A. Wolfson, *Philo*. Two vols. Cambridge, 1947. This author goes to the point of denying entirely any hellenization beyond surface in Philo. But see Erwin R. Goodenough, *By Light, Light,* New Haven, 1935.

is thoroughly Greek; the assertion is buttressed by recourse to the more recent researches in the United States and Germany in the Acts of the Apostles; it is from Acts that we get a picture of Paul as a student of Gamaliel, a speaker of Hebrew, and observant of the Jewish Law. Those scholars who contend that among the motives of the author of Luke-Acts was the delineation of both Jesus and Paul as undeviatingly faithful to Judaism; motive dictates the presentation of Paul in a portrait at great variance with that Paul writes in his epistles. Such scholars would not tend to use Acts as a source of knowledge of Paul;[19] and for them the Paul of the epistles emerges as a hellenized Jew.

If this is so, then much of Paul's doctrine has a "Greek" background, rather than a "Jewish" one. But, again, prepossession enters in at several points. First, a passage in the Fourth Gospel (4:22) contends that salvation is of the Jews; to argue for a Greek origin of a New Testament doctrine is, for some, to reduce the stature of its salvationary power. Moreover, researches of some forty years ago in hellenistic religion led scholars to identify a good many of Paul's teachings with similar or parallel ideas found in the Greek mysteries; the view was expressed with some frequency that Pauline Christianity was in essence a mystery religion.

This judgment was often made not in a descriptive sense but in an evaluative sense. It was at the culmination of over a century of effort to regain the historical Jesus—which, in other terms, meant the removal of Pauline "aberrations." In general secular historians tended to emphasize Paul's hellenization, some even to the point of denying that a historical Jesus ever lived.[20] In the interest of such secularism, the label of Mystery for Pauline Christianity was in effect a negative judgment on Paulinism.

Christian historians, affronted by the oblique attacks on Paul, tried originally to defend Paul on the basis of the reliability of Acts; it is, however, only in England that Acts continues to be regarded as historical—British scholarship is often blissfully ignorant or willfully unaware of American or German scholarship. A more prudent method was embarked on, by other scholars, in a whole series of

---

19. Cf. D. W. Riddle, *Paul, Man of Conflict.* Nashville, 1940; R. M. Hawkins, *The Recovery of the Historical Paul.* Nashville, 1943; and Knox, *Chapters in the Life of Paul.* New York, 1950.

20. Arthur C. Drews, *Christ Myth.* London, 1910.

books, of conceding Paul's hellenization, but in demonstrating that Paulinism was not a Mystery.[21]

Such judgments rested on the basic premise that the Mysteries were not only error, but also evil; Plato's praise of the Mysteries as symbolic of fundamental truth was unknown or disregarded.[22] The Mysteries were assessed solely on the basis of the licentiousness, of sexual excesses, and orgiastic frenzies. To demonstrate the lack of connection between Paul and the Mysteries was to fend off a derogation of Paul. These defenses have been interesting in the tortuous effort to find not only significant distinctions between Paulinism and Mysteries, but also in efforts to find everywhere distinctions without weighty differences.

The assertion of the absence of mystery elements from Paul cannot be accompanied by an assertion of the absence of mystery terms from his writings. But a harmonizing explanation would argue that Paul uses mystery terms but not in a mystery sense; such an explanation, too, is given in the case of Philo.

The difficulty with removing the mystery connotations from Philo and Paul is that as a result both of them would seem to be speaking from a vacuum rather than from a vibrant period of human self-search. It is only as scholars overcome the Judeo-Christian bias not only against the externals of the mysteries but also against the spiritual strivings within the mysteries, that a more balanced appraisal of the relations of both Philo and Paul to the mysteries can result. When the term mystery ceases to be a term of insult or opprobrium, but is no more than a description of historic religious approaches by means of which people have tried to penetrate to ultimate reality, then these relationships can be objectively assessed. In such a context, the goal of scholarship is not to assert superciliously or deny indignantly the relationships to mysteries, but to note the specific differences in a framework of large similarities between Philo and his Greek environment, and Paul and his.

Another aberration which needs constant correction is the failure

---

21. Cf. William Fairweather, *Jesus and the Greeks*. Edinburgh, 1924; H. A. Kennedy, *St. Paul and the Mystery Religions*. New York, 1913; S. Angus, *The Mystery Religions and Christianity*. New York, 1925. Another sample of divergent use of the same material is G. H. Gilbert, *Greek Thought in the New Testament*, New York, 1928, which admits the presence of Greek ideas but deplores them.
22. Plato, *Gorgias*, 493a.

of scholars to distinguish between the origin or genesis of a religious doctrine or ceremonial and the understanding of that doctrine or ceremonial in the mind of the adapter. People in our day who shake hands are not uniformly aware that the practice is said to have developed from the days of knights in armor who showed they were unarmed by baring their hands and clasping each other's. It is not at all inconceivable that people in our day who shake hands have no more in mind than to follow a current practice of the amenities.

There have been those scholars whose preoccupation with the background of Christian and Jewish practice has led them to equate their antiquarian discoveries with the practice of a later generation. For example, it is not to be denied that the Jewish Passover is the result of a merger of a pastoral sacrifice held at full moon and an agricultural festival of disposing of last year's grain and the consumption of some of the new crop of grain. But when Jews, after several centuries, saw in the Passover the anniversary of their release from slavery in Egypt, then what Passover meant to them was the ancient release from slavery in Egypt, and it did not mean to them the holiday merged out of two distinct primitive folk festivals.

Those who trace the origins of doctrines and customs as they are found in the rabbinic literature and Christianity often tend to confuse the origin with the view of a later day. Some scholars do not stop to consider that the authors of books of the New Testament and those statements in the rabbinic literature did not possess the recondite scholarship available in modern days, so that the person observing either the eucharist or the Festival of Tabernacles really did not know the folklore history of these observances.

Moreover, the ancient writers expressed their ideas and their convictions not in a vacuum but in a living world. While it is true that in the background of Paul's thought there are discernible reflections of the myth of dying and rising savior-god of the mystery religions, it is still another thing to say that Paul in speaking of a crucified and resurrected Christ was simply repeating a folk motif that he knew. Paul's mode of expression of his belief grew, indeed, out of his environment. But what distinguishes Paul from his environment is the singularity of the combination of background currents which he channels into one stream, and in this feat of intellectual (or, if one prefers, religious) engineering, he leaves clear traces of his own highly individual artisanship.

It is absurd to suppose that Christians of later days who accepted Paulinism were aware that the pagan myth of the dying and rising god was latent in their belief. Some scholars, on the one hand, ascribe naïveté and ingenuousness to ancient writers, and in the same breath ascribe an amazing wealth of historical learning to them. There are those who interpret the passage in II Kings 19:35, of the Assyrian hordes who went to bed and woke up in the morning to find they were dead, as an example of a slip of the pen of a naïve author—these scholars not being aware that even the ancient writers might have had a sense of humor or of the ridiculous. At the same time they will credit a supposedly naïve writer with the possession of relatively recondite data. Sometimes scholarship forgets that the authors of ancient books varied in individual character and in disposition. It is quite inconsistent, however, to credit the same author with naïveté and at the same time with erudition.

The aberration in the study of the origins, or in the study of the background, of either the study of the rabbinic literature or the New Testament is that scholars tend to confuse the origin with the facets which developed out of these origins. Relating specifically to works in the hellenistic-Jewish dispersion, whether by a Jew like Philo or by a proto-Christian like Paul, the study of the origin of doctrines may cast light on the author, but the proper question is not this: what is the background of such-and-such a passage? but, rather: in the light of such-and-such a background, what does this passage mean in its context?

The school of the Christ myth thought it was sufficient to show the folklore origin of certain doctrines and thereby to demolish them. They seemed to have given no thought to this, that somebody like Paul or Philo could hardly express himself except in a language used by people and from a background in which people lived. Can we reasonably expect Paul in giving his exposition of Christ to speak like a Chinese Confucian? Shall we expect Philo to speak like a French deist?

The issue, I repeat, is not to deny the validity of the study of origins; it is to assert that the study of origins is a supplement to the primary study, the meaning of a passage in its own context and in the light of its own purpose.

Where varying degrees of hellenization exist, and where elaborate studies in background have been made, it is not surprising that excellent lexical work has been done. One cannot overpraise the lexicographers. But scholars have occasionally carried such refinement to the point that they have attributed to a given author refinement and subtleties which are not always appropriate. Specifically, neither Paul nor Philo always utilizes precisely the same word to express precisely the same idea. Neither ever dreamt that he would be the subject of lexical studies; neither ever felt the necessity of distinguishing, let us say, between "door" and "portal," or between "soul" and "higher mind." Paul's letters are a random collection, the remnant of a larger group of letters. Philo wrote tracts. Our modern interest is to analyze, assemble, and classify the notions in these writings. Neither Paul nor Philo ever wrote analytical, systematic treatises on subjects such as God, the Logos, or the nature of man. We know their views as we bring together related passages in our own system. But ofttimes we see too much, and too many distinctions in the accidental words that the author chanced to use in given passages. We commit him to a verbal precision which none of us ever attempts in his random correspondence or in his daily oral lectures. Scholarship has often been overperspicacious in analyzing both Paul and Philo.

But still another danger inheres in such word studies. It is true that scholarship has been aware that a word such as "righteousness" means something different to the rabbis from what it means to Paul and from what it means to Philo. But what is especially true of the rabbis is also true in large measure of both Paul and Philo. Their métier was not to establish definitions or to fashion unassailable semantic fortresses. Since basically they were either expounding the Old Testament or else were rooted in the Old Testament, they conceived their views not in abstract terms but in more personal and concrete ways. For example, the rabbis tell us what a holy man is, or what a good man is, but never what are holi*ness,* good*ness,* and righteous*ness.* They illustrate these traits by pointing to Old Testament characters, Abraham, Isaac, Jacob, or others. If we are to understand their thought, then we must follow their method of thinking. The danger in lexical studies, or in analyses made on subject headings, is that they fail to do justice to the intent and conviction of the ancients. Thus, some scholars speak of rabbinic doctrines of free-will or predestination. But to interpret their views as concepts or as fully developed doctrines is to be untrue to rabbinic method. Along the same lines of reading modern analytical trends into the ancients, Professor Wolfson has given us a two volume work on Philo which can be said virtually to ignore Philo's treatment of the patriarchs and Moses; yet these characters are the medium of Philo's exposition of his views.[23] Certain German scholars have given us elaborate, and even ingenuous, analyses of rabbinic theology, always in terms of subjects and abstractions, and seldom with appreciation for the rabbinic method.[24] In dealing with Paul, many scholars have been so preoccupied with classifying the different subjects they believe Paul discussed that they pay no attention to such things as Paul's use of Scripture, Paul's deviation from the usual allegorical method, and Paul's basically unphilosophical cast of mind.[25]

It is often a little startling to read the contrasts that are said to exist between Paul's profundity and Philo's shallowness. This contrast is made not on the basis of the emotional involvement which each finds himself in where it might be said that Paul is highly emotional and Philo rather serene; it is assumed by some Christian scholars that Paul's intellectual equipment not only matched Philo's, it even exceeded it.

Such subjective judgments stem not only from a sectarian bias, from which no one is completely immune, but also from an inability to see either Paul or Philo in proper dimension and against a living background. The tendency towards a neat categorization is often as great a peril to objectivity as is antecedent evaluation.

A by-product of the effort to rescue Paulinism from the rationalist attacks of the nineteenth century has been an interesting segment of scholarly literature. Since the time of Renan, to whom is usually traced the neat phrase that Paul substituted for the religion of Jesus a religion about Jesus, there has emerged quite a spate of essays and even volumes which, in refutation, have essayed to show the congruency of the teachings of Jesus and those of Paul, and, indeed, the direct dependence of Paul on Jesus. While few scholars have gone as far as Klausner,[26] who, despite the absence of any testimony

23. Wolfson, *op. cit.*
24. F. Weber, *Jüdische theologie auf Grund des Talmud und verwandter Schriften,* Leipzig, 1897.
25. Cf. Mary E. Andrews, "Paul, Philo and the Intellectuals," *JBL, 53* (1934), 150-166.
26. J. Klausner, *From Jesus to Paul.* New York, 1943.

in any literature, believes that Paul knew the historical Jesus, other scholars have written to show that Paul was well acquainted with the details[27] of the life of Jesus. In part, such demonstrations rest on Paul's knowledge of the traditions of the death and resurrection; but there is in all the Pauline corpus but a single passage in which Paul reveals any unmistakably clear and sharpened knowledge of Jesus, the passage in which he quotes Jesus in discountenancing divorce (I Cor. 7, 10-11). Beyond this, we have only a random and scattered series of overtones.

The traditional approach towards these overtones has been to look in the Pauline corpus for congruency with or reflection of gospel materials, and then to assume that, as Jesus preceded Paul in time, so the overtones are later than Jesus and dependent on him. But modern scholarship, through the application of *sitz-im-leben* principles, and from the analyses made by form critics, is uniformly persuaded that the gospels reflect the interest and beliefs of the later church.[28] Traditional material going back to Jesus was shaped and altered by the later church; and material, reflecting constantly changing issues in or crises from the church, was created and read back into the career of Jesus. For example, the point of controversy recorded between Jesus and the Pharisees on the matter of the washing of the hands is that Jesus nullified the Jewish food laws; such implicitly is the purpose of Mark 7, 1-15 and Matthew 15, 11, while Luke 11, 41, has Jesus explicitly saying, "Behold all things are clean to you." If the question of foods had been settled in the time of Jesus, it is surprising for it to arise as though *de novo,* as it does in Galatians, or for it to be the subject of a Jerusalem council decision, as Acts 15 shows. The question of foods is but a single instance of more such problems, where modern scholarship would ascribe the priority in time of an issue and its solution to the Apostle Paul, and whatever dependency is indicated to the evangelist; in the

27. E.g., Frank C. Porter. *The Mind of Christ in Paul.* New York, 1932, pp. 18ff
28. The outstanding German names are K. L. Schmidt, *Der Rahmen der geschichte Jesu,* Berlin, 1919; Martin Dibelius, *Die Formgeschichte des Evangeliums,* Tübingen (1919) 1933; Rudolf Bultmann, *Geschichte der synoptischen Tradition,* Göttingen (1921) 1931. In America such studies were pursued by D. W. Riddle, *The Gospels, Their Origin and Growth,* Chicago, 1939; and S. J. Case, *The Evolution of Early Christianity,* Chicago, 1914; at Chicago. An excellent summary of the results and methods is to be found in a book by a Catholic author, L. J. McGinley, *Form-Criticism of the Synoptic Healing Narratives,* Woodstock, Md., 1944, written not in approval of form-criticism, but in some effort to show either its inadequacy or irrelevance. McGinley's summary is excellent.

present instance Luke is ascribing to Jesus the settlement of an issue that arose in the time of Paul.

To generalize from such a particular, where the older scholarship looked for traces of influence of Jesus on Paul, the modern turn of scholarship would be to find the reflections of Pauline doctrine in the Gospels. While some decades ago scholarship looked for Pauline doctrines in the *obiter dicta* in the Gospels, the search for such influence can legitimately be extended even to the words which the evangelists put into the mouth of Jesus. The older scholarship looked for "the mind of Christ in Paul"; an advantageous direction of modern scholarship is to look for the mind of Paul (among other early influences) in the words and events centering around Jesus.

The significant contribution of Paul was that he provided the justification for the early Christian church to make a significant departure from Judaism, namely, the abrogation of the Law of Moses; Paul emphasized faith, rather than works of the Law. Christian scholarship in general assumes not alone that Paul urged something different from his non-Christian Jewish contemporaries, but that he urged something deeper and finer. Traditional Jewish scholarship following Renan, sees Paul as a *bête noire*. In either case, evaluation has often obscured a clear understanding of just what motivated Paul, and just what his intentions were.[29]

To regard Paul as superior is inevitably to regard legal Judaism as inferior. The Epistle to the Hebrews, in addition, allocates to Judaism the role of the imperfect foreshadowing of the perfect realization, Christianity. The conviction that these evaluatory attitudes are objective judgments colors many an antecedent state of mind among the scholarly researchers. A by-product has been a series of unhappily polemical studies. A German Christian scholar, Fiebig,[30] declared that the superiority of the parables of Jesus over the parallel parables of the rabbis lay in the fact that Jesus drew on an abundance of references to nature which the rabbis totally ignored; in response, a Jewish scholar, Feldman,[31] produced a long volume of rabbinic parables limited to references to nature.

---

29. I have prepared a rather full study of the usual interpretations of Pauline antinomianism as well as suggestions of my own in an unpublished manuscript. A typescript of some of this material is available in the Yale University Library in my *Abraham in Normative and Hellenistic Jewish Tradition.*
30. Paul Fiebig, *Die Gleichnisreden Jesu im Lichte der rabbinischen Gleichnisse des neutestamentlichen zeitalters.* Tübingen, 1912.
31. Feldman, *The Parables and the Similes of the Rabbis.* Cambridge, 1924.

Moreover, the denunciation put into the mouth of Jesus of the Pharisees in Matthew 23 [32] has led to the inadvertent but natural equation of Judaism and the externals of religion, these to be contrasted with the sincere internals of Christianity. While modern Christian scholarship has largely freed itself from the prepossession that rabbinic Judaism was an arid religion of externals,[33] the residuum of the Epistle to the Hebrews attitude still abides.

An antecedent conviction that legalism is *per se* a mark of a poverty of religious expression is hardly conducive to a sober evaluation of the rabbinic literature. Many scholars forget that the genius of rabbinic literature is that it is legalistic literature, and they remain perpetually capable of being startled at finding legalism in it. What does one expect to find in the library of a law school but collections of typical cases, acute hair-splitting for the purpose of distinguishing between the factors in one case and the factors in another case, or examples of the arguments of opponents about the relevance of a mutually congenial general law as it applies to a specific point in dispute? In its good sense, casuistry is the process of applying a given principle to a succession of actual or suppositious cases, each slightly different from the other, so that the law in each of the derived specific cases can be known. The rabbinic literature is legalistic and casuistic; this is neither an accident nor fortuitous, but the natural effect of the underlying assumption basic to the rabbis, that God had revealed a Law, which needed to be known and applied in every possible human circumstance.

When one throws rabbinic literature into contrast with the New

---

32. D. W. Riddle, *Jesus and the Pharisees.* Chicago, 1928.
33. A watershed in the history of the liberal scholarship, affecting the tone of its treatment of Judaism is to be discerned in the period comprising Strack-Billerbeck and Moore's *Judaism in the First Centuries of the Christian Era.* Before them the liberal scholarship was not free from condescension or even an outright sneer at Judaism; for example, F. Weber's *Jüdische theologie auf Grund des Talmud und verwandter Schriften,* Leipzig, 1897, or G. B. Stevens' *The Theology of the New Testament,* New York (1902) 1947, and even the writings of the famous historian Edward Meyer. Against this background the Jewish dictum that higher criticism is the higher anti-Semitism is to be considered a just reaction. But the reappraisal which was indicated in the books of a Christian, Robert Travers Herford (*Pharisaism, Its Aim and Its Method,* New York, 1912, and *The Pharisees,* New York, 1924), has crucially altered the tone of scholarship and, by freeing Jews from a need of defensiveness, has encouraged them to make substantial contributions, even in the field of New Testament; see the superficial study by Thomas Walker, *Jewish Views of Jesus,* London, 1931, and the distinguished study by Gösta Lindeskog, *Die Jesusfrage im neuzeitlichen Judentum,* Uppsala, 1938.

Testament one should be aware that he is comparing and contrasting two literatures, one of which is avowedly legalistic and the other of which is predominantly basically anti-legalistic. The scholarly procrustean bed by means of which a New Testament statement is made to lie comfortably in a rabbinic bed, or a rabbinic statement in a New Testament bed, is less than infrequently to be encountered. Some Jewish scholars, eminent rabbinists, seem to feel that since the milieu of Jesus was Jewish and Palestinian, one can proceed directly from the Talmud into expounding the gospels; and some Christian scholars, personally committed to anti-legalism, utter astonishing judgments on the contents of rabbinic literature.[34]

The New Testament has come down to us in Greek. Jesus spoke Aramaic, the language of Palestine of his day, as the preservation of Aramaic terms in the New Testament demonstrates.[35] Translation of something, either of oral tradition or of written materials, took place somewhere along the line. J. Wellhausen,[36] Burney,[37] and C. Torrey[38] have made convincing cases for the presence in the Gospels of instances of faulty translation. Though some Semitists follow Torrey, almost no scholar whose approach is from the New Testament goes along with him in his view that the Gospels as we now have them were originally composed in Aramaic and that translation took place after the Gospels were written. It is only in the case of Revelation that a substantial number of scholars would concede the possibility of a whole document's having been translated.

Except for Revelation, then, the rest of the New Testament, in its recorded form, is a product of the Greek world, not the Aramaic-speaking world. While Matthew may have been composed in relative

---

34. Of the former, a good example is Klausner; of the latter, an attitude attributed to H. E. Fosdick. Rabbis named treatises after the first significant word in the treatise; their discussion of festival regulations accordingly is called "Egg"; Fosdick was reported in the *Yale Daily News* of October 13, 1948, by coincidence Yom Kippur, as having declared that Jesus was interested in the essentials of religion while the rabbis were interested only in an egg! The published version of the lecture, in *The Man from Nazareth*, New York, 1949, indicates that the undergraduate reporter did not listen with both ears. He misunderstood Fosdick's intent and spirit; but Fosdick's words lack precautions against such distortion.
35. Nazis, with obvious motive, denied that Jesus was a Jew; some scholars, without such motive, have made the serious but absurd suggestion that Greek, not Aramaic, was the language of Jesus.
36. Wellhausen, *Einleitung in die drei ersten evangelien*. Berlin, 1905.
37. F. Burney, *The Poetry of Our Lord*. Oxford, 1925.
38. C. Torrey, *Our Translated Gospels*. New York, 1936.

proximity to Palestine,[39] the rest of the New Testament comes from the more distant Dispersion, as far west as Rome.

It is curious, accordingly, that New Testament scholarship pays relatively little attention to the Graeco-Roman world. In seminaries, the usual historical courses pick up with Alexander the Great, go through the Maccabean revolt, the Hasmonean Dynasty, and get down to the time of Jesus. The Greek Dispersion of Jews is usually mentioned, but often even the mention is absent. The seminarian gets his introduction to the New Testament literature without any comparable effort to portray the conditions economic, political, social, and religious which existed in the Roman Empire out of which the New Testament books were written.

Only in studies of the later period, in which Greek philosophy and Christianity become blended, is the Greek world examined, and then almost exclusively for philosophy, and within philosophy primarily for Plato. The living religions and religious philosophies of the hellenistic period are almost totally ignored. Indeed, the Graeco-Jewish writings become the property not of the New Testament scholar but of the specialist on the periphery of the New Testament.

The greatest neglect is the religious writings of the pagans. Not that there have not been studies by eminent scholars like Reitzenstein,[40] Cumont,[41] Wilfred L. Knox,[42] Wendland,[43] A. D. Nock,[44] and Goodenough[45] who have collected and interpreted the materials of the hellenistic world. The state of mind which rejects hellenism as

---

39. Three considerations combine to form the usual view that the author of Matthew was a "Jewish" Christian. Early church tradition declares it was written in Hebrew (Aramaic); Old Testament quotations are abundant; the gospel sets up a kind of legalism. Too little notice has been taken in the scholarly world of the objections of Kenneth Clark, "The Gentile Bias in Matthew," *JBL*, LXVI (1947), 165-172, to the usual view; it is really time for it to be abandoned.

40. R. Reitzenstein, *Die hellenistichen Mysterienreligionen.* Leipzig, 1910; *Poimandres: Studien zur griechischägyptischen und frühchristlichen Literatur,* Leipzig, 1904.

41. F. Cumont, *The Oriental Religions in Roman Paganism.* Chicago, 1911.

42. W. L. Knox, *St. Paul and the Church at Jerusalem,* Cambridge, 1925; *St. Paul and the Church of the Gentiles,* Cambridge, 1939; *Some Hellenistic Elements in Primitive Christianity.* London, 1944.

43. P. Wendland, *Die hellenistisch-römische kultur in ihren Bezeihungen zu Judentum und Christentum.* Tübingen, 1912.

44. Principally Nock's *Conversion,* London, 1933.

45. Principally Goodenough's *By Light, Light,* which despite some occasional overstatement is a landmark which points towards the fullest knowledge of the meaning of hellenistic Judaism. In it one finds a rarity in scholarship: the utilization of the significant Hermetic Literature, overlooked and ignored despite a fine translation in a good edition in four volumes by Walter Scott, *Hermetica.* Oxford, 1924-36.

unworthy of Christianity I have spoken of above; in the present context, the issue is that the basic materials for understanding the environment out of which the New Testament books were composed are ignored, even though they are available. This is much more true of American scholarship than of German, yet it applies to the Germans, too.

The testimony of the non-literary papyri, and the inscriptions on gravestones, are important sources for our knowing the people whose religious inclinations led to the creation of the books of the New Testament. Not alone Plato himself, but Plato as intermediated in his successors is highly significant for New Testament study.

V

It is my conviction that the center of gravity of New Testament studies needs some drastic shifting. To understand, as far as it can be recovered, the Palestinian background of Jesus, Apocrypha and rabbinic literature are focal. But to understand the gospels (as distinct from Jesus) and the rest of the New Testament, it is the Graeco-Jewish writers who are focal, and these writers, Philo, Aristeas, and Aristobulus, can be most clearly understood only against the wider background of Gentile hellenism.

That the mastery of all these disciplines by a single individual is a staggering task is to be conceded. It is at the same time an unavoidable necessity. A single person cannot be a pin-point specialist in each of these pursuits. The lament made here is that the work of the specialists is by our day relatively readily available, but is nevertheless not utilized. It needs to be used, if what is desired is well-rounded scholarship, rather than fractional scholarship.

VI

The Graeco-Roman world did not know the arbitrary boundaries that modern departmentalizing in most universities occasions. Hillel, a celebrated rabbi shortly before the time of Jesus, devised a legalistic formula by means of which a direct requirement of the Pentateuch was set aside, this not capriciously but out of a social need; the formula was known not by a Hebrew or Aramaic term, but by the Greek word *prosboule*. An assembly of elders, which functioned both before and after his time, is known by the Greek term *synhedrion*.

Can the dimensions of this man, a great sage, a great teacher,

249

a religious personality whose impression on his contemporaries was vivid in the extreme, be known without our knowing the Greek factor in his life? How extensive were the Greek influences to which he was exposed, and was there any measure in which he responded to these, to accept or repel them? Did his *prosboule* rest on a native, Jewish dialectic method, or was he in some way influenced by Greek rhetoric? The fullness of the man can be recovered only as we fill in as much as the sources permit us the range of environmental factors. Out of these Hillel will speak not as a disembodied voice, but as a living and breathing human being.

So, too, the writers of the New Testament can cease to be the impersonal voices of unspecified times and places, but rather warm and yearning people whose confrontation of the problems of life and its meaning are always of significance to other human beings.

However elusive the final bits of data may be, and however we may, by the absence of complete information, have to look at things darkly, *en ainigmati,* surely a more rounded scholarship, sensitive to a full array of considerations, and mindful of inevitable variables, can be able to see that crucial period more clearly, and to meet its people face to face.

XV

PETRARCH'S DOCTRINE OF MEDITATION

By DAYTON PHILLIPS

(Associate Professor of History)

PETRARCH, who made himself the subject of so much of his writing, bequeathed to later ages an image of himself which is full of inconsistencies and unresolved contrasts.[1] Because he was preoccupied with ethical issues, the nature of his ideals and attitudes has been the subject of much debate, and at the center of this discussion has been the little Latin prose treatise frequently referred to as his "confessions" but which he himself called *Secretum meum* or *De secreto conflictu curarum mearum.*[2] Here, under the guise of three imagined dialogues between "Franciscus" and "Augustine," Petrarch examined his own inner life with reference to the theme that meditation upon death is the root of salvation. The first dialogue is more abstract and impersonal than the other two. Whereas the latter call forth the image of a reluctant penitent debating his predispositions with a father confessor, the first dialogue suggests a venerable teacher expounding to an untrained but sincere student the thesis that moral reformation springs from earnest meditation. Although this doctrine has been taken as symbolic of ascetic ideals in conflict with Petrarch's literary activities, its exact significance and its relation to the self-examination for which it provides an introduction and framework

---

1. For the literature on Petrarch, cf. *Cornell University Library: Catalogue of the Petrarch Collection bequeathed by Willard Fiske,* compiled by Mary Fowler (N. Y., 1916); N. Sapegno, *Il Trecento* (Milan, 1942); C. Calcaterra, *Nella selva del Petrarca* (Bologna, 1942); U. Bosco, *Petrarca* (Turin, 1946); *Studi Petrarcheschi* (Bologna, 1948 ff.).
2. Franciscus Petrarcha, *De contemptu mundi, colloquiorum liber, quem Secretum suum inscripsit,* in *Opera omnia* (Basle, 1554), I, 374-416; Francesco Petrarca, *Il mio segreto,* trn. E. Carrara (Florence, 1942); W. H. Draper, *Petrarch's Secret, or The Soul's Conflict with Passion* (London, 1911). Few have written about Petrarch without devoting some attention to the *Secretum.* Calcaterra, *op. cit.,* chs. 1, 8, has, I believe, best indicated the attitudes (although not the ideas) underlying the *Secretum,* and the views there stated are a necessary corrective for much that has been written about Petrarch in English and German. Also important is P. P. Gerosa, "L'umanesimo agostiniano del Petrarca," *Didaskaleion,* III-VII (1925-29). G. Voigt, *Die Wiederbelebung des classischen Alterthums* (Berlin, 1893), I, 133, declared that the *Secretum* was "der Schlüssel zu allen andern Werken Petrarcas und die Krone derselben." Cf. E. Carlini-Minguzza, *Studio sul Secretum di Francesco Petrarca* (Bologna, 1906), p. 96: "Il Secretum è il centro e l'anima delle opere petrarchesche."

are not clear.[3] It is the aim of the following discussion to examine the course of Petrarch's thought in the first dialogue of the *Secretum* in order to explain the meaning of this theme. This is a necessary prelude to any satisfactory understanding of the *Secretum* and of Petrarch's ethical interests and conceptions.

That passion, desire, and volition are deeply influenced by concentrated reflection is suggested at many points in Petrarch's works. Indirectly, there is a hint of the idea in his own voluminous consideration of the vicissitudes of life in the *De remediis utriusque fortunae*. Similarly, it is suggested by his praise of leisure, solitude and literary study in the *De vita solitaria* and *De otio religiosorum*. In his letters, the idea is more explicit when he writes, "Although salvation may not lie in literature, nevertheless, there is and has been a way to salvation there for many." [4] In another letter, he declared:

> I would not hope easily to explain how valuable to me in solitude are those familiar words and letters by which I am wont to arouse my sleeping spirit not merely by silent study but by reading them aloud, or how much pleasure it gives me to mull over the works of others or myself, or how much I feel myself freed from gross and bitter annoyances by that reading.[5]

In attacking excessive concern with dialectic, Petrarch stated in the *Invectiva contra medicum quendam:*

> In truth, to meditate upon death, to arm oneself against it by indifference and patience, to combat it if necessary, and in the name of eternal life, happiness, and glory, to endure this brief and miserable existence with high spirit, this in the end is the true philosophy, that which has aptly been said to be nothing but a contemplation of death.[6]

---

3. G. Koerting, *Geschichte der Litteratur Italiens im Zeitalter der Renaissance*, I: *Petrarca's Leben und Werke* (Leipzig, 1878), p. 629, has said with reference to the *Secretum* as a whole: "Ja, fast ist es geradezu unmöglich, eine einigermassen verständliche Analyse zu geben. . . ."

4. Francesco Petrarca, *Le familiari*, ed. V. Rossi, 4 vols. (Florence, 1933-42). Hereafter, only the book, letter, and paragraph in which the reference occurs will be cited, as follows: *Fam.*, XVII, 1, 3: "Quamvis enim in literis non sit salus, est tamen fuitque iam multis ad salutem via. . . ."

5. *Fam.*, I, 9, 11: "De me autem, quid mereantur in solitudine quedam voces familiares ac note, non modo corde concepte, sed etiam ore prolate, quibus dormitantem animum excitare soleo; quam preterea delectet vel aliorum vel mea nonnunquam scripta revolvere; quantum ve ex ea lectione exhonerari me sentiam gravissimis acerbissimisque molestiis, non facile dicturum me speraverim."

6. Quoted from the Italian translation in Sapegno, *op. cit.*, p. 220.

Especially interesting is the note recording Laura's death in his own handwriting on a much-prized Vergil manuscript, in which he asserted:

> It is time to flee from Babylon, and this will be facilitated by God's prevenient grace and by sharp and forceful thinking about the vain endeavors, empty hopes, and unwelcome accidents of former times.[7]

Petrarch, however, was not interested in rational doctrines; he was concerned about the immediate attributes of experience itself. It is not, therefore, an idea about meditation but the fact that it was ethically significant to him which stands out in his works. Yet there is an exception to this rule in his discussion of the theme that meditation is the root of salvation in the first dialogue of the *Secretum*.

In general, the *Secretum* reflects Petrarch's sense of the contrast between spiritual ends and his own worldly aims. In the second and third dialogues, he scrutinized his tendencies with reference to the seven mortal sins and then analyzed the evils of his desire for love and fame. From a statement in the third dialogue that it was sixteen years since Franciscus had first fallen in love with Laura, the book appears to have been conceived in 1343. This was the year in which Petrarch's second illegitimate child was born, and that it was a time of spiritual crisis is also suggested by the *Psalmi mei septem* and by certain sections of the *Rime sparse*.[8] But the ideas and interests which shaped Petrarch's sense of conflict are not clear. Inevitably, one looks to the doctrine which holds the discussion together for some explanation of the author's thought, but the theme of meditation upon death allows varied interpretations. For some, it has appeared to be a literary device for defining a standard of otherworldly values in terms of which his inclinations and activities were to be measured and within which there were reverberations of Platonism, Stoicism, or

---

7. P. de Nolhac, *Pétrarque et l'humanisme* (Paris, 1907), II, 286: "Tempus esse de Babilone fugiendi crebra horum inspectione ac fugacissime etatis estimatione commonear, quod, previa Dei gratia, facile erit preteriti temporis curas supervacuas spes inanes et inexpectatos exitus acriter ac viriliter cogitandi." Cf. *Francisci Petrarcae Vergilianus Codex,* pubblicato in fassimile fototipico dall' editore U. Hoepli (Milan, 1930).

8. Cf. H. Cochin, *Pétrarque, les psaumes pénitentiaux* (Paris, 1929); E. Chiorboli, *Le rime sparse e i trionfi* (Bari, 1930), nos. 120, 189, 264; A. Foresti, *Aneddoti della vita di Francesco Petrarca* (Brescia, 1928), pp. 98 ff.; A. Foresti, "La data dei *Salmi penitenziali* del Petrarca e la sua crisi spirituale," *Convivium*, III (1931), 39-55; H. Cochin, *Le frère de Pétrarque et le livre* Du repos des religieux (Paris, 1903).

medieval mysticism.[9] For others, the emphasis upon meditation is primarily a reflection of the Stoic belief that desire can be swayed by the mind's power to alter the view of its object, and it is supposed that Petrarch tried to reinforce this influence by giving a pseudo-immediacy to the goal of perfection and by emphasizing the hopes and fears connected with death. "Kill the appetite for the things of this world by the smell of their dissolution: that is the medieval-Christian in Petrarch," J. H. Whitfield has declared.[10] Most agree that Petrarch's conscience dictated that he reflect upon sin, renounce the world, and meditate upon death.[11] Since Franciscus does not in the end decide to become a monk, the whole treatise is looked upon as an essentially tragic record of unresolved conflict and spiritual frustration, a vain attempt to influence choice through intellectual appreciation.[12] But why should Petrarch have prepared his reflections for publication if they pertained merely to vain endeavors and a perennial sense of frustration?

The reference and organization of Petrarch's thought has been obscured by the assumption that he believed that he should become a monk. The fourteenth century was an age of conflicting ideas about moral conduct and about the relation of the secular life to ethical aims and values. Hybrid forms of renunciation went hand in hand with a new emphasis upon the subjective aspects of morality in the works of Dante, Eckhart, Wycliffe, Groote, and others. Indeed, the trend was not toward an extension of monasticism but toward a deepening of secular morality, and secularism in other realms was accompanied

9. Calcaterra, *op. cit.*, ch. 1, has outlined the general trends in the interpretation of Petrarch's attitudes. For emphasis upon Petrarch's Stoic tendencies, cf. H. W. Eppelsheimer, *Petrarcha* (Bonn, 1926); G. A. Levi, "Pensiero classico e pensiero cristiano nel *Secretum* e nelle *Familiari* del Petrarca," *Atene e Roma*, XXXV (1933), 68; XXXIX (1937), 78. With reference to Platonism, cf. G. Saitta, *L'umanesimo* (Bologna, 1949), pp. 71-115. For medieval mysticism, cf. Carlini-Minguzza, *op. cit.*, p. 60.

10. *Petrarch and the Renascence* (Oxford, 1943), p. 53. For Stoic influence, cf. A. Bobbio, "Seneca e la formazione spirituale e culturale del Petrarca," *La Bibliofilia*, XLIII (1941), 254.

11. Cf. Calcaterra, *op. cit.*, p. 295: "In fondo all'animo il Petrarca, allorché scrisse il *Secretum*, sentiva che la soluzione ideale era quella a cui stava per volgersi il fratello Gherardo, rompere cioè ogni relazione col mondo, chiudersi a penitenza, non essere più che di Dio; e perciò nell' opera l'intima sollecitudine di un distacco dal mondo è espressa con severo e trepido sentimento, poiché rispondeva a un' ansia sincera. . . ."

12. Cf. E. Razzoli, *Agostinismo e religiosità del Petrarca* (Milan, 1937), p. 3: "Il Petrarca, uomo di malferma volontà, oscillasse, invece, incerto per lungo tempo fra gli allettamenti della passione e la fuga dalla colpa."

by what might be called a secularization of monastic ideals of perfection. Petrarch's *Secretum* was written, then, in an atmosphere of widespread concern about the essentials of moral effort, and when an author brings his experience to bear upon matters of contemporary interest, his book must be read for what it has to say about these matters as well as for what it says about the author himself. There is evidence in the *Secretum* that, instead of idealizing monasticism, Petrarch looked upon meditation as something of a substitute for it. The soul is brought into line with its true nature and destiny not by a renunciation of worldly ties but by an inward turning of the mind in meditation. Although Petrarch did not attack monasticism, the function he attributed to it was peripheral rather than central to moral effort. Monasticism was for him an admirable means of devoting oneself fully to meditation and contemplation, but this conception made it something of an incidental adjunct to the higher stages of spiritual life. On the other hand, Petrarch's praise of meditation pointed toward higher standards of secular morality by applying to secular life practices earlier believed to require a monastic environment. By suggesting that perfection might be achieved even without renouncing the world, it encouraged individual moral effort. Thus, Petrarch's ethical point of view might be called individualistic in contrast to the medieval exaltation of group discipline, but since all moral effort has an individualistic character, it would be truer to say that his outlook emphasized subjective, at the expense of objective, aspects of morality and, consequently, diminished the contrast between secular and monastic ideals. These implications of the *Secretum* have been obscured, however, not by any lack of precision in Petrarch's own thought but by neglect of medieval ideas about the mechanisms of moral effort.

Although scholars have stressed the medieval character of Petrarch's concern with meditation upon death, the intellectual significance of his ideas has not been carefully investigated. Yet his notions bear a strong resemblance to the psychological and ethical theories of the medieval Augustinians, and in terms of those theories, a definite idea about the function of meditation can be perceived in the first dialogue of the *Secretum*. In meditation, the mind takes cognizance of the dictates of the heart and allows the inner bent of the will to emerge into consciousness as the center of the true life of the soul. Meditation is, therefore, a way of achieving some unity of desire. The exposition of this notion in the first dialogue of the *Secretum* centers upon three main topics. In an introductory section, the meaning of meditation is developed by relating it to the Augustinian problem of influencing the structure of volition. A second section indicates that the efficacy of meditation lies in the development of an ever-expanding area of self-possession through the inner cooperation of the mind with the deepest urges of the will. In a final section, the author points out that intuitive understanding of the soul itself is the proper substance of ethical meditation. Recognition of these ideas suggests that Petrarch's ultimate reason for working his self-examination into literary form for publication was that he believed it significant both as a revelation of spiritual realities and as material for the meditations of others. The following discussion will be divided into four parts. In the first, indications of Petrarch's use of medieval ideas will be briefly considered, and then in subsequent divisions, each of the three main sections of the first dialogue of the *Secretum* will be examined.

I

Giuseppe Rotondi has recently remarked that we should not be deceived by Petrarch's studious avoidance of reference to medieval writers, and he has shown that Petrarch at times took his quotations of the classics from the works of Hugh of St. Victor, John of Salisbury, Vincent of Beauvais, and others rather than from the classics themselves.[13] Petrarch annotated the books of Richard of St. Victor, Abelard, and Cassiodorus, and in notes on the latter's *De anima,* he cited the *De spiritu et anima,* a twelfth-century compendium of Augustinian psychology probably written by Alcher of Clairvaux, although attributed in Petrarch's day to Augustine.[14] The *Secretum* itself suggests that Petrarch was in far closer touch with the devotional literature of the Middle Ages than has been supposed. Its Prologue recounts how Franciscus, lost in meditation, once came face to face with Truth, a beautiful and gracious lady, who called upon

13. G. Rotondi, "Note alle *Familiari* del Petrarca," *Rendiconti del reale istituto lombardo di scienze e lettere, Classe di lettere e scienze morali e storiche,* LXXVI (1942), 123. A. Viscardi, *Francesco Petrarca e il medio evo* (Naples, n.d.), deals with attitudes rather than ideas.
14. L. Delisle, "Notice sur un livre annoté par Pétrarque," *Notices et extraits des manuscrits de la Bibliothèque nationale et autres bibliothèques,* XXXV (Paris, 1896), 17.

Augustine to speak with him in human voice, that is, the voice of conscience, and to give him aid, while Truth remained a silent auditor in the background. Reminiscent of the visit of Lady Philosophy to Boethius, this setting also suggests the medieval idea that when conscience turns inward, it is in the presence of truth, since self-knowledge is the surest form of verity. In the light of the fact that Petrarch's brother Gerard became a Carthusian early in 1343, when the *Secretum* was probably conceived, it is interesting to note the opening of one of the classics of monastic literature, the *Meditationes* of Guigo, the fifth prior of the Carthusians:

> Truth, like beauty, must be placed in the middle between extremes. . . .
> The beginning of a return to truth is displeasure with falsehood in
> yourself. . . . In whatever effort you make for your salvation, no
> measure or remedy is more useful to you than to censure and despise
> yourself. Indeed, anyone who does this is your helper, for he does what
> you were or should have been doing so that you might be saved.[15]

The phrases of another medieval writer are called to mind at the end of the Prologue when Franciscus declares that he has written this book:

> not because I wish to include it among my other works or seek any
> glory through it, but for the greater reason that I want to experience
> as many times as possible through reading it that pleasure which I once
> received from the talk itself. You, then, little book, will not seek the
> resorts of men but will be content to stay with me, true to your title,
> for you are and shall be called *My Secret,* and you who record what
> was once said in secret will remind me of it in secret in my meditations.[16]

These words seem to echo the introduction of an anonymous manual of monastic meditation which was frequently ascribed to Augustine, Bernard, or Hugh of St. Victor:

---

15. Guigo, *Meditationes* (*Pat. Lat.*, CLIII, 601, 604), chs. 1-2: "Veritas ponenda est in medio, tanquam pulchrum aliquod. . . . Initium redeundi ad veritatem, est displicere sibi in falsitate. . . . In omni cura quam pro salute tua geris, non est ullum officium vel medicamentum utilius tibi quam teipsum vituperare atque contemnere. Quicunque ergo hoc facit, adjutor est tuus. Hoc enim agit quod tu agebas, aut agere debuisti, ut salvus fieres."

16. *Secretum*, p. 373 (page refers to the Basle, 1554, edition of the *Opera omnia*): "Hoc igitur tam familiare colloquium, ne forte dilaberetur, dum scriptis mandare instituo, mensuram libelli huius implevi, non quem annumerari aliis operibus meis velim, aut unde gloriam petam, maiora quaedam mens agitat, sed ut dulcedinem, quam semel ex collocutione percepi, quotiens libuerit ex lectione percipiam, tuque ideo libelle conventus hominum fugiens, mecum mansisse contentus eris, nominis proprii non immemor, Secretum enim meum es et diceris, mihique in altioribus occupato, ut unum quodque in abdite dictum meministi, in abdito memorabis. . . ."

257

I have worked on this little book not with rash ambition but for love and praise of my God so that I might always have with me a brief and convenient word about my God taken from the most expressive statements of the fathers in order to light with fire my love of Him by reading it whenever I may grow cold.[17]

There is also a strong medieval note in the opening of the first dialogue. Augustine asks Franciscus:

What is your life, poor man? What do you dream? What do you wait for? Do you forget that you are mortal?[18]

When Franciscus declares that his condition terrifies him, Augustine asserts:

There is no more efficacious measure for scorning the enticements of life and for bringing peace to the soul amid the tempests of the world than the memory of one's own misery and assiduous meditation upon death, provided that such consideration be not light and superficial, but sink down into the very marrow of the bones.[19]

The term "misery" has been used above to translate the Latin *miseria*, which in the Middle Ages specifically designated the sinful condition of man and called to mind the contrast between the frustrations of the world and the glory of the hereafter. The importance of meditating upon the misery of life and of taking thought about oneself was a common theme in medieval moralizing. The *De spiritu et anima*, for example, stated:

We should exercise the spirit in continuous meditation and consider our miseries and wants, our labors and sorrows. . . . We should think how short our life may be, how uncertain is the way, how sure is death, and how unsure is the hour of its coming.[20]

Hugh of St. Victor asked in his treatise on prayer:

17. *Manuale* (*Pat. Lat.*, XL, 951), I, Preface: "Idcirco non praesumptionis temeritate, sed magis Dei mei dilectione, huic opusculo ad laudem ejus operam dedi, ut ex elegantioribus dictis sanctorum Patrum breve et manuale verbum de Deo meo mecum semper haberem, ex cujus lectionis igne, quoties tepesco, in ejus accendar amorem."

18. *Secretum*, p. 374: "Quid ais homuncio? Quid somnias? Quid expectas? an non te mortalem esse meministi?"

19. *Ibid.*: "Ad contemnendas vitae huius illecebras, componendique inter tot mundi procellas animum, nihil efficacius reperiri, quam memoriam propriae miseriae, et meditationem mortis assiduam, modo non leviter aut superficie tenus serpat, sed in ossibus ipsis ac medullis insideat. . . ."

20. Alcher of Clairvaux, *De spiritu et anima* (*Pat. Lat.*, XL, 816), ch. 49: "Jugi ergo meditatione animum nostrum exerceamus, et consideremus miserias et necessitates nostras, labores et dolores. . . . Cogitemus ergo quam sit brevis vita nostra, quam via lubrica, quam mors certa, et hora mortis incerta."

What, indeed, is more efficacious for stimulating man to zealous prayer than the misery and misfortune of so many evils which oppress him?[21]

And similarly, William of St. Thierry declared:

There is no more worthy nor more useful exercise for man who is a rational creature than the use of mind and spirit in which he surpasses other creatures and other aspects of his own nature.[22]

The resemblance of these to Petrarch's statements certainly invites consideration of the meaning of his ideas from the medieval point of view.

II

The ethical problem which is indicated at the opening of the *Secretum* is that of achieving Christian perfection, for the advice which Augustine gives Franciscus goes beyond mere repentance for actual sin and points toward the adoption of a positive program for moral reformation. The very ideal of freedom from sinfulness, *libertas a miseria,* to which the discourse refers, was, indeed, a definition of Christian perfection.[23] This explains the relation of the argument to ideas about grace. Sanctifying grace was a prerequisite for, and consequently implied in, any impulse toward self-improvement. Because Franciscus asserts a desire to improve, grace can be taken for granted. Moreover, when the soul does what it can, then further grace comes to its aid. Hence, the problem is what man himself should do to improve the state of his soul.

The traditional medieval program was to renounce the world and become a monk. The subjective aspects of morality, however, were not neglected. Whereas the proper relationship of the soul to God was defined in objective terms as avoidance of actual sin and action in conformity with the divine plan, this relationship was also conceived in subjective terms as an inner transformation passing through purgative, illuminative, and unitive stages of spiritual development. Yet a strong sense of the contrast between worldly pleasures and religious aims early led to identification of the elementary, purgative phase of

---

21. Hugh of St. Victor, *De modo orandi* (*Pat. Lat.,* CLXXVI, 977), ch. 1: "Quid enim efficacius hominem ad orandi studium excitaret quam miseria et calamitas tantorum malorum, quibus addictus premitur?"
22. M. M. Davy, *Un traité de la vie solitaire: Epistola ad fratres de Monte-Dei de Guillaume de Saint-Thierry* (Paris, 1940), no. 90, p. 132: "Nullum vero dignius et utilius exercitium est homini eam habenti, quam in eo quod melius habet, et in quo ceteris animalibus, et ceteris partibus suis preeminet, quae est ipsa mens vel animus."
23. Cf. Bernard of Clairvaux, *Tractatus de gratia et libero arbitrio* (*Pat. Lat.,* CLXXXII, 1007), chs. 11, 14.

moral effort primarily with certain types of action: penance and avoidance of sin for people living in the world or, in the case of full effort toward perfection, renunciation of worldly ties and preoccupation with ascetic exercises.[24] The early medieval tendency, then, was to associate subjective processes of devotion especially with the higher stages of the contemplative life and to consider them primarily the concern of the monk.

In the *Secretum,* Augustine's praise of meditation as a means to peace of soul obviously seems to belong in the sphere of interest traditionally connected with monasticism. But medieval ethical thought and practice were not so uniform nor static as has sometimes been assumed. In the objective sphere, there was increasing variety in the kind of renunciation thought appropriate for an effort toward perfection, especially in Petrarch's day, when devotees of poverty, beguines, heretics of the "Free Spirit," Friends of God, and others were emphasizing various forms of action, while tertiaries and other laymen were adopting programs of penitence which verged upon traditional monastic practices. Moreover, with reference to the inner reformation of the soul, Aristotelians and Augustinians held conflicting views about the kind of effort which influences the inner life of the soul.[25] This disagreement was sharpest with reference to the elementary stages of spiritual development. Whereas Augustinians leaned toward emphasis upon subjective exercises of prayer and meditation, Thomistic moral theology tended toward an emphasis upon rational choice and objective discipline. Because, then, of the very fluidity of medieval thought about perfection, the meaning of the statements in the *Secretum* cannot be perceived without careful analysis.

The outstanding characteristic of the advice offered by Augustine to Franciscus is that it approaches the problem of morality from the point of view of an inner transformation of spirit. The objective relationships involved in spiritual progress are not considered. Indeed, even with reference to the inner life of the spirit, the discussion is peculiarly focused upon the psychological, as opposed to the ultimate ontological, aspects of inner transformation. In traditional terms, Petrarch was interested in the purgative rather than in the

---

24. Cf. Vacant et Mangenot, *Dictionnaire de théologie catholique,* arts., "Contemplation," "Perfection," and "Vertu."
25. Cf. O. Lottin, *Psychologie et morale aux XIIe et XIIIe siècles* (Louvain, 1942-49), I, 226-31; 382-89; III, 539-75.

higher stages of spirituality, but this means that he was more concerned about some sense of his own integrity than about ultimate
union with God. In the *Secretum,* the argument turns upon how an
inner change of spirit is to be achieved. Augustine declares that,
despite Franciscus' profession that he realizes his sinfulness and,
consequently, intends to change, he deceives himself about his appreciation and intention because, otherwise, he would not neglect the
means that could raise him out of his state:

> For just as the man who has learned through deep and intensive medi-
> tation that he is miserable should desire not to be miserable, so he
> should pursue what he has begun to desire in such a way that he may
> also arrive at what he has been pursuing. But because it is clear that
> the third step is hindered only by lack of the second; the second, only by
> absence of the first; it is the first step which it is necessary to take
> as the root of salvation.[26].

Franciscus assumes that what Augustine means is that deep appreciation will lead to certain choices and actions which, in turn, will
lead to spiritual peace, and he objects that this claims too much for
meditation since there are many things that men cannot achieve no
matter how ardently and earnestly they desire them. But Augustine
gives a hint that he does not mean what Franciscus supposes by replying that, with reference to the end in question, the case is different
and that a real desire to leave one's faults behind will not be disappointed. Franciscus insists that "all have certainly willed to lay down
this burden of misery but very few have been able to." [27] Augustine,
however, forces him to admit that men have at least the negative
power not to act, for otherwise there would be no responsibility for
sin; but Franciscus stubbornly continues to object that although men
fall through their own choices, they do not voluntarily remain in their
fallen condition. The author, in short, has brought the argument to
the very issue which divided Aristotelian from Augustinian views of
morality, the question of the influence of choice and outer action
upon the inner spirit.

With implicit humor, Petrarch ascribed to Franciscus the assump-

---

26. *Secretum,* p. 374: "Ut sicut qui se miserum alta et fixa meditatione cognoverit,
cupiat esse non miser, et quid optare coeperit, sectetur sic, ut quod sectatus
fuerit, possit etiam adipisci. Enim vero tertium huiusmodi, sicut non nisi ex
secundi, sic secundum, non nisi ex primi defectu impediri posse, compertum est
itaque primum illud, ceu radix humanae salutis subsistat oportet."

27. *Ibid.*: "hanc miseriae sarcinam omnes quidem deponere voluisse, rarissimi
autem potuisse, notissimum est."

tion that Augustine is an Aristotelian believing that men can influence their desires through their choices. This Aristotelian conviction represented a particular psychology and, consequently, a particular definition of the problem of spiritual change. It was held that freedom of choice is not only a negative power not to act but also a positive way of influencing future desire because desire or will is itself actualized and determined through the very act of choosing. Franciscus, on the other hand, adopts the point of view of the medieval Augustinians who, with an eye to the organization of personality as a whole, stressed the fact that the inner bent of desire seems to elude and, indeed, control choice rather than to be shaped by it. For the Augustinians, the problem of inner change did not ultimately pertain to the functioning of choice at all; it was a problem of the tendencies in will and desire which create and influence the very occasions of choice. It was the problem of willing, as it were, the will itself. As the real St. Augustine asked in the *Confessions:*

> Whence is this anomaly and why? Mind commands body, and there is instant obedience; mind commands mind, and there is rebellion.
> . . . Mind commands mind to will and, though it is one, it will not hear. Whence and why is this anomaly? I say it commands to will; and it would not command unless it did will, and yet its command is inoperative.[28]

Because grace, not human effort, was recognized by the Augustinians as the ultimate source of the inner bent of the will, freedom of choice was sharply distinguished from the power to choose the good freely and easily. In Bernard's terms, free choice, by which we initiate our actions, gives *libertas a necessitate* but it does not give *libertas a peccato,* which depends upon choice guided by reason, and above all, it does not give *libertas a miseria,* which depends upon the power to will the good wholly and freely.[29]

Having brought the argument of the *Secretum* around to Franciscus' assertion that men cannot correct their inner tendencies by their own choices, the author does not ascribe to Augustine the opposite view that choice is a remedy for sin. Indeed, given the author's demonstrable awareness of the Augustinian problem of influencing

28. Augustine, *Confessions,* VIII, 10.
29. Bernard, *op. cit.* (*Pat. Lat.,* CLXXXII, 1012), ch. 6: "Ut ergo velle nostrum, quod ex libero arbitrio habemus, perfectum habeamus, duplici gratiae munere indigemus, et vero videlicet sapere, quod est voluntatis ad bonum conversio, et pleno etiam posse, quod est ejusdem in bono confirmatio."

the will, it is hardly possible to believe that he would have attributed to his spokesman, Augustine, the Aristotelian doctrine that choice guided by intellectual appreciation is the key to inner change. Petrarch clearly stated in the *De remediis:*

> I would not have you trust earthly philosophy which promises virtuous dispositions through repetitious actions, for the wise know how much faith to put in this promise.[30]

Hence, when Augustine is made to reiterate his original thesis that it is meditation which is the root of salvation, the implication is that the significance of meditation does not lie in its influence upon choice but in some more direct type of influence upon inner tendencies of desire and will. In short, Petrarch's view of the problem of moral reformation is essentially Augustinian, and it is the Augustinian context of his thought which explains the meaning which he sees in meditation.

Augustine's thesis means, then, that meditation is a form of self-determination through which man can influence his own desires. Because meditation has this power, Augustine insists that intention can realize itself and that failure to improve must be attributed to lack of intention rather than to the impossibility of influencing the will. "Instead of saying you cannot, you ought to say you will not." [31] As proof that there is an inner power of self-determination in meditation, Augustine paraphrases the statement of the real St. Augustine in the *Confessions* that his conversion began "when deep reflection brought forth from its secret stores the whole cloud of my misery. . . ." [32] By emphasizing the fact that the real St. Augustine discovered this connection, Augustine claims, as it were, an empirical basis for his theory about the spiritual efficacy of meditation. This passage concludes the introductory section of the first dialogue.

Did this doctrine imply some form of ascetic retirement from secular ties? Literally the ideal to which Augustine refers can be

---

30. Franciscus Petrarcha, *De remediis utriusque fortunae libri duo,* 4th ed. (Paris, 1610), II, dial. 104: "quod sic accipias velim, non ut terrenae philosophiae, quae ex frequentatis actibus habitum spondet, cuius quanta sit promissi fides, experti sciunt. . . ."

31. *Secretum,* p. 376: "verba vero, quibus te uti velim haec sunt, ut ubi te non posse dixisti, ultra te nolle fatearis. . . ."

32. Augustine, *Confessions,* VIII, 12. This is paraphrased in the *Secretum,* pp. 376-7: "Et tamen haec inter idem ille quod fueram, mansi, donec alta tandem meditatio, omnem miseriam meam ante oculos congessit. Itaque postquam plene volui, ilico et potui, miraque et foelicissima celeritate transformatus sum in alterum Augustinus."

identified with repentance, renunciation of the world, and meditation upon death, but although the literal form allows this interpretation, Augustine's emphasis points in a different direction. Monasticism was traditionally regarded as the means for developing a "real" desire for perfection because, by freeing the soul from the world, it allowed it to turn to God. But Augustine seems to identify monasticism with the second or illuminative stage of spiritual development, as though it implied a certain degree of perfection already achieved. Emphasis falls on meditation as the means to a "real" desire. This notion also appears at the very end of the *Secretum* in a statement which is commonly cited as proof that Petrarch was trying to argue himself into becoming a monk. Franciscus declares:

> I know, as you pointed out a few moments ago, that it would be much safer for me to devote myself to this one concern [meditation upon death], and, relinquishing bypaths, to seize the right road to salvation, but I am not able to control my desire.[33]

But this very statement suggests that Franciscus (and, consequently, the author) was not thinking about monasticism as the one step most necessary for restraining desire. The *Secretum,* in short, seems to make meditation a substitute for ascetic action in purgative effort, and Augustine's statements can actually be interpreted as a new way of outlining the contemplative life. It is to be remembered that, at the beginning of the *Secretum,* Augustine emphasized three essential steps:

> For just as the man who has learned through deep and intensive meditation that he is miserable should desire not to be miserable, so he should pursue what he has begun to desire in such a way that he may also arrive at what he has been pursuing. But because it is clear that the third step is hindered only by lack of the second; the second, only by absence of the first; it is the first step which it is necessary to take as the root of salvation.[34]

Here, the first or purgative stage is meditation which leads to "real" desire; the second or illuminative stage is action appropriate to such desire, and this was traditionally conceived to be full devotion to discursive contemplation; the third or unitive stage is the achievement of spiritual perfection. Petrarch seems, then, to have applied ideals

---

33. *Secretum,* p. 416: "Non ignarus (ut paulo ante dicebas) multo mihi futurum esse securius studium hoc unum sectari, et de viis praetermissi, rectum callem salutis apprehendere, sed desiderium frenare, non valeo."
34. Cf. note 26 above.

and practices previously associated with monasticism to secular morality and to have opened the door to perfection, as it were, to men in the world.

III

This clarifies the ethical reference of Petrarch's ideas, but how could meditation be conceived as an influence upon the intrinsic bent of desire? [35] Was his psychology Stoic or Augustinian? Petrarch's classical studies were undoubtedly a factor leading him to see an ethical influence in meditation. Cicero pointed out that "meditation and exercise allow many to endure a natural defect." [36] He also declared that "consideration . . . not only holds in check the passions but even lessens pain itself, I know not by what pact." [37] Seneca held similar views:

> It is clear to you, Lucilius, I know, that no one can live happily or even tolerably without devotion to wisdom. Perfect wisdom makes a happy life and even elementary wisdom makes it tolerable. But this realization must be strengthened and more deeply rooted by daily meditation because it takes more effort to keep a resolution than to adopt it. You must persevere and gain force through constant effort until your good intention becomes a will to the good. [38]

---

35. Others have answered this question as follows: P. Mazzei, *La vita e opere di Francesco Petrarca* (Livorno, 1927), p. 74: "Il nucleo centrale del primo dialogo è questo: Perchè—domanda il poeta—io che ho cercato di governarmi secondo la ragione e i precetti dei filosofi e degli asceti, non riesco a liberarmi dalle catene del peccato?—Sant' Agostino risponde che in lui c'è stato sì il desiderio, ma è mancata la volontà di liberazione.—Che cosa deve dunque fare? —In primo luogo è necessario che abbia coscienza delle sue colpe, e, perchè, l'*intelletto* possa muovere la *volontà* alle cose divine, dietro la *coscienza* delle miserie umane deve armarsi di *volontà buona*. Per uscire dalla selva dei vizi, gli è necessario dunque: 1° Meditare sull' umana miseria e sulla morte; 2° Volere fortemente fuggire il male e seguire il bene." Cf. E. Carlini-Minguzza, *Studio sul Secretum di Francesco Petrarca* (Bologna, 1906), p. 60: "Quattro gradi dunque per giungere a Dio: volere, desiderare fortemente, desiderare sempre, seguire la ragione. . . . E però la ragione non basta perchè siamo uomini e la carne e il mondo sono viziati: ecco gli ultimi due gradi, che soprastanno agli altri quattro, primo cioè: la meditazione in genere; secondo: la meditazione della morte in particolare. Qui siamo in pieno misticismo."

36. Cicero, *De divinatione libri*, II, 96: "Multi etiam naturae vitium meditatione atque exercitatione sustulerunt."

37. Cicero, *Tusculanae disputationes*, II, 22, 53: "atque haec cogitatio, quid patientia, quid fortitudine, quid magnitudine animi dignissimum sit, non solum animum comprimit, sed ipsum etam dolorem, nescio quo pacto, mitiorem facit."

38. Seneca, *Epistulae morales*, XVI, 1: "Liquere hoc tibi, Lucili, scio, neminem posse beate vivere, ne tolerabiliter quidem sine sapientiae studio et beatam vitam perfecta sapientia effici, ceterum tolerabilem etiam inchoata. Sed hoc, quod liquet, firmandum et altius cotidiana meditatione figendum est: plus operis est in eo, ut proposita custodias quam ut honesta proponas. Perseverandum est et adsiduo studio robur addendum, donec bona mens sit, quod bona voluntas est."

Petrarch, however, interpreted this emphasis in contemporary Christian terms. He had more respect for the inner autonomy of the will than is revealed in ancient thought. He insisted in the *De remediis,* for example, that the essential quality of virtue is not wisdom but rather something which the will imparts to the soul:

> The attribute of virtue is to be concerned not with what has been achieved but with what remains to be achieved. . . . Virtue, if I may so speak, is avaricious or has points of resemblance with avarice. . . . and therefore, it is never still but always on the march; it always strives as though just beginning.[39]

In the light of Petrarch's Augustinian approach to ethical problems, it is interesting to note that the medieval Augustinians laid great stress upon the ethical function of meditation. Bernard, William of St. Thierry, Guigo the Carthusian, Hugh and Richard of St. Victor, Bonaventura, and others made it a factor in all devotion, and their treatises abound in discussions of it. Underlying this interest was the notion that through meditation the mind cooperates with the inner bent of the soul. Grace imparts to the soul an impulse which might be called a "higher will" to fulfill the soul's capacity for unity in an all-embracing type of understanding and desire which find their fruition in God. Meditation allows the higher will to take possession of the life of the soul. The will first manifests itself by leading the mind to turn away from the world to a truer appreciation of the soul's nature and destiny. Meditation, however, permits the inner will to fuse with these new appreciations and become, as it were, the conscious center of the life of the soul. Turning inward in meditation also cuts off the passing influence of sense impressions upon desire. Thus, meditation reinforces the will and paves the way for wider appreciations and subsequent consolidation of the will, until the latter embraces the whole intellectual and affective life of the soul.

The idea of an inner life of the soul stemming from a sort of circular interplay of mind and will is elusive. Petrarch suggested it by stressing the necessity for both understanding and desire in meditation. Augustine declares:

> What I set out to do with you was to show you that to escape the bonds

---

39. *De remediis,* I, dial. 10: "Proprium est virtutis, non quid actum, sed quid agendum sit. . . . Dicerem, si liceret, avaram, aut certe avaritiae similem esse virtutem. . . . atque adeo nunquam torpet, et semper in actu est: semper, quasi nunc incipiens, accingitur."

of this mortal life and to raise oneself above it, the first step, so to speak, is meditation upon death and human misery, the second, in truth, an intensive desire and effort to arise. Given these conditions, I promised an easy ascent to that toward which our intention aspires.[40]

Hugh of St. Victor created the image of an upward flight of the mind produced by an inner cooperation of mind and will:

> Prayer is carried upward on these two wings, the wretchedness of man and the mercy of the Redeemer. For as long as the mind constantly inspires itself to devotion by alternate consideration of these things, spiritual desire imparts an impetus which raises it above itself and enables it to soar. Such meditation is necessary to prayer and prayer can never be perfect unless it is accompanied or preceded by meditation.[41]

For Bernard, the soul discovers its own "life" in contrast with the life it gives the body when the mind turns inward in harmony with the higher will.[42] Alcher of Clairvaux and William of St. Thierry called the soul, as vivifying principle of the body, the *anima;* but as a subjective unity of mind and will, the *animus*.[43] William declared:

> When the soul passes from mere capacity for reason to participation in perfect reason, then it casts off the feminine character of *anima* and becomes *animus,* that is, reason capable of ruling the body or spirit in possession of itself.[44]

In a manner closer to Petrarch, Bonaventura emphasized the double aspect of the higher life of the soul in the *Soliloquium* which is a dialogue between the soul and "the inner man." In the first part of the discourse, the inner man points out that "the soul ought to learn to focus the beam of conscience upon its inner self in order to

---

40. *Secretum,* p. 375: "Id agere tecum institueram, ut ostenderem ad evadendum huius vitae mortalitatis angustias, attollendoque se altius, primum veluti gradum obtinere, meditationem mortis humanaeque miseriae: secundum vero desiderium vehemens studiumque surgendi, quibus exactis, ad id quo nostra suspirat intentio, ascensum facilem pollicebar."
41. Hugh of St. Victor, *De modo orandi* (*Pat. Lat.,* CLXXVI, 977), ch. 1: "Istis duabus alis, miseria scilicet hominis et misericordia Redemptoris, oratio sublevatur, quia dum mens alterna horum consideratione se ad devotionem incessanter excitat, quodam spiritualis desiderii impetu sursum levata volat. Sic ergo orationi sancta meditatio necessaria est, ut omnino perfecta esse oratio nequeat, si eam meditatio non comitetur aut praecedat."
42. G. B. Burch, *The Steps of Humility of Bernard, Abbot of Clairvaux* (Cambridge, 1942), p. 8.
43. Alcher of Clairvaux, *De spiritu et anima* (*Pat. Lat.,* XL, 781), chs. 1-2.
44. Davy, *op. cit.,* no. 85, p. 130: "Quae ubi perfectae rationis incipit esse, non tantum capax, sed et particeps, continuo abdicat a se notam generis feminini, et efficitur animus particeps rationis, regendo corpori accomodatus, vel se ipsum habens spiritus."

see how it has been formed by nature, deformed through sin, and reformed by grace." [45] In a second part of the dialogue, the soul awakens to a real desire for purification and for God. This is a consequence of the new understanding emphasized in the first part. In the *De triplici via,* Bonaventura explained the psychological process by which meditation brings the life of the soul into line with the innermost bent *(pondus naturale* or *synderesis)* of the will:

> In meditation of this type, the whole soul ought to be intent, using all its faculties: reason, *synderesis,* conscience, and will. For in this kind of meditation, discursive reasoning raises some question [about the good]; *synderesis* intuitively inclines toward [the good]; conscience understands its implications; and the will shapes itself accordingly. If anyone, aided by grace, wishes to enter the purgative way through meditation, reason should inquire, "What ought to happen to the man who has violated the temple of God?" *Synderesis* will reply that he deserves to be destroyed unless he is purified through repentance and sorrow. Conscience says to itself, "Such are you! Certain is your damnation if the need for penitence does not strike and spur you." Thence the will shapes its course, for, since it shrinks from eternal damnation, it voluntarily takes upon itself to repent in sorrow.[46]

Bonaventura's point is not that a rational weighing of consequences influences practical judgment and choice but that, if mind lends itself to the deep urges of the will, then certain judgments and choices follow like the conclusions of a syllogism.

A different explanation of the influence of meditation was offered by the Franciscan Hugo Panziera in a treatise on perfection. Panziera, who died in the Eastern Empire about 1330, wrote a number of devotional works. With reference to purgative, illuminative, and unitive steps toward perfection, he regarded "mental action" as appropriate to the first, meditation to the second, and contemplation to the third:

45. Bonaventura, *Soliloquium,* in *Opera omnia* (Quaracchi, 1882-1902), VIII, 29: "anima per mentale exercitium debeat radium contemplationis reflectere ad interiora sua ut videat, qualiter sit formata per naturam, deformata per culpam, et reformata per gratiam."
46. Bonaventura, *De triplici via,* in *Opera omnia,* VIII, 7: "In huiusmodi autem meditatione, tota anima debet esse intenta, et hoc secundum omnes vires suas, scilicet secundum rationem, synderesim, conscientiam et voluntatem. Nam in huiusmodi meditatione ratio percunctando offert propositionem, synderesis sententiando profert definitionem, conscientia testificando infert conclusionem, voluntas praeeligendo defert solutionem. Verbi gratia, si quis velit meditari circa viam purgativam, debet ratio quaerere, quid debeat fieri de homine, qui templum Dei violaverit; synderesis respondet, quod aut debet disperdi, aut lamentis poenitentiae purgari; conscientia assumit: Tu es ille, ergo vel oportet te damnari, vel poenitentiae stimulis affligi; deinde voluntas praeelegit, scilicet, quia recusat damnationem aeternam, assumit voluntarie poenitentiae lamenta."

Mental action is often referred to by the terms meditation and contemplation. Yet there is a certain difference between mental action and meditation; a great difference between mental action and contemplation. Perfect mental action is the way which leads to perfect meditation and contemplation when all conditions are right. Its office is to appeal so strongly to the imagination that the latter impresses its object continuously upon the corporeal affections which go with passing thoughts. When the mind has in the end communicated Christ to the imaginative faculties by exercising itself in Christ, Christ will not allow himself to lose the active and corporeal virtue inherent in the spirit.

In the first stage, when the mind begins to think about Christ in conformity with the conditions required by Christ, Christ seems to be written into the mind and imaginative faculties; in the second, he appears to be outlined; in the third, outlined and shaded; in the fourth, colored and lifelike; and in the fifth, he seems to be sculptured in the flesh. And because virtue rules the body, the virtue of the spirit is all the more perfect. This active and virtuous condition of the spirit, combined with the virtuous action of the body, merits the gift of meditation and contemplation in conformity with divine justice.[47]

Petrarch's ideas belong in this tradition. He attributed significance to meditation not because the mind has the power to influence choice through an understanding of conditions and consequences, but because there is a central urge in the soul which can become the center of the soul's own life through the deep, inward turning of the mind. And because the pressure to realize the inner circle of the soul's own life is so real, Augustine can claim that Franciscus deceives himself when he declares that he wants to improve but cannot. As Petrarch has pointed out in his letters, the outer life is, indeed, a sort of deception of the inner.[48] Although these notions may have had distant roots in certain aspects of Stoicism, the explicit emphasis upon the importance of striving and desire in connection with meditation was not Stoic but Augustinian.

This consideration of Petrarch's psychology provides a basis for understanding the structure of a second section of the *Secretum* where Petrarch indicated the psychology underlying efficacious meditation. Under the guise of describing the characteristics of ideal meditation, the author emphasized the need for bringing the mind into contact with the inner kernel of the will. Yet the psychological reference of Petrarch's thought is obscured by the literary device of translating ideas into a discourse where Franciscus and Augustine

47. Quoted from the French translation in J. Chuzeville, *Les mystiques italiens* (Paris, 1942), pp. 108-9.
48. Cf. *Fam.*, II, 9, 2; XVII, 10, 28.

discuss the concrete and specific attributes of meditation upon death. Augustine begins by attempting to explain, with reference to the will, that ideal meditation must be aimed at realizing the inner urge of the soul for God. He declares literally that "a perfect knowledge of one's misery will beget a perfect desire to be rid of it, if only desire will yield to power." [49] This appears to mean that "perfect knowledge will beget perfect desire if only transient impulse will yield to the inner bent of the will." It reminds one of the words of St. Augustine quoted by Petrarch in one of his letters. " 'In truth, there are two wills because one of them is not the whole will and because the other has what this one lacks.' This," Petrarch declared, "is the pure, naked truth." [50] In the *Secretum,* Augustine's problem is to define what kind of desire the higher will is. The first characteristic of the higher will is that it corresponds to something deep and permanent in the soul and is not merely a passing urge. Augustine brings this out by citing Ovid's dictum: " 'To wish is little; it is necessary to will in order to arrive.' " [51]

The second trait of a total will is that it can be distinguished from other desires only through self-examination. Hence, Augustine advises Franciscus to consult his conscience. The meaning of this injunction is explained by William of St. Thierry:

> The man who wishes to love God or who loves Him already ought always to consult the inner life (*animus*) of the soul and examine his conscience to know what the soul really and fully desires (*quod in totum vult*) and why it so desires (*propter quod vult*) and to understand all that the spirit wills and hates and what the flesh desires in opposition to it. For incidental and transitory inclinations, which come, so to speak, from outside, and which, in a way, one wills without willing, ought not to be attributed to the will itself but rather to idle thoughts. Even if at times they delight the inner spirit (*animus*), the spirit quickly shakes them off and regains mastery of itself. With reference to that which man desires with his whole will, he ought to consider first what he desires, then, how much he desires it, and finally, the way in which he desires it . . . whether even at the expense of con-

49. *Secretum,* p. 377: "Recognoscis ne igitur veram illam fuisse sententiam, graduumque progressum, ut miseriarum suarum perfecta cognitio, perfectum desiderium pariat assurgendi, si desiderium potentiae obsequatur." In F. P., *Il mio segreto,* p. 19, Carrara has translated the latter part: "che la perfetta conoscenza delle proprie miserie produca un perfetto desiderio di risorgere. Al desiderio segue la forza di farlo."
50. *Fam.,* XVII, 10, 20: " 'et ideo sunt due voluntates, quia una earum tota non est, et hoc adest alteri quod deest alteri.' Hec est nuda et pura veritas, amice. . . ." Cf. Augustine, *Confessions,* VIII, 9.
51. *Secretum,* p. 377: " 'Velle parum incipias, ut re potiaris oportet.' " Cf. Ovid, *Ex Ponto,* III, 1, 35.

tempt for himself and of all that is or might be, and not only according to rational judgment but also with such desire that his will is already more than will. . . .[52]

Finally, Augustine emphasizes that the kind of desire in question is exclusive and incompatible with other ordinary desires. "And yet, besides the objects at which this desire is aimed, infinite are those which its fulfillment displaces. . . . No one can fully attain this desire without making an end to all others."[53] It has been supposed that the author was here recommending to himself an ascetic type of renunciation.[54] But in reality, his effort was to describe the higher will with which the mind must make contact in meditation.

The discussion then turns to the intellectual characteristics of perfect meditation. First, because it must be a broad appreciation of the whole significance of life, reflection upon death is peculiarly appropriate. Secondly, it must be permeated by real understanding, and in a long passage, Augustine denounces the vain prattling and hackneyed phrases of dialecticians. Finally, it must have emotional depth. "If in meditation itself, you grow stiff, tremble, turn pale, and feel as if you were already in the throes of death . . . then you may be assured you have not meditated in vain."[55] Ideal meditation, then, is that which aims at an inner unity of mind and will.

---

52. Davy, *op. cit.*, no. 104, p. 143: "Ideo homini amare volenti Dominum vel iam amanti, suus semper consulendus est animus, examinanda conscientia, quid sit quod in totum vult, et propter quod vult; quicquid aliud vult spiritus vel odit, quicquid contra illud caro concupiscit. Incidentes enim quasi extrinsecus et decedentes et pretervolitantes voluntates, quibus modo vult, modo non vult, nequaquam inter voluntates, sed pene inter otiosas deputandae sunt cogitationes. Nam etsi aliquando fiunt usque ad delectationem animi, cito tamen se inde excutit animus compos sui. Quod autem in totum vult, primo considerandum est quid illud sit quod sic velit; deinde, quantum velit, et quomodo velit . . . utrum usque in contemptum sui ipsius, omniumque quae sunt vel esse possunt; et hoc non tantum ex iudicio rationis, sed etiam ex affectu mentis ut iam voluntas plus quam voluntas sit. . . ."

53. *Secretum*, p. 378: "Atqui ut ea sileam, ex quibus desiderium istud constat, quam multa sunt ex quorum eversione conficitur . . . . Nulli potest desiderium hoc absolute contingere, nisi qui aliis omnibus desideriis finem fecit. . . ."

54. Cf. E. H. R. Tatham, *Francesco Petrarca*, 2 vols. (London, 1925), II, 248: "At this point we reach the kernel of the first dialogue. The director has laid an unerring finger upon the chief mark which distinguishes asceticism from humanism; he has made the demand which Petrarch is never really ready to concede. . . . He is told, not that he must subordinate the lower desires to the highest, but that he must 'make an end' of the former in order to accomplish the latter. St. Augustine's ideal is that of the cloister. . . ."

55. *Secretum*, p. 380: "ac si in ipso cogitatu obrigueris, contremueris, expalluetis, tibique iam huic laborare visus fueris, medias inter mortis angustias . . . non frusta te meditatum esse confide."

IV

The final section of the first dialogue of the *Secretum* extends the psychological conceptions just discussed, but its essential function is to indicate the relation of Petrarch's ideas about meditation to the more concrete and personal reflections presented in subsequent dialogues. As in other portions of the book, the author's intention is not explicitly stated. Here, it is implied in an analysis of why the previous meditations of Franciscus have not been efficacious. He has fallen short because he has not had adequate motives and because his meditations have not had the proper content. The conclusion is that a reformation of particular tendencies is required and this leads to a specific examination of Franciscus' inner life in the two remaining dialogues. But the implications of this conclusion can be grasped only through analysis of the discussion.

With reference to motives, Franciscus has not appreciated the dependence of meditation upon the inherent hunger of the soul for the good. When he claims that he has meditated upon death and been driven almost to distraction by his fears and yearning for peace, he reveals that he was motivated by emotion rather than by the inner bent of the will. Augustine merely comments that at least his effort checked evil impulses. Similarly, meditation fails when it is nothing but an intellectual consideration of death from afar without any turning of the mind inward toward the roots of the soul. And finally, Augustine hints that Franciscus has not realized that the type of motive in question depends ultimately upon divine grace, for he reminds Franciscus that he ought to be grateful to God for the urge to self-improvement. In short, "two factors enter into human acts, and if one is lacking, any effect is barred. There must be a will, and this so intense that it may be called desire." [56] Although this seems to involve the paradox of making desire a prerequisite for desire, the meaning is that the wish or intention which leads to meditation must spring from central tendencies which have deep roots so that the more the wish is considered, the stronger it becomes.

Inadequate motives are not the only cause of falling short. Meditation may lack the proper content, and Augustine proceeds to point out that the meditations of Franciscus have been inadequate in three

---

56. *Secretum*, p. 381: "Sed in actibus humanis duo versantur, quorum si deest alterum, praepedire constat effectum, voluntas igitur praesto sit, eaque tam vehemens, ut merito desiderii vocabulum sortiatur."

respects because he has neglected the origin, nature, and destiny of the soul. First, the mind forgets its divine creator and heavenly origin. Secondly, it loses sight of the nature of the soul:

> Inasmuch as innumerable images and impressions of visible things enter through the senses and are admitted one by one into the recesses of the soul, they collect there in a horde, overburdening and baffling the soul which has no place within itself for them and cannot cope with such meaningless chaos. . . .[57]

Petrarch cites St. Augustine's *De vera religione* as the source of this conception, but there is no close resemblance between the pertinent sections of that work and his own, whereas his statements follow almost literally the discussion of these topics in the *De spiritu et anima* of Alcher of Clairvaux.[58] In the latter work, however, these ideas are part of a more or less rational metaphysical system in contrast to the subjective orientation of St. Augustine's thought. A third cause of inefficacious meditation is failure to grasp the aim and destiny of the soul.

> These phantasms are the evil which plagues you; this will lead you to perdition if you do not fight against it. For, overwhelmed by sense impressions and oppressed by many, varied, and conflicting cares, the distraught spirit cannot determine what it should first attack, nourish, destroy, or repel, and all the strength and all the time that a sparing hand has conceded are not sufficient for such a task. Thus, just as seeds which are sown in a narrow space impede each other's growth, so in your own too crowded soul nothing useful takes root and nothing fruitful comes forth, and without a standard of judgment you roll along, now here, now there, in astonishing fluctuation, never spotless, never whole. . . .[59]

The faults which Augustine finds in the workings of the mind indicate that efficacious meditation must be centered upon truths pertaining to the soul itself: its origin, its true nature, and its destiny. This seems to contradict the earlier emphasis upon death as the

---

57. *Secretum*, p. 382: "Conglobantur siquidem species innumerae et imagines rerum visibilium, quae corporeis introgressae sensibus, postquam singulariter admissae sunt, catervatim in animae penetrabilibus densantur, eamque nec ad ingenitam, nec tam multorum difformium capacem praegravant, atque contundunt. . . ."
58. Cf. Augustine, *De vera religione* (*Pat. Lat.*, XXXIV, 139 ff.), chs. 40-41, 45; Alcher of Clairvaux, *op. cit.*, (*Pat. Lat.*, XL, 784, 801), chs. 4, 31-32.
59. *Secretum*, p. 382: "Haec tibi pestis nocuit, haec te nisi provideris, perditum ire festinat, siquidem phantasmatibus suis obrutus, multisque et variis ac secum sine pace pugnantibus curis animus fragilis oppressus, cui primum occurrat quam nutriat, quam perimat, quam repellat exanimare non potest, vigorque eius omnis ac tempus parca quod tribuit manus ad tam multa non sufficit, quod igitur evenire solet in angusto multa serentibus, ut impediant se fata concursu, idem tibi contingit, ut in animo nimis occupato, nihil utile radices agant, nihilque fructiferum coalescat, tuque inops consilii, modo huc, modo illuc mira fluctuatione volvaris, nusquam integer, nusquam totus. . . ."

most important subject for meditation. But it is to be remembered that Augustine also stressed realization of man's "misery," that is, his actual state, and that, in the words of Cicero quoted by Petrarch, "what we call our life is death." [60] Petrarch frequently declared that "philosophy is nothing but meditation on death." [61] It is not far-fetched, then, to assume that by meditation on death Petrarch meant consideration of the essential meaning of life. This meaning was contained in truths about the soul itself. But what are such truths and how are they known? Because Petrarch establishes a sharp contrast between the life of the soul and that of the body with its passions and sense impressions and because there is no hint that the soul is part of a vast system of metaphysical relations, he does not seem to have had in mind as material for meditation those insights embedded in ontological conceptions which fill the works of Bernard, Richard of St. Victor, and Bonaventura. True spiritual values are revealed by the experienced attributes of the soul; they are those toward which the inner bent of the soul itself is turned. Hence, knowledge of what is truly desirable has the somewhat paradoxical character that it comes only from observing the process of deep and true desiring. This idea appears in the *De remediis:*

> Philosophy does not offer wisdom but the love of wisdom. Whoever loves wisdom achieves it by loving. This matter is not, as some think, heavy and difficult; if you love true wisdom with true love, you will be a true philosopher.[62]

The main reason Franciscus has failed in previous meditations, then, is that he has lacked insight into the nature of true knowledge, true values, and the soul itself. He has not understood the very nature of meditation. But to appreciate that the soul achieves peace and unity by turning inward requires that type of insight which is the soul's first step toward taking possession of itself. Hence, instead of saying that Franciscus does not understand the soul or meditation, it would be more to the point to say that his soul is not in a condition to allow the mind to make contact with the higher will. The next step in the discourse is, therefore, for Augustine to attempt to show Franciscus exactly what is wrong with his present

---

60. G. Fracassetti, *Lettere senili di Francesco Petrarca* (Florence, 1869), I, 5.
61. *De otio religiosorum*, in *Opera omnia*, p. 356.
62. *De remediis*, I, dial. 46: "Philosophia non sapientiam, sed amorem sapientiae pollicetur. Quisquis hanc igitur vult, amando consequitur. Non est, ut quidam putant, operosus, aut difficilis hic titulus; dummodo verus amor sit, et vera, quam ames, sapientia; philosophus verus eris."

tendencies. This supplies the immediate framework for Petrarch's examination of his inner life. This perspective, however, is merely part of a larger one, that of understanding the very nature of the soul, and this in turn part of the problem of grasping the function of meditation. Moreover, since the psychology outlined in the first dialogue pertains to the inner structure of the soul, it provides a pattern for analyzing the nature of evil tendencies and determines the organization of the discussion. In short, Petrarch's doctrine of meditation upon death explains both the intellectual reference and the actual organization of the remainder of the book.

Petrarch's theme also offers a clue to the author's intentions in working his reflections into literary form and publishing them. His book is an exposition of profound ethical insights. In terms of his conviction that the attributes of experience are a guide to the true nature of values, the awareness of his own incidental frivolities, deep inconsistencies, and ultimate yearnings had significance as a clue to spiritual truth. Moreover, because such reflections were the very type of material which he believed necessary for efficacious meditation, they offered material for the meditations of others. But as a source of new insights drawn from his own experience, the *Secretum* has more the character of Augustine's *Confessions* than that of a manual like the *Imitation of Christ* or the *Spiritual Exercises*.

In conclusion, it may be pointed out that Petrarch's ideas about meditation seem to be much more closely related to his literary attitudes than has been supposed. They were rooted in that interest in the introspective study of experience which is manifest in so many of Petrarch's writings. His poetry was largely a study of his own soul. He regarded the classics as a source of truth about the inner life; and his letters are dominated by an introspective awareness of his own perplexities, annoyances, achievements, and rewards. Literary study itself seems to have been for him a source of insight into the significance of traditional ethical teachings. It is not surprising, however, that in an intellectual environment colored by religious interests, Petrarch's literary thought should have taken an ethical turn. To recognize this aspect of his ideas is, indeed, to place them within the context of medieval attitudes and interests, but without denying their novelty and significance for what is called the Renaissance.